Wissenschaftliche Untersuchungen
zum Neuen Testament · 2. Reihe

Herausgeber / Editor
Jörg Frey (Zürich)

Mitherausgeber / Associate Editors
Markus Bockmuehl (Oxford) · James A. Kelhoffer (Uppsala)
Hans-Josef Klauck (Chicago, IL) · Tobias Nicklas (Regensburg)
J. Ross Wagner (Durham, NC)

434

Sławomir Szkredka

# Sinners and Sinfulness in Luke

A Study of Direct and Indirect References in
the Initial Episodes of Jesus' Activity

Mohr Siebeck

Sławomir Szkredka, born 1974; 2001 MDiv and MA in Theology; 2005 MA in Philosophy; 2008 PhD in Comparative Religions (Buddhism); 2012 Licentiate in Sacred Scripture; in 2016 defended a doctoral dissertation at the Pontifical Biblical Institute, Rome; since 2015 Assistant Professor of Biblical Studies at Saint John's Seminary, Camarillo, CA, USA.

ISBN 978-3-16-155057-7
ISSN 0340-9570 (Wissenschaftliche Untersuchungen zum Neuen Testament, 2. Reihe)

Die Deutsche Nationalbibliothek lists this publication in the Deutsche Nationalbibliographie; detailed bibliographic data are available on the Internet at *http://dnb.dnb.de*.

© 2017 Mohr Siebeck Tübingen, Germany. www.mohr.de

The book was printed by Laupp & Göbel in Gomaringen on non-aging paper and bound by Buchbinderei Nädele in Nehren.

Printed in Germany.

# Preface

This study is a revised version of my doctoral thesis presented to the Pontifical Biblical Institute in Rome. The thesis was submitted in October 2015 and defended in January 2016.

It is appropriate that I take the opportunity here to express my gratitude to some of the many people without whose support this study would not have been possible. In the first place, I wish to thank my doctoral supervisor, Professor Dean Béchard, SJ. With scholarly diligence as well as personal generosity and patience he both guided and inspired this work from its inception. The second reader, Professor Luca Pedroli, offered his careful and critical feedback. To them and to all at the Biblicum I remain deeply grateful.

Among my friends and fellow students of Saint Luke in Rome, I wish to acknowledge the Reverends Luke Macnamara, OSB and Piotr Kot. Their friendship and love for Scripture have nurtured my work. At Saint John's Seminary in Camarillo, CA, I had the good fortune of having Fr. Patrick Mullen as my mentor. He knows, I hope, how much I have valued his support and wise counsel. Finally, I cannot forget Mary Jane Bartee who graciously proofed the text at its various stages.

In preparing the thesis for publication I have profited from comments offered by Professor James Kelhoffer. He has helped me to clarify my argument as well as to avoid some errors. My gratitude goes to him and to the editorial staff at Mohr Siebeck.

The roots of this project lie in Los Angeles. It was Cardinal Roger Mahony and then Archbishop José Gómez who directed me to the study of Scripture and offered constant encouragement during the years of doctoral work. In thanking them, I wish to thank the entire Church of Los Angeles without whose assistance this thesis would not have been written.

*Camarillo, October 18, 2016*                                    *Sławomir Szkredka*

# Table of Contents

# List of Abbreviations

The abbreviations for the biblical books and for ancient authors and literature, with the exception of the Gospel of Luke abbreviated here as Lk, are drawn from P. H. ALEXANDER et al. (ed.), *The SBL Handbook of Style for Ancient Near Eastern, Biblical, and Early Christian Studies* (Peabody, MA 1999). The abbreviations for periodicals and collections are as listed in S. M. SCHWERTNER, *Internationales Abkürzungsverzeichnis für Theologie und Grenzgebiete / International Glossary of Abbreviations for Theology and Related Subjects* (IATG²) (Berlin – New York ²1992), supplemented by S. BAZYLIŃSKI, *A Guide to Biblical Research* (SubBi 36; Rome ²2009) 222–232. Other abbreviations that do not appear in these works are quoted below:

| | |
|---|---|
| AncBRL | The Anchor Yale Bible Reference Library |
| ANTC | Abingdon New Testament Commentaries |
| BDAG | BAUER, W. – DANKER, F. W. – ARNDT, W. F. – GINGRICH, F. W., *A Greek-English Lexicon of the New Testament and Other Early Christian Literature* (Chicago – London ³2000). |
| BDF | BLASS, F. – DEBRUNNER, A. – FUNK, R. W., *A Greek Grammar of the New Testament and Other Early Christian Literature* (Chicago 1961). |
| BDR | BLASS, F. – DEBRUNNER, A. – REHKOPF, F., *Grammatik des neutestamentlichen Griechisch* (Göttingen ¹⁴1976). |
| BECNT | Baker Exegetical Commentary on the New Testament |
| BHGNT | Baylor Handbook on the Greek New Testament |
| EDNT | BALZ, H. – SCHNEIDER, G. (ed.), *Exegetical Dictionary of the New Testament* (Edinburgh 1990, 1991, 1993) I–III. |
| *Hist. Conscr.* | LUCIAN, *Quomodo Historia Conscribenda sit.* |
| LSJ | LIDDELL, H. G. – SCOTT, R. – JONES, H. S. – MCKENZIE, R., *A Greek-English Lexicon* (Oxford – New York ⁹1940, 1985). |
| NTA.NF | Neutestamentliche Abhandlungen. Neue Folge |
| ÖTNT | Ökumenischer Taschenbuchkommentar zum Neuen Testament |
| SBLEJL | Society of Biblical Literature. Early Judaism and Its Literature |
| TDNT | KITTEL, G. – FRIEDRICH, G. (ed.), *Theological Dictionary of the New Testament* (Grand Rapids, MI 1964–76; Ger orig, *TWNT*, 1933–79). |
| WUNT 2.R | Wissenschaftliche Untersuchungen zum Neuen Testament. 2. Reihe |

Chapter 1

# Introducing the Study and Its Presuppositions

This chapter briefly presents the nature and goal of the study. It situates it in the context of previous research on the subject and spells out methodological assumptions on which the study is based. It provides a reconstruction of the implied reader's pre-existing beliefs pertaining to the studied subject, and it justifies concentration on Lk 5:1–6:11 on the grounds of its place in the composition of Luke-Acts.

## 1.1. A Brief Presentation of the Nature of This Study

This study is about reading Lk 5:1–6:11 and examining its portrayal of sinners. It is about *reading* in that it traces the implied reader's progressive reactions to the first cycle of episodes narrating Jesus' public ministry. It is about *examining the portrayal of sinners* in that, within that cycle, it uncovers and explains the textual strategy of confronting the reader with multiple direct and indirect references to the literary characteristic of sinfulness.

Thus formulated, this study hopes to contribute to the scholarly discussion about the literary and theological roles of sinners in the Gospel of Luke. The contribution it hopes to make rests on the assumption that the role of sinners in Luke is properly assessed not just by examining sinner texts, that is, the pericopae containing the word "sinner" or its cognates, but also by uncovering and assessing all the textual strategies that prompt the reader to infer the characteristic of sinfulness, even in the absence of its direct textual referent. Motivation and justification for such a working assumption come from phenomena detectable in Luke's Gospel: upon close reading of the text, the characters known as sinners are found to be distinct from other characters such as, for instance, the disciples or the Pharisees, in that their defining characteristic is often found inadequate, rendered inapplicable, and transferred to another character. It departs from them, as it were, by attaching itself to other inhabitants of the narrative world. An eloquent example of that phenomenon is found in 5:27–39. The sinners (ἁμαρτωλοί) spoken of in 5:30 are, according to Jesus, no longer sinful; in their table fellowship with him their repentance is accomplished. They have met their physician. At the same time, however, by repeatedly directing himself to the Pharisees and by identifying himself as the one sent to call sinners to repentance, Jesus treats the Pharisees as the sick in need of a physician. It appears that the Pharisees are marked by sinfulness, since it is to them that Jesus directs his attention. Multiple direct and indirect references to sinfulness in the Gospel reflect similar shifts in the identification of sinners and invite an inquiry into the likely effect of such operations. As a result, in this study, the Lukan portrayal of sinners is examined more as a process than as a final product. It is analyzed and explained in light of the function Luke ascribes to its various components as they emerge in the temporal unfolding of the narrative of Lk 5:1–6:11.

The assessment of Luke's presentation of sinners in Lk 5:1–6:11 is preceded by an examination of the ways in which the narrative prior to 5:1 frames the reader's understanding of sin and sinners, and it is completed by an inquiry into how Lk 5:1–6:11 conditions Luke's presentation of the sinner theme in the remaining portion of the Galilean ministry of Jesus.

In the end, what the reader understands about sinners is that he or she must discover and assimilate Jesus' perception of them. Interpretive effort implied by that task is employed productively by Luke. He deploys the references to sinfulness in a way that engages the reader in a search for the normative view of Jesus. By untangling crisscrossing viewpoints formed around sinfulness – implied, inferred, directly stated, overcome, or rejected – the reader's *coming* to know Jesus is enacted.

## 1.2. A Sinner in Luke and in Lukan Scholarship

The Greek term ἁμαρτωλός appears eighteen times in Luke while only five times in Matthew (9:10,11,13; 11:19; 26:45) and six times in Mark (2:15,16[twice],17; 8:38; 14:41). Of the eighteen Lukan uses, four have parallels in the other Synoptic Gospels (Lk 5:30 = Mark 2:16 = Matt 9:11; Lk 5:32 = Mark 2:17 = Matt 9:13; Lk 7:34 = Matt 11:19; Lk 24:7 = Mark 14:41 = Matt 26:45), and the remaining fourteen are uniquely Lukan. Among them one finds three elaborate scenes of encounter between Jesus and a sinner: at the beginning of his Galilean ministry, in 5:1–11, Jesus meets Simon, described as a "sinful man" in verse 8; in 7:36–50 Jesus meets the "sinful" woman characterized as such in verses 37 and 39; and at the final stage of the Travel Narrative, in 19:1–10, Jesus meets Zacchaeus, referred to as a sinner in verse 7. Apart from that, the word "sinner" (ἁμαρτωλός) is found again in the following pericopae: in the Sermon on the Plain (6:32,33,34[twice]); in the warning to repent or perish in 13:2; in the parables about the lost sheep, coin, and son (15:1,2,7,10); and the story about the Pharisee and the tax collector (18:13).

Luke's frequent mention of sinners has triggered inquiries into their literary and theological functions within his oeuvre.[1] The role of sinners in the final text of Luke's Gospel has been the object of explorations conducted by D. Neale,[2] H. Adams,[3] and, most recently, by A. Pesonen,[4] although in his case in combination with questions of the origin and development of the sinner texts. Many of the sinner texts in Luke have also been analyzed by G. D. Nave and F. Méndez-Moratalla in their respective works on the themes of repentance and conversion.[5] The study of Lukan soteriology by H. J. Sellner[6] and the investigation of Lukan anthropology by J. W. Taeger[7] similarly overlap with many sinner texts, although without tracing their meaning at the level of the complete text's narrative strategies, but rather by locating it in the author's redactional intentions.

In terms of the function of sinners in the final form of the Lukan text, two major results emerge from these studies. Neale affirms that the sinners in Luke are an ideological category employed in order to fuel the conflict – the engine of the plot – and ultimately to exemplify "the right response to Jesus  in counterpoint to the uncomprehending and bigoted 'Pharisees.'"[8] Luke then uses sinners to bring about a reversal of all expectations: in a bipolar world of religious discourse, it is the category of sinners, not the Pharisees, that represents those who are saved. Adams, on the other hand, concludes that the sinner theme fulfills Isaiah's promise about "all flesh" seeing God's salvation

---

[1] For a survey of the patristic, early modern, and modern interpretations of the "sinner" in Luke, see H. ADAMS, *The Sinner in Luke* (The Evangelical Theological Society Monograph Series; Eugene, OR 2008) 1–20.

[2] D. NEALE, *None but the Sinners*. Religious Categories in the Gospel of Luke (JSNT.S 58; Sheffield 1991).

[3] ADAMS, *The Sinner in Luke*.

[4] A. PESONEN, *Luke, the Friend of Sinners* (Diss. University of Helsinki; Helsinki 2009).

[5] G. D. NAVE, *The Role and Function of Repentance in Luke-Acts* (SBL Academia Biblica 4; Atlanta, GA 2002); F. MÉNDEZ-MORATALLA, *The Paradigm of Conversion in Luke* (JSNT.S 252, London 2004). Nave stresses the ethical-social dimension of repentance relegating the religious aspect, in the sense of the change of beliefs, to secondary concerns. Méndez-Moratalla, on the other hand, puts the religious experience in the center. The belief in Jesus as Christ stands for him as the central concern of the Lukan conversion texts. Our present investigation will give further support to the conclusions reached by Méndez-Moratalla. Of limited value to the present project is the work by D. S. MORLAN, *Conversion in Luke and Paul*. An Exegetical and Theological Exploration (LNTS 464; London 2013), as its analysis of the Lukan texts is restricted to Luke 15; Acts 2; and Acts 17:16–34.

[6] H. J. SELLNER, *Das Heil Gottes*. Studien zur Soteriologie des lukanischen Doppelwerks (BZNW 152; Berlin – New York 2007).

[7] J. W. TAEGER, *Der Mensch und sein Heil*. Studien zum Bild des Menschen und zur Sicht der Bekehrung bei Lukas (StNT 14; Gütersloh 1982).

[8] NEALE, *None but the Sinners*, 193.

(Isa 40:5; Lk 3:6), and prepares for the mission to the Gentiles in the Acts of the Apostles.[9] Luke then uses sinners to illustrate the far-reaching scope of Jesus' messianic mission through which the OT promises of salvation are fulfilled. Both Neale and Adams come to their conclusions by first examining the socio-religious content of the idea of sinners detectable in the first-century Jewish and Greek cultural milieu, and then by applying the results of that examination to their study of Lukan sinner texts. Although they differ in what they see to be the meaning of the term ἁμαρτωλός in the first-century world – Neale tends to see it mostly as an ideological label, while Adams demonstrates that certain moral and religious behaviors constituted, in fact, its content – they reach conclusions that appear more complementary than contradictory. While Adams reads the sinner texts through the promise-fulfillment scheme anchored in Isa 40:5, Neale might be said to be more of a structuralist in that he focuses on elements of contrast and reversal in the conceptual system underlying Luke's story. Adams treats all of the 18 Lukan occurrences of the term ἁμαρτωλός, whereas Neale limits his study to five scenes: the Call of Levi, the Story of the Sinful Woman, the Gospel for the Lost (Luke 15), the Pharisee and the Tax Collector, and the Story of Zac-chaeus. Both Neale and Adams dedicate about 90 pages each to the analysis of the Gospel passages, and they both claim to give a comprehensive view of what literary and theological values are to be ascribed to the Lukan use of the term sinner.[10]

That said, the theoretical tools afforded by narrative criticism prompt us to question the adequacy of Neale's and Adam's results. As it has been observed, the relative frequency with which the term "sinner" punctuates Luke's narrative deserves consideration. But what also deserves consideration is the fact that the criterion of lexicography, that is, the selection of texts that use the term ἁμαρτωλός, does not fully account for the way the narrative evokes for the reader the idea of sinners. In other words, sinners as literary characters are evoked, not only when they are directly labeled as such, but also each time the text provokes the reader to apply such a labeling to a given character in the story. Are not those who receive John's baptism of repentance in 3:6–14 to be considered sinners? Are not criminals (κακοῦργοι) mentioned in 23:32,33,39 to be counted among sinners? An adequate treatment of the sinner material in Luke must take into account numerous instances in which various textual indicators (epithet, description of

---

[9] ADAMS, *The Sinner in Luke*, 195–196.

[10] What Pesonen discovers about the literary function of sinners can be described as a combination of Neale's and Adams' results. Like Neale, with whom he dialogues throughout his work, Pesonen stresses the conflict-fueling function of sinners. Going beyond Neale, he notices in the sinner texts a preparation for the positive reception of Gentiles in Acts, an insight developed independently by Adams. PESONEN, *Luke, the Friend of Sinners*, 225–228.

profession, description of action, direct speech) point to the possibility of identifying a given character as a sinner. This identification may take a form of allusion, accusation, or objective narratorial description, and the subsequent narrative may affirm, deny, or leave it in suspense. Still, every occurrence of such identification always contributes to the way the text structures the reader's understanding of sinners. In other words, every emergence of the literary trait of sinfulness, that is, that characteristic by which a given character is subsumed under the category of sinners, needs to be considered.[11]

What makes the need for such a consideration even more evident is our recognition of the degree to which the reading conventions operative among the addressees of Luke's Gospel were supportive of perceiving the *same* characteristic of sinfulness through *various* direct (epithet) and indirect (action, self-revealing expression) indications. That such support is to be expected comes, first of all, from the realization that the ability to infer characters' traits is fundamental to the process of reading in general.[12] Secondly, inasmuch as the ancient Greek reading conventions assumed that one's character (ethos), even though often amounting to nothing more than just a type, was revealed through one's actions (praxis), they encouraged inference of characteristics from that person's words and actions.[13] Finally, to give an affirmative answer to the question of the Lukan reader's ability to infer the same characteristic from various types of indicators, we need to recall the ancient Greco-Roman perception of the way words work. Downing's study of this very problem reveals that ancient semantics was governed by the model of "naming" – meaning was thought to reside in the mind, not in the words. Word served to name, that is, to evoke an otherwise unspecified mental im-

---

[11] The same could be said, *mutatis mutandis*, with regard to the characteristic of faith. Faith as a trait of a given character is more often than not indirectly predicated. When Elizabeth describes Mary in 1:45 as "one who believed that there would be a fulfillment of what was spoken to her by the Lord," the reader is invited to see Mary's answer in 1:38 as an act of faith, even though the term "faith" does not appear in the scene of the Annunciation. It is the explicit naming of faith at some points that invites its recognition at other moments in the narrative.

[12] Chatman discerns the following correlation between a trait, which he calls a narrative adjective, and its direct textual referent, that is, an actual verbal adjective: "The actual verbal adjective, of course, need not (and in modernist narratives will not) appear. But whether inferred or not, it is immanent to the deep structure of the text. [...] We must infer these traits to understand the narrative, and comprehending readers do so. Thus the traits exist at the story level: indeed, the whole discourse is expressly designed to prompt their emergence in the reader's consciousness." S. CHATMAN, *Story and Discourse*. Narrative Structure in Fiction and Film (Ithaca, NY – London 1980) 125.

[13] See F. W. BURNETT, "Characterization and Reader Construction of Characters in the Gospels", *Semeia* 63 (1993) 11, who follows D. A. RUSSEL, "On Reading Plutarch's *Lives*", *Greece and Rome* 13 (1976) 144, and G. N. STANTON, *Jesus of Nazareth in the New Testament Preaching* (MSSNTS 27; New York 1974) 122.

pression. Words then were not expected to be precise.[14] The widespread modern expectation of clear lines between possible connotations of particular words was foreign to ancient readers and writers.

Since the previous treatments of the sinner theme in Luke have not sufficiently explored the role of frequent direct and indirect references to sinfulness, there arises the need for a study that would remedy this omission.[15] The present study answers that need and takes a step toward a fuller understanding of Luke's portrayal of sinners. That said, the investigation conducted in this study is limited by the methodological principles assumed in it, historical reconstructions exploited by it, and a single narrative cycle selected as its basis. All these factors – method of literary analysis, reconstruction of relevant historical background, and concentration on a selected portion of the Lukan text – inasmuch as they both limit and define the nature of this study, need to be explained and justified.

## 1.3. Methodological Assumptions Governing This Study

The present study utilizes methods of investigation developed within modern[16] narrative criticism. Given the variety of approaches to the biblical text that are informed by modern narrative criticism, it is necessary to clarify the methodological assumptions on which this study is based. The following is a presentation of the basic theoretical principles we assume and of the necessary tasks they entail for this project.

### 1.3.1. The Reader as Produced by the Text

The meaning of the Gospel is understood as the sum of the effects the implied author intends for the story to have upon the implied reader, with the implied author being the subject of the narrative strategy used in the text, and the im-

---

[14] Downing's examination of ancient theory of metaphor and allegory allows him to conclude: "if names are seen as exchangeable, and the transferred one likely as evocative as (or better than) the common one, there is nothing 'in' a name that affords precision." F. G. DOWNING, "Ambiguity, Ancient Semantics, and Faith", *NTS* 56 (2009) 152.

[15] It is worth noting that Taeger's brief treatment of sinners in Luke overcomes some of the above-mentioned limitations. He investigates the notion of sinners by treating not just the term ἁμαρτωλός, but the entire word group by which various dimensions of sin are lexicalized in the Gospel. Traeger does not ask about implicit references to sinners nor does he consider the effects of the sequential reading of the sinner texts. TAEGER, *Der Mensch und sein Heil*, 31–44.

[16] For a criticism of the fallacious assumption that ancient literary work can be adequately judged only in terms of ancient literary criticism, see D. FEENEY, "Criticism Ancient and Modern", *Ancient Literary Criticism* (ed. A. LAIRD) (Oxford Readings in Classical Studies; Oxford 2006) 440–454.

plied reader being the ideal receiver of that strategy.[17] It will be our task to uncover the narrative strategies – configurations of plot, setting, characters, point of view – by which the text elicits responses from its reader[18] and to describe the effects (on the reader) which correspond to a maximal realization of these strategies.

### 1.3.2. The Reader as Assumed by the Text

If the implied author is the subject of the narrative strategy used in the text, and the implied reader is the ideal receiver of that strategy, then the task of decoding the biblical text involves the task of reconstructing "the capacities for knowledge, attitudes, preoccupations, reactions which the author (rightly or wrongly) attributes to his future reader, and which condition the development of his narrative."[19] To put it differently, the implied reader comes to engage a given pericope with knowledge, skills, and expectations formed not only by the part of the narrative prior to it, but also by the cultural milieu that frames and conditions the communication between the implied author and the implied reader even before the reading commences. The implied reader of a given pericope has both pre-existing and narrative-formed beliefs.[20] Thus, before we analyze the literary effects of the references to sinfulness, we must ask what notion of sinfulness was the reader expected to have before engaging the text of the Gospel. That is, we must explore the pre-existing beliefs about what made one sinful.

---

[17] The categories of implied author and implied reader were first developed by W. ISER, *Der implizite Leser*. Kommunikationsformen des Romans von Bunyan bis Beckett (UTB 163; München 1972) [English translation: *The Implied Reader*. Patterns of Communication in Prose Fiction from Bunyan to Beckett (Baltimore 1974)]; *Der Akt des Lesens*. Theorie ästhetischer Wirkung (UTB 636; München 1976) [English translation: *The Act of Reading*. A Theory of Aesthetic Response (Baltimore 1978)]. As a matter of convenience, the name "Luke" and masculine pronouns referring to "Luke" will be used in this study as shorthand for the implied author of Luke-Acts.

[18] In the words of Grilli, "il testo cerca un proprio lettore, il quale sia capace di comprendere dei riferimenti specifici, gli indici letterari, gli schemi comunicativi, gli impulsi, ecc." M. GRILLI, "Evento comunicativo e interpretazione di un testo biblico", *Gregorianum* 83 (2002) 675.

[19] D. MARGUERAT – Y. BOURQUIN, *How to Read Bible Stories*. An Introduction to Narrative Criticism (tr. J. BOWDEN) (London 1999) 14. [Originally published in French as *Pour lire les récits bibliques* (Paris 1998)].

[20] On the difference between pre-existing and narrative-formed beliefs, see Booth's observation: "As a rhetorician, an author finds that some of the beliefs on which a full appreciation of his work depends come ready-made, fully accepted by the postulated reader as he comes to the book, and some must be implanted or reinforced." W. C. BOOTH, *The Rhetoric of Fiction* (Chicago [2]1983) 177. For an example of further theoretical elaboration of that distinction see P. DANOVE, *The Rhetoric of Characterization of God, Jesus, and Jesus' Disciples in the Gospel of Mark* (JSNT.S 290; New York 2005) 10–11.

### 1.3.3. Temporal Ordering and a First-Time Reading

The forming of the implied reader's knowledge, skills, and convictions is understood here to take place along the time-continuum of the reading process. The fact that the text is grasped successively is one of the factors determining its meaning. The segments of the narrative acquire their meaning depending on where in the text-continuum they appear: along the temporal production of the narrative's effects on the reader, what comes first (the "primacy" effect) may be subsequently frustrated, reinforced, or simply modified by what comes later (the "recency" effect).[21] To capture adequately the temporal dynamic of effects produced by the text, our analysis will proceed sequentially through the text in an attempt to reconstruct the effects of a first-time reading by the implied reader.[22]

### 1.3.4. Literary Form and Narrative Function

Our attempt to decipher the reading of the implied reader involves reconstruction of interpretive frameworks within which the elements of the story cohere best. Next to pieces of information regarding cultural and religious

---

[21] "The nature of a literary work, and even the sum total of its meanings, do not rest entirely on the conclusions reached by the reader at the end-point of the text-continuum. They are not a 'sifted,' 'balanced,' and static sum-total constituted once the reading is over, when all the relevant material has been laid out before the reader. The effects of the entire reading process all contribute to the meaning of the work: its surprises; the changes along the way; the process of a gradual, zig-zag-like build-up of meanings, their reinforcement, development, revision and replacement; the relations between expectations aroused at one stage of the text and discoveries actually made in subsequent stages; the process of retrospective re-patterning and even the peculiar survival of meanings which were first constructed and then rejected." M. PERRY, "Literary Dynamics: How the Order of a Text Creates its Meanings", *Poetics Today* 1 (1979) 41. (A Hebrew version of this article was written in 1973 and published in Israel.). On the primacy-recency effect, see "Chapter Four" of M. STERNBERG, *Expositional Modes and Temporal Ordering in Fiction* (Baltimore 1978), 90–128.

[22] The first-time reading by the implied reader differs from the actual first time reading in that, while the latter entertains multiple possibilities for further development, the former discards possibilities not supported by the development of the plot. Perry's description of his own method of reading illustrates that difference well: "The reading process described in this article is therefore from the vantage-point of the whole. It is a process of a 'reconstructed first reading'. Only from this vantage-point can one make the selection between relevant and accidental surprises. An actual first reading of a text is a gradual process of selection. The more the construction of the whole nears its completion, the more the reader is able to tell accidental surprises from functional ones" (PERRY, "Literary Dynamics", 357). G. YAMASAKI, *John the Baptist in Life and Death.* An Audience-Oriented Criticism of Matthew's Narrative (JSNT.S 167; Sheffield 1998) 53, is correct when he observes that "Perry's 'reconstructed first reading' – that is, a first-time reading with accidental surprises eliminated – is functionally equivalent to a first-time reading by the implied reader."

knowledge assumed by the text (such as pre-existing beliefs about sinfulness), the interpretive frames consist in the knowledge of the formal segmentation of the text. The text's effects on the reader depend on the literary composition the reader is expected to assume in the text. It will be necessary then to ask about the place of Lk 5:1–6:11 in the formal segmentation of the Gospel. Since the narrative function depends on the literary form, and conversely the determination of the literary form depends on the narrative function (the Proteus Principle),[23] our initial reconstruction of the literary composition must be taken as a working hypothesis to be reevaluated later in light of the function assigned to Lk 5:1–6:11 at the end of our study.

## 1.4. The Implied Reader's Pre-existing Beliefs about Sin and Sinners

By asking about the implied reader's pre-existing beliefs about sinfulness, we are concentrating on that part of the conventional knowledge presupposed in Luke's readers that relates to sin and sinners. We want to know who was considered a sinner and, by extension, what kind of offense rendered someone sinful. Traditionally, biblical scholarship has broached this topic by asking about the historical sinners thought to be represented in the Synoptic Tradition.[24] Our interest lies not in the historical sinners, but in the ways sin, sin-

---

[23] Strictly speaking, the Proteus Principle postulates the many-to-many correspondence between form and function. That is, a given form can perform more than one function; a given function can be achieved by more than one form. It follows that the determination of form depends on the determination of function. See M. STERNBERG, "Proteus in Quotation-Land", *Poetics Today* 3 (1982) 107–156; in particular his blunt statement: "In discourse, typology is less than useless where divorced from teleology" (*ibid.* 130).

[24] Two scholars have shaped the discussion of the historical sinners more than others: J. Jeremias and E. P. Sanders. In his influential article "Zöllner und Sünder", *ZNW* 30 (1931) 293–300, Jeremias held that, although from the perspective of the Pharisees the common people, the *'am hā-'āreṣ*, would be labeled as sinners, the general public saw sinners as a narrower category, namely, as those who were notoriously immoral and/or the members of the rabbinically designated "despised trades." In his other writings, however, Jeremias came to use "sinners" and *'am hā-'āreṣ* almost as synonyms, at least when speaking of the point of view of the opponents of Jesus. See J. JEREMIAS, *Neutestamentliche Theologie. Erster Teil. Die Verkündigung Jesu* (Gütersloh 1971) 114. Sanders accepted Jeremias' view of sinners as immoral or practitioners of despised trades, but offered a convincing criticism of Jeremias' linking of "sinners" to the uneducated masses. See E. P. SANDERS, *Jesus and Judaism* (Philadelphia 1985) 174–211. We may add that Sanders, in turn, came to be criticized for too easily equating *hamartolos* with the term *rāšā'* and for his contention that Jesus did not seek repentance from sinners. See N. H. YOUNG, "'Jesus and the Sinners': Some Queries", *JSNT* 24 (1985) 73–75; B. D. CHILTON, "Jesus and the Repentance of E. P. Sanders", *TynB* 39 (1988) 1–18; *idem*, "Jesus and Sinners and Outcasts",

ners and sinfulness were conceptualized in the discourse that shaped the presupposed convictions of Luke's readership. Since Neale and Adams have not
only summarized the history of the research in this field but also conducted a
fresh analysis of the evidence, we shall draw on their findings.

Neale investigates references to sinners in Second Temple literature. His
research centers on the Greek Psalms, first of all because the sinner theme is
most frequent in the Psalter, and secondly because of the prominent role of
the Psalter in the religious life of the Jews during the Gospel formation period. The study of the Greek Psalms brings Neale to two conclusions: the level
of information about the identity of the sinner conveyed through the Psalms
is quite general; that is, there are many attitudes and behaviors considered
typical of sinners. Sinners are described as men of violence (Ps 11:5–6; 58:2;
140:4), cruel and unjust (71:4), workers of evil (28:3; 36:11–12; 92:7; 101:8;
141:5). They befriend thieves and adulterers (50:18), slander (50:19–20),
forsake the law (119:53,109–10,119,155), oppress the poor (10:2–3,12–15;
37:14–16; 82:2–4; 94:1–7; 109:16; 146:9; 147:6) have dispossessed the meek
of their land (37:7,9–11,22,34; 73:3–12,16–20). They are also identified as
Israel's national enemies (9:15–16; 10:15–16; 94:3–5; 129:3–4).[25] For Neale,
these descriptions do not reflect historical information about actual sinners
but rather represent the ideology of the author of the Psalms; they are a foil
against which the values promoted by the author are favorably contrasted.
Neale's second conclusion is that sinners, while representing everything that
stands in opposition to righteousness, are portrayed as the ones for whom
repentance and salvation are not possible. It is only in the first century CE
that Jewish literature exhibits a semantic shift in the notion of sinners: they
are now spoken of in a penitential context, that is, as an object of God's mercy.[26]

Since, in his interpretation of the evidence, Neale tends to focus on general
trends in the characterization of sinners, particularly their function as the ideological opposite of the righteous, what he uncovers about historical sinners
is that they are not so much an identifiable social group as a category in the
bipolar world of religious discourse. Adams finds such conclusions inadequate. While not in disagreement with the notion that sinners performed a
necessary contrastive role to the righteous in the religious discourse of the
time, he attempts to recover more the referential content of the category of
sinners. He points to Acts 4:25 and notes how Peter applies Psalm 2 to Herod,

---

*Handbook for the Study of the Historical Jesus.* Volume 3. The Historical Jesus (ed. T.
HOLMÉN – S. E. PORTER) (Leiden – Boston 2011) 2815–2824. For more on sinners in con-
temporary historical Jesus research, see PESONEN, *Luke, the Friend of Sinners*, 3–12.

[25] NEALE, *None but the Sinners*, 80.

[26] Neale notes that such new developments tend to date from the post-destruction period. The only known case predating the destruction of the temple is, according to him, the
*Prayer of Manasseh* (*ibid.* 91).

Pilate, the people of Israel and the Gentiles who joined in opposition to Jesus, the Lord's anointed.[27] Adams then reads various descriptions of sinners in the Psalms as capable of reflecting actual sinners and their concrete sinful acts. In addition, Adams looks for various references not just to sinners but also to those of whom sin is predicated, that is, those indirectly described as sinful. A telling illustration of his expanded approach is his discussion of Psalm 51 (LXX 50) in which the offer of repentance is made to the one whose sin is clearly seen (ἡ ἁμαρτία μου ἐνώπιόν μού ἐστιν διὰ παντός, verse 5) but who is never called a sinner (ὁ ἁμαρτωλός).

Adams expands the field of research beyond the Psalms and finds that the theme of mercy to sinners is present, albeit infrequently, already in the OT. Moreover, his expanded study[28] of the OT, in combination with his investigation of intertestamental Jewish material as well as Rabbinic literature, permits him to inject the category of sinners with other more specific historical referents. Thus he demonstrates how the concept of a sinner functions in relation to concrete religious and moral failures: sinners are the ones who neglect God's law but also the ones who violate the rules of human relationships flowing from the nation's covenantal relationship with God (e.g. Lev 19).[29] Three other characteristics of the discourse about sinners emerge from Adam's analysis: sinners are judged to be sinners by God, and stand under his wrath; sometimes Gentiles were designated as sinners, particularly in later Jewish literature (e.g., *Jub.* 23.24); and the righteous were called upon to distance themselves from those publicly acknowledged as sinners, not simply for fear of being ceremonially defiled, but for fear of being influenced by them (e.g., Psalm 1).[30]

What Neale and Adams do not treat directly, and what constitute an essential aspect of the discourse on sin and sinners, are the metaphors used to convey the notions of sin and its removal. Anderson's study of the development of the metaphors for sin in the early Jewish and Christian tradition describes how, by the Second Temple period, the dominant early biblical metaphor for sin, burden or weight, was replaced by the metaphor of debt.[31] As a result, the economic concepts of credits, loans, and redemption were frequently used to describe the situation of those who commit a sin. A sinner was depicted as a debtor; the removal of sin was described as satisfaction of a debt. We may add that out of many other metaphors kept alive by the Jewish literary tradi-

---

[27] ADAMS, *The Sinner in Luke*, 33.

[28] Chilton considers this to be a competent overview of the evidence. See B. D. CHILTON, review of D. H. ADAMS, *The Sinner in Luke* (The Evangelical Theological Society Monograph Series; Eugene, OR 2008), *RBLit* 1 (2009) 370.

[29] ADAMS, *The Sinner in Luke*, 31.

[30] ADAMS, *The Sinner in Luke*, 66–67.

[31] G. A. ANDERSON, *Sin. A History* (New Haven, CT 2009).

tion,[32] two are of particular interest: sin was often depicted as sickness, and its forgiveness as healing (e.g., Sir 38:9,15);[33] it was also described as a stain and its removal as a purifying wash (Isa 1:16; Ps 51:4,9). Lukan narration will make use of these two metaphors.

Finally, the sinner's detachment from sin often entailed not just moral repentance – ceasing to sin and returning to God and his commands – but also rituals and ascetic practices. Next to sacrificial means of atonement (Lev 16), practices such as almsgiving, (Dan 4:24; LXX 4:27), suffering (Isa 40:2), or some righteous deed such as honoring one's father (Sir 3:14) were considered meritorious and guilt removing.[34] Recitation of penitential prayer, an established genre in Jewish literature,[35] often functioned as a necessary ritual com-

---

[32] See the discussion of the NT sin metaphors and their OT background in G. RÖHSER, *Metaphorik und Personifikation der Sünde*. Antike Sündenvorstellungen und paulinische Hamartia (WUNT 2.R 25; Tübingen 1987) 29–102; H. J. KLAUCK, "Heil ohne Heilung? Zu Metaphorik und Hermeneutik der Rede von Sünde und Vergebung im Neuen Testament", *Sünde und Erlösung im Neuen Testament* (ed. H. FRANKEMÖLLE) (QD 161; Freiburg 1996) 18–52; M. WOLTER, "Die Rede von der Sünde im Neuen Testament", *Theologie und Ethos im frühen Christentum*. Studien zu Jesus, Paulus und Lukas (WUNT 236; Tübingen 2009) 475–481. For a phenomenological reading of the symbolism of sin, defilement, and guilt, see P. RICOEUR, *The Symbolism of Evil* (tr. E. BUCHANAN) (Religious Perspectives 17; New York 1967) 25–151.

[33] Another problem is the relationship between suffering and sin. The OT gives more than one answer to this question. See, for example, F. LINDSTRÖM, *Suffering and Sin*. Interpretations of Illness in the Individual Complaint Psalms (CB.OT 37; Stockholm 1994). Lindström points to a lack of any causal relationship between personal sin and sickness in the theology common to the individual complaint psalms. He notes, however, that the affliction described in Psalms 51, 86, and 130 "has a different character than the one which dominates in the individual complaint psalms. To the understanding of life which is presupposed in these three psalms belongs the conception that sin and the experience of guilt is a permanent problem because of man's divided heart" (*ibid.* 450). This observation strengthens Adam's criticism of Neale's construal of sinners in Psalms as one-sided.

[34] ANDERSON, *Sin*, 43–54, 135–151. See also the section titled "Possibility of the Removal of Guilt" in B. D. SMITH, *The Tension Between God as Righteous Judge and as Merciful in Early Judaism* (Lanham, MD 2005) 75–86. For a general treatment of the theme of forgiveness of sins in ancient Judaism, see H. THYEN, *Studien zur Sündenvergebung im Neuen Testament und seinen alttestamentlichen und jüdischen Voraussetzungen* (FRLANT 96; Göttingen 1970) 16–130; P. FIEDLER, *Jesus und die Sünder* (BET 3; Frankfurt – Bern 1976) 19–96; C.-H. SUNG, *Vergebung der Sünden*. Jesu Praxis der Sündenvergebung nach den Synoptikern und ihre Voraussetzungen im Alten Testament und frühen Judentum (WUNT 2.R 57; Tübingen 1993) 1–182. For a reconstruction of a general theological message about sin in the context of the present canonical shape of the OT, see M. J. BODA, *A Severe Mercy*. Sin and Its Remedy in the Old Testament (Siphrut, Literature and Theology of the Hebrew Scriptures 1; Winona Lake, IN 2009).

[35] See R. A. WERLINE, *Penitential Prayer in Second Temple Judaism*. The Development of a Religious Institution (SBLEJL 13; Atlanta, GA 1998) 2–4; S. VON STEMM, *Der*

ponent demanded from those who wanted to repent and reenter the true Mosaic covenant (*Rule of the Community* 1QS I, 22–25; Philo, *Praem.* 163).[36] Significantly, some prayers, by necessitating the need for divine assistance in liberating and safeguarding from sin (11Q5 XXIV, 11–13a) or by acknowledging divine assistance (4Q434 1 I, 2–4), presented the human inclination to sin as innate and inevitable.[37]

To summarize, the recent research allows us to affirm that the term *sinner* would have evoked for Luke's readers a continuum of meanings ranging from metaphorical to specific historical referents. Neale's work explores one of the ends of this continuum and demonstrates the ideological labeling performed by the term *sinner*. Adams' study, on the other hand, points to juridical guilt and various kinds of moral failure as specific historical referents of the term *sinner*, signaling its occasional identification with Gentiles, association with mercy, and the need for the righteous one's dissociation from those known to be sinners.[38] Finally, the readers would have been familiar with the metaphor of a debtor as a popular means of conveying the meaning of one's sinfulness.

## 1.5. Lk 5:1–6:11 as a Narrative Section

Historically, examination of literary structure has taken into account a number of factors: from chronological and geographical data, traditionally considered decisive, through the classical *Literarkritik*'s attention to literary criteria, theological themes, and the influence of Luke's sources on the overall shape of his work, to structural patterns such as chiasmus and concentric structures pondered by promoters of a more formal aesthetic approach. Narrative methodologies added dramatic criteria: changes of place, time, *dramatis*

---

*betende Sünder vor Gott.* Studien zu Vergebungsvorstellungen in urchristlichen und frühjüdischen Texten (AGJU 45; Leiden 1999) 218–223.

[36] T. HÄGERLAND, "Jesus and the Rites of Repentance", *NTS* 52 (2006) 172–173.

[37] See the discussion of these two prayers and other texts representing various understandings of the human inclination to sin in M. T. BRAND, *Evil Within and Without. The Source of Sin and Its Nature as Portrayed in Second Temple Literature* (Journal of Ancient Judaism. Supplements 9; Göttingen 2013) 37–146.

[38] Adams does not list the breaking of the purity laws among sins. This agrees with the basic approach of the Hebrew Bible where ritual impurity was considered natural, unavoidable, and not sinful. See J. KLAWANS, *Impurity and Sin in Ancient Judaism* (New York 2000) 160. But see also *ibid.* 67–91 for Klawans' view of the Qumran sectarian writings in which moral and ritual impurity were to meld into a single conception of defilement. M. HIMMELFARB, "Impurity and Sin in 4QD, 1QS, and 4Q512", *DSD* 8/1 (2001) 9–37, questions the view that the Qumran community conflated the categories of impurity and sin. She argues for a non-literal use of purity language in reference to moral failures.

*personae*, dramatic action, and so forth. [39] As different scholars give different weight to these factors, divergent results in determining the structure of Luke are reached. [40] In agreement with our methodological assumption that the literary form and narrative function are mutually dependent (§1.3.4.), we assume a segmentation of the Gospel that, in accounting for the variety of indicators present in Luke's text, permits us to incorporate an additional criterion in its favor, namely, the narrative function of the characters known as sinners. Ó Fearghail has produced a study that does that. Taking into account various indicators of the literary arrangement of Luke-Acts, he affirms that Lk 1:5–4:44 constitutes a literary unit, "a preliminary narrative section in the gospel," [41] and that the narrative proper of the Gospel begins with Lk 5:1, that is, with an account of the first encounter between Jesus and someone described as a sinner. In our current reconstruction of the implied reader's ability to match the form and the function, [42] we can only proceed by way of assumptions whose effectiveness is to be proved by the explanatory power of the results reached at the end of this study. And so, in assuming the literary structure proposed by Ó Fearghail, we assume that this structure becomes even more evident once the narrative function of the Lukan references to sinners is explored. At this point let us utilize Ó Fearghail's arguments to determine the place of Lk 5:1–6:11 in the structure of Luke.

All agree that the distinct style and content of Lk 1:1–4 mark it as a self-contained proemium. It is also commonly accepted to perceive a separate Infancy Narrative unit in Lk 1:5–2:52. What Ó Fearghail argues is that the parallel between John and Jesus, which governs the structure of Lk 1:5–2:52, governs also the presentation of the material in Lk 3:1–4:44. He detects the following parallels in the Lukan presentation of the infancies of John and Jesus: [43]

---

[39] See A. DENAUX, "The Delineation of the Lukan Travel Narrative within the Overall Structure of the Gospel of Luke", *Studies in the Gospel of Luke. Structure, Language and Theology* (Tilburg Theological Studies; Berlin 2010) 4–5.

[40] See a similar observation by PERRY, "Literary Dynamics", 43, n. 7: "Different principles of continuum-structure determine different divisions into stages; since there exists, in a text, a series of ordering principles for the continuum, there cannot be a single division into stages, – rather, each principle has its own stages."

[41] F. Ó FEARGHAIL, *The Introduction to Luke-Acts. A Study of the Role of Lk 1,1–4,44 in the Composition of Luke's Two-Volume Work* (AnBib 126; Rome 1991) 38. See the discussion of the use of preliminary narratives in ancient literature in *ibid.* 153–154.

[42] As PERRY, "Literary Dynamics", 43, n. 7, puts it, "the division into segments and the determination of the ordering principle are mutually dependent, and neither takes precedence over the other: they take place simultaneously."

[43] Ó FEARGHAIL, *The Introduction*, 16. Within this structure, Ó Fearghail postulates an additional parallelism between Elizabeth's (1:42–45) and Mary's (1:47–55) hymns of praise. J. B. GREEN, *The Gospel of Luke* (NICNT; Grand Rapids, MI 1997) 50, views the parallelisms slightly differently:

*Table 1:* John-Jesus parallel in Luke 1–2

| | | | |
|---|---|---|---|
| Announcement of Conception, etc. | 1:5–25 | | 1:26–38 |
| Visitation | | 1:39–56 | |
| Birth | 1:57–58 | | 2:1–20 |
| Circumcision and Naming | 1:59–66 | | 2:21 |
| Praise & Prophecy | 1:67–79 | | 2:22–39 |
| Growth; Life prior to public ministry | 1:80 | | 2:40–52 |

And he discerns, in the beginnings of the ministries of John and Jesus, the same unbalanced parallel as in the beginnings of their lives: [44]

| | | |
|---|---|---|
| The Introduction of Parents | 1:5–7 | 1:26–27 |
| The Annunciation | 1:8–23 | 1:28–38 |
| The Mother's Response | 1:24–25 | 1:39–56 |
| The Birth | 1:57–58 | 2:1–20 |
| Circumcision and Naming | 1:59–66 | 2:21–24 |
| Prophetic Response | 1:67–79 | 2:25–39 |
| Growth of the Child | 1:80 | 2:40–52 |

The differences between the dispositions of the text proposed by Green and Ó Fearghail do not negate the existence of parallels; they simply differently reflect their unbalanced nature. For the purposes of our study, it is enough to note that the structural organization of Lk 1:5–2:52 invites the reader to compare, that is, to note the similarities and the differences between the origins of John the Baptist and of Jesus at every point of the Infancy Narrative. No part of the narrative functions outside this parallel structure. A brief critical comment regarding a competing structural proposal will further illustrate this point. A. GARCÍA SERRANO, *The Presentation in the Temple. The Narrative Function of Lk 2:22–39 in Luke-Acts* (AnBib 197; Rome 2012) 226, following E. BURROWS, "The Gospel of the Infancy: the Form of Luke Chapters 1 and 2", *The Gospel of the Infancy and Other Biblical Essays* (ed. E. F. SUTCLIFFE) (Bellarmine Series 6; London 1940) 4–6, J. DRURY, *Tradition and Design in Luke's Gospel. A Study in Early Christian Historiography* (London 1976) 64, C. PERROT, *Les récits d'enfance de Jésus: Matthieu 1–2; Luc 1–2* (CEv 18; Paris 1976) 38, G. PÉREZ RODRÍGUEZ, *La infancia de Jesús (Mt 1–2; Lc 1–2)* (Teología en diálogo 4; Salamanca 1990) 57, and T. STRAMARE, *Vangelo dei misteri della vita nascosta di Gesù. Matteo e Luca 1–2* (BeOS; Bornato in Franciacorta 1998) 316, proposes to structure Luke 1–2 along three diptychs, that is, along three parallels found in adjacent episodes: (1) diptych of announcements (to Zechariah and to Mary, including the visitation); (2) diptych of nativities (of John and of Jesus); and (3) diptych of Temple mysteries (presentation and finding). In such a configuration, the last diptych, as García Serrano puts it, "breaks the narrative parallelism between John the Baptist and Jesus in favor of Jesus who is the only one who has two passages in the Temple" (*ibid.* 223–224). We must qualify this proposal by saying that the communicative force of the John-Jesus parallel does not disappear in the last diptych; it continues to exert its interpretive influence in what now becomes an unbalanced juxtaposition of John and Jesus. It is not the parallel that is broken, but the symmetry of that parallel.

[44] Ó FEARGHAIL, *The Introduction*, 30. As he admits (*ibid.* 29), an existence of such a parallel, in at least part of chapters 3 and 4, had been noted by R. MORGENTHALER, *Die*

*Table 2:* John-Jesus parallel in Luke 3–4

| 3:2b | 'Commission' | 3:21–22 | 'Commission' |
|------|--------------|---------|--------------|
| 3:2c | Son of Zachariah | 3:23–28 | Son of Joseph; genealogy |
| 3:2d | In the desert | 4:1–13 | In the desert; temptation |
| 3:3–20 | Ministry | 4:14–44 | Ministry |
| 3a | Scene of ministry | 14f,44 | Scene of ministry |
| 4–6 | Fulfills Isaian Prophecy | 18f,21 | Fulfills Isaian Prophecy |
| 7–19 | Words (Deeds implied) | 14–44 | Words and Deeds |
| 18 | εὐηγγελίζετο τὸν λαόν | 43 | εὐαγγελίσασθαί ... τὴν βασιλείαν τοῦ θεοῦ |
| 20 | ἐν φυλακῇ | 44 | ἦν κηρύσσων ... Ἰουδαίας |

Consequently, Jesus' words and deeds described in 4:14–44 do not mark the beginning of his Galilean ministry. Rather, while 4:14–44 completes the parallel with the ministry of John the Baptist, it represents an anticipation of Jesus' entire activity.[45] The mention of Judea in 4:44, which Ó Fearghail argues must be taken in the sense of Palestine, indicates that the portrayal of Jesus' complete ministry, expanding from Galilee to Palestine (Lk 23:5; Acts 10:37), is recounted here.[46] Similarly, the fact that in the further narrative the beginning (ἀρχή) of Jesus' ministry is associated with the motifs of αὐτοψία and the twelve (Acts 1:21–22; 10:37–39), suggests that the beginning of the narrative proper must be found after 4:44, that is, when Jesus' association with his disciples is first described.[47] Lk 4:14–44 belongs to 1:5–4:44 and together with it forms a preliminary narrative unit preparing the reader for the narrative proper.

Another reason for treating 1:5–4:44 as a literary unit comes from the realization that 5:1–24:53 forms a literary unit in its own right. The ordering principle behind the unity of 5:1–24:53 is the relationship between Jesus and his disciples. Their continual contact with Jesus runs from 5:1–11 to 24:51,

---

*lukanische Geschichtsschreibung als Zeugnis.* Gestalt und Gehalt der Kunst des Lukas (Zürich 1949) I, 154–155, and W. GRUNDMANN, *Das Evangelium nach Lukas* (ThHK 3; Berlin [2]1961) 119. GREEN, *The Gospel of Luke,* 49, n. 5, points to an argument by W. WILKENS, "Die Theologische Struktur der Komposition des Lukasevangeliums", *TZ* 34 (1978) 1–3, who, while finding cycles of three throughout the Gospel, postulated three parallels between John and Jesus in the first section of the Gospel: Announcement (1:5–56), Birth (1:57–2:52), and Debut (3:1–4:44). The structuring function of Jesus-John parallelism in Luke 3–4 is noted and explored by P. BÖHLEMANN, *Jesus und der Täufer.* Schlüssel zur Theologie und Ethik des Lukas (MSSNTS 99; Cambridge 1997) 44–66.

[45] "The unit 4,14–44 does not narrate the 'beginning' of Jesus' ministry but represents an anticipation of that ministry which does not stand in a chronological relationship with what follows" (Ó FEARGHAIL, *The Introduction,* 38).

[46] Ó FEARGHAIL, *The Introduction,* 27–28.

[47] Ó FEARGHAIL, *The Introduction,* 27–28.

the moment of Jesus' ascension.[48] As has been widely recognized, geography serves as an organizing factor for the division of Jesus' ministry into the ministry in Galilee, the travel narrative, and the final activity in Jerusalem. The Galilean part is further held together by the theme of apostleship.[49] Three successive stages in Jesus' relationship to his disciples mark the triple division of the Galilean section: Jesus gathers his disciples in 5:1–6:11; he chooses and prepares the twelve in 6:12–8:56; he entrusts to them a mission in 9:1–50.[50] When it comes to 5:1–6:11,[51] the placing of the conclusion at 6:11 is additionally supported by the fact that the opposition to Jesus, first voiced in the scene of the Healing of the Paralytic (5:21,30), reaches its initial climax in 6:11.[52]

To sum up, Lk 5:1–6:11 constitutes the first cycle of episodes within the narrative proper of the Gospel. In the progression of Jesus' relationship with his disciples, Lk 5:1–6:11 marks the stage at which Jesus gathers the ones from whom, at the next stage, he will form the twelve.

---

[48] Ó FEARGHAIL, *The Introduction*, 39.

[49] Four of the eight Gospel references to the twelve are found here (6:13; 8:1; 9:1,12) as well as two of the six uses of the term ἀπόστολος (6:13; 9:10). See Ó FEARGHAIL, *The Introduction*, 40.

[50] Ó FEARGHAIL, *The Introduction*, 44.

[51] Ó FEARGHAIL, *The Introduction*, 43, n. 20, lists Godet, Schanz, Plummer, Lagrange, Schürmann, Ernst and Evans among the commentators who consider 5:1–6:11 a section. Among those who place the conclusion of a section at 6:11 he lists Knabenbauer and J. Weiss (4:14–6:11); Ellis (4:31–6:11); Hauck, Marshall and Schweizer (5:12–6:11); Schmid, Staab, Harrington and Karris (5:17–6:11).

Recently, Y. MATHIEU, "Pierre, Lévi et les douze apôtres en Luc 5,1–6,19. Les conséquences théologiques d'une mise en discours", *ScEs* 60 (2008) 101–118, has advanced structural arguments in support of linking the Calling of Simon in 5:1–11 and the Calling of the Twelve in 6:12–16. The two calling scenes frame the account of Jesus' initial activity in Galilee creating a chain of seven episodes, with the Calling of Levi (5:27–39) in the center and two healing stories (5:12–16 and 5:17–26) and two Sabbath controversies (6:1–5 and 6:6–11) before and after Jesus' encounter with Levi. As the title indicates, Mathieu proposes to extend the block to 6:19, strengthening the frame of two calling episodes with the frame of two crowd scenes in 5:1–3 and 6:17–19. In this he follows M. THEOBALD, "Die Anfange der Kirche: zur Struktur von Lk 5:1–6:19", *NTS* 30 (1984) 91–108. The problem with this proposal is that it fails to account for the progressive character of Jesus' relationship with his disciples. The gathering of the disciples and the forming of the twelve are best seen as two distinct stages in the process that spans the entire Galilean ministry of Jesus. Secondly, the elegant chiastic structure proposed by Theobald and Mathieu cannot carry the weight of the segmentation they propose. Other chiastic structures could be discerned. See R. MEYNET, *L'Évangile de Luc* (Rhétorique sémitique 1; Paris 2005) 251, who advocates the following compositional arrangement: two healings (5:17–26 and 6:6–11) frame two controversies (5:27–35 and 6:1–5) leaving the parable about old and new (5:36–39) in the center.

[52] As Ó FEARGHAIL, *The Introduction*, 45, notes, the conclusion of the travel narrative in 19:48 is marked by the same motif of opposition.

In itself, Lk 5:1–6:11 constitutes a total of 50 verses. NA$^{28}$ groups them into nine paragraphs (5:1–3; 5:4–11; 5:12–16; 5:17–26; 5:27–32; 5:33–35; 5:36–39; 6:1–5; 6:6–11). Two additional smaller divisions separate 5:4–7 from 5:8–11 and 5:27–28 from 5:29–32 elevating the number of sense-units to eleven. As it shall be argued in more detail in the course of the narrative analysis to follow, the dramatic criteria of place, time, *dramatis personae*, and dramatic action, permit binding together Jesus' preaching from Simon's boat (5:1–3) with the miraculous catch (5:4–7) and the calling of Simon Peter (5:8–11), as well as construing as one scene the disputes and sayings (5:29–32; 5:33–35; 5:36–39) set within the context of a single meal at Levi's house. Thus one can speak of seven narrative episodes (5:1–11; 5:12–16; 5:17–26; 5:27–28; 5:29–39; 6:1–5; 6:6–11) in Lk 5:1–6:11. Still, because of the close narrative connection that makes of the meal scene at Levi's house (5:29–39) a continuation of the scene of his call (5:27–28), and because of the many narrative links that bind the two consecutive Sabbath disputes scenes (6:1–5 and 6:6–11) together, our final analysis will combine the seven episodes into five chapters dealing with 5:1–11; 5:12–16; 5:17–26; 5:27–39 and 6:1–11 respectively.

## 1.6. The Task Ahead

A cursory look at the story narrated in Lk 5:1–6:11 reveals that, with the exception of the Cleansing of a Leper (5:12–16), the characteristic of sinfulness emerges in every single episode of the cycle, that is, in 5:1–11; 5:17–26; 5:27–28; 5:29–39; 6:1–5 and 6:6–11. From the self-characterization of Simon Peter as a sinful man in 5:8, and a surprising reference to the paralytic's association with sin ("your sins are forgiven you") in 5:20, through Levi's possible association with sin in virtue of his profession in 5:27, and the scandalizing presence of the company of sinners at Levi's house recalled in 5:30, to the indirect labeling of Jesus and his disciples as sinners in virtue of breaking the Sabbath law in 6:2,7, the trait of sinfulness repeatedly makes its way into the fabric of the narrated world. The closer the reading, the more urgent the need to ask about many other possible references to sinfulness. Are not the disciples of Jesus sinful by eating and drinking with tax collectors and sinners, yet are they not simply following Jesus in this regard? Are not the Pharisees and the scribes sinful, or to use Jesus' expression "the sick ones," since it is to them that Jesus, the physician, addresses himself? The references to sinfulness are not only frequent, they are also frequently unclear.

Traits, whether overtly verbalized by the narrator or dramatically evoked through action, are a constitutive feature of the narrated world and an eloquent tool in an array of communicative factors. What is it that the text communicates to its reader by a frequent recourse to the characteristic of sinfulness and, we must add, by the ambiguity that often surrounds its correct predication? It is to this question that our analysis will address itself in the manner of a close reading of Lk 5:1–6:11. Such a reading will be conducted in Chapters Three to Seven. In Chapter Two, however, a preliminary step must be accomplished. We must discover how the narrative of Lk 1:5–4:44 frames the reader's understanding of sin and sinners and concomitantly sets the expectations for the protagonist's first encounter with sinful humans at the onset of his public ministry. Chapter Eight will bring the results of our investigation to bear on the interpretation of the remaining sinner texts within the Galilean ministry of Jesus.

Chapter 2

# Sin and Sinners in Luke 1–4

Simon Peter is the first character in the Gospel to be directly characterized as a sinner (ἁμαρτωλός). The scene of his calling (5:1–11) constitutes the first instantiation of a relationship of discipleship, which in reference to Peter and subsequent others will be sustained and developed through the rest of Luke-Acts. The first stage of that relationship, narrated in 5:1–6:11, will be marked by repeated references to the characteristic of sinfulness, predicated directly or indirectly and from various points of view. Before we ask about the effect the repeated references to sinfulness are likely to have on the reader of 5:1–6:11, we must account for the ways in which the preparatory narrative of Luke 1–4 frames the reader's understanding of sin and sinners. That is, we need to observe how, within the structure of the unbalanced parallel between the life origins (1:5–2:52) and ministry origins (3:1–4:44) of John the Baptist and Jesus, the theme of sinfulness is introduced and elaborated: in connection with what themes and at the service of what narrative developments. Since the compositional structure invites the reader to constantly weigh the similarities and differences between the presentations of John the Baptist and Jesus,[1] attention must be paid not only to references to sin and sinners but also to their lack in places where in virtue of the overarching parallelism they would be expected. In our analysis, we will move sequentially through the story disclosing the strategies by which the text evokes for the reader the notion of sinfulness. At the end, we will consider two mutually illuminating interactions: the way in which the deployment of thus identified references to sinfulness contributes to the principal effects the preliminary narrative of Luke 1–4 has on the reader, and the way in which the principal effects color the reader's perception of sinfulness.

---

[1] For a detailed parallel disposition of the text of Luke 1–2 and Luke 3–4, see §1.5.

# 2.1. References to Sin and Sinners in the Infancy Narrative of Luke 1–2

## 2.1.1. John's Birth Announced (1:5–25)

Beginning with Lk 1:5, the readers, persuaded by an elevated style of the preface (1:1–4) to expect a work of Hellenistic historiography,[2] find themselves instead in a distinctively Jewish story-world that now will appropriate the Hellenistic historiography's claim to greatness.[3] The announcement of

---

[2] As has been widely recognized, seminally by H. J. CADBURY, "Commentary on the Preface of Luke", *The Acts of the Apostles*, Vol. 2. Prolegomena II: Criticism (ed. F. J. FOAKES JACKSON – K. LAKE) (The Beginnings of Christianity 1; London 1922) 489–510, the style, content, and formal organization of the preface aligns it with the works of Hellenistic historiography. While other types of resemblance can be detected in the preface, such as, for example, the features of a technical/scientific work [see L. ALEXANDER, *The Preface to Luke's Gospel*. Literary Convention and Social Context in Luke 1,1–4 and Acts 1,1 (MSSNTS 78; Cambridge 1993) 103–105], the dominant features of the preface – it is a narrative (διήγησις) about past events (περὶ τῶν...πραγμάτων) – make its affinity with Hellenistic historiographical style unmistakable. Cf. Dionysius Halicarnassus, *Ant. rom.* I,7.4 (...περὶ τίνων ποιοῦμαι πραγμάτων τὴν διήγησιν...); Josephus, *Ant.* 20.157 (ἐπανήξω τοίνυν ἐπὶ τὴν τῶν οἰκείων πραγμάτων διήγησιν); in addition see J. MOLES, "Luke's Preface: The Greek Decree, Classical Historiography and Christian Redefinitions", *NTS* 57 (2011) 463; M. WOLTER, "Die Proömien des lukanischen Doppelwerks (Lk 1,1–4 und Apg 1,1–2)", *Apostelgeschichte im Kontext antiker und frühchristlicher Historiographie* (ed. J. FREY – C. K. ROTHSCHILD – J. SCHRÖTER) (BZNW 162; Berlin – New York 2009) 477; GREEN, *The Gospel of Luke*, 1–6. Scholars have attempted to narrow this broad historiographical character of the preface and to identify the kind of Hellenistic historiography that Luke-Acts resembles most. The types such as apologetic historiography [G. E. STERLING, *Historiography and Self-definition*. Josephos, Luke-Acts and Apologetic Historiography (NT.S 64; Leiden 1992) 16–19], kerygmatic history [Ó FEARGHAIL, *The Introduction*, 173–180], or biography for Luke, biography-historiography for Luke-Acts [D. FRICKENSCHMIDT, *Evangelium als Biographie*. Die vier Evangelien im Rahmen antiker Erzählkunst (TANZ 22; Tübingen 1997) 478–500] have been proposed. But these proposals result from bringing the weight of the entire Luke-Acts to bear on the understanding of the historiographical type announced in the preface. The first-time reader must limit himself or herself to the recognition of the broad historiographical convention and be ready to receive what follows in light of this historiographical expectation.

[3] MOLES, "Luke's Preface", 474–475, notes the progressive emergence of this effect in Luke-Acts: "Many commentators find the relationship between Preface and narrative problematic, on the ground that the Preface advertises a work of Classical or Hellenistic historiography, whereas the narrative is held to assume a distinctively Jewish tone and perspective. [...] Then in the narrative, while elements congenial to Classical or Hellenistic taste continue all the way through, the Classical reader (particularly the Gentile reader) progressively grasps that this Jewish-Christian perspective, which seems small and provincial, that of a mere 'corner' of the world, actually extends both to the end of the earth and to the end of time (Acts 1.8), and is therefore the greatest of all possible historical themes, indeed, a

John's birth (1:8–23), preceded by the introduction of his parents (1:5–7) and followed by the confirmation of his conception (1:24–25), depicts nothing less than God's redemptive intervention. Even though it meets with an insufficient response (Zachariah's lack of faith), God's plan moves forward inciting the reader's interest in its outcome. On the one hand, God acts on behalf of a childless couple, and thus in continuity with a known pattern.[4] On the other hand, his intervention acquires an eschatological character clearly seen in the type of relationship Luke establishes between John the Baptist and the prophet Elijah.

Eschatology is a modern theological term. It refers both to the expectation of situations and circumstances that will mark the culmination of history or the end of individual lives (a future-oriented eschatology), and to the process of fulfillment and realization of the expected realities in the present historical moment (a present-oriented eschatology).[5] The process of consummation and fulfillment, whether still awaited or already experienced, is understood to have a final character. It cannot be undone.[6] That Luke wants his readers to see God's intervention as final and decisive, that is, as eschatological, is to be inferred from the intertextual link forged in 1:16–17. Here John is related not to the Elijah narratives of the Deuteronomistc History but rather to the figure

---

very special, Christian, kind of universal history." An early indication of the transvaluation of Hellenistic history is Luke's subordination of the figure of Emperor Augustus to the workings of the divine plan of salvation. See C. BLUMENTHAL, "Augustus' Erlass und Gottes Macht: Überlegungen zur Charakterisierung der Augustusfigur und ihrer erzählstrategischen Funktion in der lukanischen Erzählung", *NTS* 57 (2011) 1–30.

[4] The motif of barrenness, as seen in the stories of Sarah (Gen 18), Rebekah (Gen 25), Rachel (Gen 30), the mother of Samson (Judg 13), and Hannah (1 Sam 1–2), is linked with the fulfillment of God's redemptive plans. "The presence of God for his people is therefore the underlying theme behind these narratives." D. W. PAO – E. J. SCHNABEL, "Luke", *Commentary on the New Testament Use of the Old Testament* (ed. G. K. BEALE – D. A. CARSON) (Nottingham 2007) 256.

[5] See J. Frey's application of this notion of eschatology to biblical studies: "[…] New Testament exegesis […] has to distinguish between two 'lines' of eschatological expressions or ideas in early Christian texts: first the reference to events, situations or circumstances that were traditionally expected in the future or linked with the end of the individual life or the end of time, and second the idea that at least some of those elements of traditional expectation are now made present or fulfilled (in Christ, in the Christian community, or the individual life of the Christian)." J. FREY, "New Testament Eschatology – An Introduction. Classical Issues, Disputed Themes, and Current Perspectives", *Eschatology of the New Testament and Some Related Documents* (ed. J. G. VAN DER WATT) (WUNT 2.R 315; Tübingen 2011), 7–8.

[6] Which, of course, does not mean that in the final situation effected by the process of eschatological consummation there is no room for change and alterations. See M. WOLTER, "Eschatology in the Gospel According to Luke", *Eschatology of the New Testament and Some Related Documents* (ed. J. G. VAN DER WATT) (WUNT 2.R 315; Tübingen 2011), 93.

of Elijah as presented in the book of the prophet Malachi. According to Malachi's widely shared prediction,[7] Elijah would return before "the great and glorious day of the Lord" (Mal 3:1,22–23 LXX), paving the way for God's final eradication of evil (Mal 3:19 LXX).[8] John is then presented as someone whose mission will initiate the realization of God's conclusive redemptive intervention. What is more, the prediction of John's mission comes from an angelic figure who "stands in the presence of God" (1:19). God is not just about to intervene through the mission of John the Baptist; he is already intervening through the mission of his angel.[9]

John's task of "turning" (ἐπιστρέφω) the people to the Lord is expressed in language used in the OT for the repentance of God's people (Deut 30:2; 1 Sam 7:3; Hos 3:5; 7:10). This "turning" is further specified in 1:17 as turning "the hearts of fathers to their children" (ἐπιστρέψαι καρδίας πατέρων ἐπὶ τέκνα) and as turning "the disobedient to the wisdom of the righteous." The former is a clear evocation of the eschatological mission of Elijah[10] described in Mal 3:23 LXX (ἀποκαταστήσει καρδίαν πατρὸς πρὸς υἱόν), and with an even more exact parallel in Sir 48:10 (ἐπιστρέψαι καρδίαν πατρὸς πρὸς υἱόν). The latter may reflect the juxtaposition of "the righteous" (δίκαιος) and "the wicked" (ἄνομος) in Mal 3:18 LXX,[11] reaffirming Malachi's prophecy as an interpretive frame for John's ministry.

Neither sin nor sinners are directly mentioned. Nevertheless, the sinfulness of the people seems to be implied. Both the language of "turning" and the context of Mal 3:19–24 LXX, where the eschatological eradication of evil, as well as the threat of destruction of the unrepentant, are mentioned, reflect the sinful condition of Israel.[12] The reader is led to conclude that God's interven-

---

[7] See, for instance, Sir 48:10; *Liv. Pro.* 21.3 (Epiphanii Recensio Altera); *4 Ezra* 6.26; *Sib. Or.* 2.187–189; cf. M. WOLTER, *Das Lukasevangelium* (HNT 5; Tübingen 2008) 80.

[8] Elijah's return precedes the fiery punishment of the wicked in *Sib. Or.* 2.285–310; it is connected with the obliteration of evil in *4 Ezra* 6.27–28.

[9] Angelic appearance (1:11), renewal of prophecy (1:17), and activity of the Holy Spirit (1:15) signal end-time anticipation. For a detailed discussion of the eschatological character of the birth narrative, see J. B. CHANCE, *Jerusalem, the Temple, and the New Age in Luke-Acts* (Macon, GA 1988) 49–56.

[10] As W. WINK, *John the Baptist in the Gospel Tradition* (MSSNTS 7; Cambridge 1968) 43 observes, "the reference to Mal. 4:5f. is unmistakable, yet Luke resists identifying John as Elijah *redivivus* who will restore all things; he will only be *like* Elijah, i.e. a mighty prophet of repentance." For an overview of the current discussion on John-Elijah association, see J. RINDOŠ, *He of Whom It Is Written. John the Baptist and Elijah in Luke* (ÖBS 38; Frankfurt am Main 2010) 16–27.

[11] GREEN, *The Gospel of Luke*, 77.

[12] PAO – SCHNABEL, "Luke", 258. See also J. A. FITZMYER, *The Gospel According to Luke I–IX.* Introduction, Translation, and Notes (AncB 28; New York 1981) 326, who sees a possible echo of Mal 2:6 (καὶ πολλοὺς ἐπέστρεψεν ἀπὸ ἀδικίας) in Lk 1:16 (καὶ πολλοὺς ... ἐπιστρέψει). This possibility creates intertextual resonances between the

tion, in general, and John the Baptist's mission, in particular, are to address the sinful state of the people of Israel.

### 2.1.2. Jesus' Birth Announced (1:26–38)

References to sin and sinners are absent from the parallel annunciation of Jesus' birth (1:26–38), a scene that affirms Jesus' higher status as divine son and Davidic king, while depicting Mary's readiness to collaborate with God's plan. That Mary's child will reign over the house of Jacob *for ever* (εἰς τοὺς αἰῶνας) and that of his kingdom there will be *no end* (οὐκ ἔσται τέλος) further confirms the final, eschatological character of God's intervention.

### 2.1.3. Meeting of the Mothers (1:39–56)

The subsequent meeting of the mothers (1:39–45) brings about the first exercise of John's prophetic ministry: his leaping in Elizabeth's womb is interpreted by his Spirit-filled mother as joy over the coming of the Lord, Mary's unborn child.[13] If God's purpose is to address the sinful state of his people, Mary's unborn son is now recognized as an agent of God's intervention. How that intervention is to be understood will now be pronounced by Mary.

In the unfolding of Luke 1–2, in which what is announced (John's birth in 1:5–25; Jesus' birth in 1:26–38) will quickly come to be fulfilled (their births and namings in 1:57–66 and 2:1–21 respectively), Luke suspends the flow of narration and shifts to a poetic mode of expression. He allows Mary, Zechari-

---

"iniquities" referred to in Mal 2:6, the sinful condition of Israel painted in Mal 4, and the presumed sinful state of the addressees of John's mission described in Lk 1:16–17.

[13] As Green accurately observes, "even from the womb he prophesies, implicitly transferring the designation of 'Lord' to Mary's unborn baby, recognizing in this baby the eschatological coming of God" (GREEN, *The Gospel of Luke*, 95). Green's observation harmonizes well with what K. A. KUHN, "The Point of the Step-Parallelism in Luke 1–2", *NTS* 47 (2001) 38–49, considers to be the main Christological point of the step parallelism of Luke 1–2. Kuhn states: "Yahweh, rather than Jesus, is the express subject of John's preparatory role. It is only by implication developing throughout the following narrative – and largely through the step-parallelism Luke composes – that the evangelist indicates that Jesus is (also) the one for whom John prepares" (*ibid.* 42). For a detailed discussion of the narrative effects produced by Luke's use of the term κύριος in reference to Jesus in 1:43 see C. K. ROWE, *Early Narrative Christology. The Lord in the Gospel of Luke* (BZNW 139; Berlin – New York 2006) 34–49, particularly his statement: "Taking into account Luke's frequent use of κύριος for the God of Israel (both within and outside of biblical citations) and the movement of the Lukan narrative, it becomes possible to draw the conclusion that the dramatic moment of 1:43 in the narrative bespeaks a kind of unity of identity between YHWH and the human Jesus within Mary's womb by means of the resonance of κύριος" (*ibid.* 45). For an argument that Mary is indeed pregnant in the scene of Visitation, see G. NASSAUER, "Gegenwart des Abwesenden. Eidetische Christologie in Lk 1.39–45", *NTS* 58 (2012) 69–87, especially 75–80.

ah, and later Simeon, to become interpreters of the events being fulfilled.[14] As we shall see, there will be a notable progression in the themes foregrounded by the three[15] canticles. In the *Magnificat*, God will be celebrated as the one who has shown himself as a Savior; in the *Benedictus*, John the Baptist's mission will be inscribed into God's salvific plan; in the *Nunc Dimittis*, the spotlight will be directed to Jesus as the embodiment of God's salvation.[16]

Mary's song of praise centers on God.[17] Her word of praise (46b–47) is followed by the reasons for praise. The reasons are God's actions toward Mary (48–49a), toward groups of people – the proud, the powerful, the lowly, the hungry, the rich (51–53) – and toward Israel (54–55). Thus Mary's (τῆς δούλης αὐτοῦ) own experience of God's action appears as emblematic of Israel's (παιδὸς αὐτοῦ) experience of God's graciousness.

For Mary, God is a savior who acts in a warrior-like fashion against the proud, powerful, and rich. He acts out of covenantal mercy for the lowly; both Mary and Israel are beneficiaries of his acts. Are the proud, powerful, and rich to be considered sinners? Or is sinfulness rather to be ascribed to Israel, in continuity with the idea of the sinful condition of Israel implied in the announcement of John's birth? The text does not move along the lines of thought pondered by these questions. There is no interest in making the category of sin into a dominant characteristic of either those whom God resists or those he favors. What is central, instead, is the opposition between the categories of power and privilege on the one hand, and lowliness and hunger on the other. This opposition is not at the service of a reversal where the lowly would simply take the place of the powerful; it rather points to the efficacy of God's covenantal mercy in transforming the social order as a whole.[18] Mary's

---

[14] R. C. TANNEHILL, "The Magnificat as Poem", *JBL* 93 (1974) 265, captures well the effect created by the poetic interruptions of the narrative flow: "Viewed in its narrative context, the Magnificat is like an aria in opera. The artistic conventions of opera allow the composer to stop the action at any point so that, through a poetic and musical development exceeding the possibilities of ordinary life, a deeper awareness of what is happening may be achieved."

According to T. KAUT, *Befreier und befreites Volk*. Traditions- und redaktionsgeschichtliche Untersuchung zu Magnifikat und Benediktus im Kontext der vorlukanischen Kindheitsgeschichte (BBB 77; Frankfurt am Main 1990) 96, the poetic passages perform a meta-syntax function in narration: far from being only loosely connected with narrated events, they offer poetic-theological condensation of these events.

[15] Hymnic properties and structure can be discerned also in the Angel's Song in 2:14.

[16] GARCÍA SERRANO, *The Presentation in the Temple*, 247.

[17] "Es gibt [...] nach der doxologischen Redeeröffnung (V. 46b.47) und wiederum mit Ausnahme von 48b kein Prädikat, dessen Subjekt nicht Gott (bzw. Sein Name und sein Erbarmen [49b.50]) ist." WOLTER, *Das Lukasevangelium*, 100.

[18] As GREEN, *The Gospel of Luke*, 105, correctly observes, when God acts on behalf of the lowly "this is not to obliterate the powerful so that the lowly can achieve the positions of honor and privilege to which they previously had no access. Rather, God is at work in

song makes God's mercy into an interpretive key of God's redemptive intervention. As the addressees of God's action were first indirectly characterized
as sinful, now God's action is characterized as merciful.

### 2.1.4. Birth of John and Praise of Zachariah (1:57–80)

The first time the reader is directly confronted with the notion of sin is in
1:77, that is, in the prophetic song of Zachariah. Mary's song was pronounced when the first signs of the fulfillment of God's promises – the conceptions of John and Jesus – had taken place. Zachariah sings God's praise
following the birth of his son. As the fulfillment of God's promises advances,
God's purpose becomes more clearly defined. The Song as a whole moves
from the proclamation of God's visitation (68–75) – described in past tense
with Exodus typology (liberation for the sake of serving God) and a Davidic
agent of deliverance – to the anticipation of God's further acts (76–79) – described in future tense with terms evocative of Jeremiah's promise of forgiveness (Jer 31:31–34) and Isaianic language of revelatory light (Isa 42:6;
49:6; 60:1,19).[19] The future-oriented part of the Song specifies the roles that
John (76–77) and "the dawn from on high" will play in the unfolding of
God's plan.

In the first part of the Song, Zachariah, like Mary, recognizes in the recently transpired events God's acts of covenantal mercy aimed at the redemption
and salvation of his people, the central act being the raising of "a horn of salvation" in the house of David (1:69). The enemies (1:71,74), from whose
hands God saves, are identified as "all who hate us" (1:74). It is significant
that despite frequent identification of enemies with sinners, particularly in the
Psalms,[20] Zachariah's song does not exploit this connotation. Instead,[21] it
reverts to the language of sin in 1:77, that is, while describing the effects of
John's mission on God's people.

---

individual lives (like Mary) and in the social order as a whole in order to subvert the very
structure of society that supports and perpetuates such distinctions."

[19] See the discussion of the poem's structure in GREEN, *The Gospel of Luke*, 112–114.

[20] For identification of an enemy (ἐχθρός) with a sinner (ἁμαρτωλός) see LXX Ps
36:20; 54:4; 67:2–3. For an enemy as synonym of someone unjust (ἄδικος) and deceitful
(δόλιος) see LXX Ps 42:1–2; for enemies as workers of lawlessness (ἀνομία) see LXX Ps
58:2–3; 63:2–3; 91:10; for enemies as those who do evil (πονηρεύομαι) see LXX Ps 63:2–
3; 91:9.

[21] On how the gospel narrative anchors itself in canonical scripture, receiving weight
and legitimacy from it, and how at the same time it differentiates from the Hebrew Bible in
order to present unprecedented modes of relationship between God and his people, see B.
FISCHER, "Dialogic Engagement between the Birth Stories in Luke 1 and 2 and selected
Texts from the Hebrew Bible: A Bakhtinian Investigation", *Scriptura* 94 (2007) 128–142.

When Zachariah describes John's mission, he first reaffirms John's prophetic ministry of preceding the Lord and preparing his way.[22] Then he specifies John's mission. John is "to give knowledge of salvation to his people by the forgiveness of their sins" (1:77). On the one hand, John's ministry has already been described as a mission of effecting repentance, and thus its orientation toward forgiveness of sins seems natural.[23] On the other hand, not much beyond that can be said. Zachariah's lyrical statement offers no precise description of how forgiveness is to be imparted. Syntactically, ἐν ἀφέσει ἁμαρτιῶν can complement τοῦ δοῦναι or σωτηρίας.[24] If the granting (τοῦ δοῦναι) of knowledge of salvation is done by means of the forgiveness of sins, then John's ministry must be seen as mediating forgiveness of sins. If, however, ἐν ἀφέσει ἁμαρτιῶν modifies salvation (σωτηρίας), then John mediates not forgiveness but knowledge of salvation, though it is still the knowledge of that salvation which consists in the forgiveness of sins. Depending on how theoretical ("knowing that") or practical ("experiencing") this knowledge is, John's task can range from making people know that salvation comes from forgiveness to making people experience salvation through forgiveness.[25] This ambiguity beckons for explanation. What is more, John is not the "horn of *salvation*," nor is he "the light from on high," so the precise relationship between the intended result – people's experience of salvation through forgiveness of sins – and the ministries of the one who prepares the Lord's ways (ὁδούς) and the one destined "to guide our feet into the way (εἰς ὁδόν) of peace" remains unclear.[26] What is clear is that Lk 1:77

---

[22] Zachariah's words in 1:76 recall and confirm Gabriel's announcement in 1:17: προφήτης ὑψίστου recalls ἐν πνεύματι καὶ δυνάμει Ἡλίου, while προπορεύσῃ γὰρ ἐνώπιον κυρίου ἑτοιμάσαι ὁδοὺς αὐτοῦ recalls προελεύσεται ἐνώπιον αὐτοῦ ... ἑτοιμάσαι κυρίῳ λαὸν κατεσκευασμένον.

[23] According to WOLTER, *Das Lukasevangelium*, 116, "giving knowledge" corresponds to "turning" people to the Lord (1:16), that is, it functions as a notion of conversion.

[24] NAVE, *Repentance in Luke-Acts*, 33, opts for the former when he translates 1:77 as: "to give knowledge of salvation to his people by means of the remission of their sins." Most commentators, however, postulate the latter. See D. L. BOCK, *Luke* (BECNT 3; Grand Rapids, MI 1994) I, 190; BÖHLEMANN, *Jesus und der Täufer*, 26; H. KLEIN, *Das Lukasevangelium* (KEK 1/3; Göttingen 2006) 125; H. MARSHALL, *The Gospel of Luke. A Commentary on the Greek Text* (NIGTC; Grand Rapids, MI 1978) 93; H. SCHÜRMANN, *Das Lukasevangelium*. Kommentar zu Kap. 1,1–9,50 (HThK 3/1; Freiburg 1969) 91, n. 69; TAEGER, *Der Mensch und sein Heil*, 32, n. 111; WOLTER, *Das Lukasevangelium*, 116.

[25] See SELLNER, *Das Heil Gottes*, 55–56.

[26] For FITZMYER, *Luke*, I, 386, "John's role here is cast in terms of the effect of the Christ-event itself, and John is thus portrayed as spreading salvation in a form that will be characteristic of Jesus' role." But this ignores the sequential nature of reading; the meaning developed later for the salvation through forgiveness of sins in the ministry of Jesus cannot be projected back into an earlier stage. We shall see that the missions of John and Jesus will reveal different configurations of salvation-forgiveness relationship. Jesus' ministry will be similar but not identical to John's.

confirms the link between salvation and forgiveness of sins.[27] Now both John
and Jesus need to enact it and thereby elucidate its nature by means of their
respective ministries.

### 2.1.5. Birth of Jesus and Jesus in the Temple (2:1–50)

The parallel accounts of birth, circumcision, naming, and prophetic response
to Jesus (2:1–39) reaffirm his superior status:[28] he is savior, messiah, and the
Lord (2:11). His mission has a universal reach (2:30–32).[29] But it will not be
universally accepted: he will be opposed and will cause the falling and the
rising of many in Israel (2:34). Could moral failure, that is, sin, be intended
here by the language of falling (πτῶσις)?

The verb "to fall" (πίπτω) is certainly capable of designating a moral failure.[30] In addition, the context in which this word appears here – Jesus is destined to be a sign that will be opposed, with the effect that "the inner thoughts
of many will be revealed" (2:35) – suggests that it is because of opposition to
Jesus that the fall will take place. Thus the pairing of ideas – opposition to
Jesus being the cause of a fall and the resulting revelation of anti-Jesus intentions – can potentially refer to those who by opposing Jesus prove themselves
to be sinners. But we need to follow the subsequent narrative to see if this
potentiality is realized, if those who oppose Jesus are characterized as sin-

---

[27] Scriptural allusions in this passage have been noted. MARSHALL, *The Gospel of Luke*,
93 states: "Thus Je. 31:34 with its promise of knowledge of God and forgiveness is fulfilled." SCHÜRMANN, *Das Lukasevangelium*, I, 91, n. 71, sees the reference to Jer 31:34
only as a possibility. A less widely discussed OT text echoed in the Benedictus is Mic 7:8–
20. R. J. DILLON, "The Benedictus in Micro- and Macrocontext", *CBQ* 68 (2006) 470,
points to the following cluster of ideas common to Micah 7 and Lk 1:68–79: "God's oath
to Abraham and the ancestors (the last words of the prophecy, Mic 7:20), God's compassionate forgiveness of people's sins (7:18–19), the rout of their enemies (7:10, 16–17), and
– especially noticeable – God's bestowal of light on the one who 'sits in darkness' (7:8–
9)."

[28] Jesus' superior status does not take away from John's greatness. It rather assumes it.
See Verheyden's perceptive statement: "[...] the one principle that seems to dominate the
whole of the Infancy Narrative, as told in Luke 1–2, could be formulated as follows: the
greater the first, the greater still the second." J. VERHEYDEN, "Creating Difference
Through Parallelism: Luke's Handling of the Traditions on John the Baptist and Jesus in
the Infancy Narrative", *Infancy Gospels*. Stories and Identities (ed. C. CLIVAZ – A. DETT-
WILER – L. DEVILLERS – E. NORELLI) (WUNT 281; Tübingen 2011) 160.

[29] That the Presentation in the Temple (2:22–39) constitutes a climax of a cumulative
characterization of Jesus in Luke 1–2 is demonstrated by GARCÍA SERRANO, *The Presentation in the Temple*, 211–261. He calls it "the broadest and most complete characterization
of Jesus" (*ibid.* 261).

[30] Moral overtones can be detected in the language of falling in Prov 24:16 and Sir 1:30.
They are more clearly present in *T. Gad* 4.3 as well as in Heb 4:11 and Rom 11:11.

ners.[31] The story being told so far has not described anyone who would oppose Jesus. And those who oppose God – the proud, powerful, and rich mentioned in the *Magnificat*, as well as the enemies described in the *Benedictus* –
have not been categorized as sinners. Thus, in the present context the "falling" as contrasted with "rising" is best understood in a broad sense of destruction, failure, or change for the worse. Jesus is thus destined to perform a
type of action (lifting up and bringing down) that has been attributed to God
in 1:52.[32]

To recapitulate, the reader of Luke 1–2 is placed in the midst of the events
that both initiate God's final redemptive intervention and provoke various
degrees of human collaboration (Zachariah, Mary). God's action, grounded in
his covenantal mercy and aimed at fulfilling ancient promises, brings about
the birth of God's agent, designated as savior, messiah, and the coming Lord.
As the story progresses and as the first prophetic announcements come to be
fulfilled, the reader's interest in the final outcome of God's redemptive intervention becomes inextricably bound with the person and mission of God's
agent. The story of God's action becomes the story of God's agent. The reader's interest in Jesus is heightened by the prophetic foretelling of the opposition and conflict God's agent will have to face (2:34). Finally, the fact that
even Mary, a privileged recipient of angelic and Spirit-inspired revelations
about Jesus, struggles to understand the mystery of her son (2:50) demonstrates that God's normative point of view, made manifest now in and
through Jesus, is not easily perceptible. God's intervention and the human
capacity to grasp it are at odds.

It is within this large frame of the reader's exposure to God's action,
God's agent, and the human responses they elicit, that the theme of sinfulness
is first introduced and then elaborated. As we have seen, the literary trait of
sinfulness enters the fabric of the narrative world at the very beginning of the
story, but in an indirect way. Its emergence in the consciousness of the reader
is prompted by the intertextual link with Malachi's vision of the eschatological mission of Elijah. The reader is led to assume that the addressees of God's

---

[31] Similarly, whether the falling and the rising refer to successive experiences of the
same group, or designate disjunctively two different categories of Jesus' addressees, can be
answered only from the vantage point of the entire story of Luke-Acts.

[32] When F. BOVON, *Luke 1. A Commentary on the Gospel of Luke 1:1–9:50* (tr. C. M.
THOMAS) (Hermeneia; Minneapolis, MN 2002) 104, considers Isa 8:14 as a possible OT
background of Lk 2:34, he postulates a similar transposition of activity from God to Jesus,
although from a different interpretive angle. He states: "Though Isa 8:14 is not cited, as
often in these chapters it remains in the background. According to Isa 8:18, the prophet
and his children will become signs and portents in Israel. Thus the image of falling and
rising is also inspired by Isaiah 8; there (8:14) God himself reveals both through the sign
of his prophets. In Luke, Jesus plays both the roles of the prophetic sign (Isa 8:18) and of
the divinity himself (8:14)."

redemptive intervention are in a sinful state. This assumption is affirmed when in 1:77 an explicit link is forged between the sinful condition of the people and the salvation to be prepared by John and worked out by Jesus.

Sinfulness as a literary characteristic is predicated of the people in general. No detailed descriptions of concrete sins are given. As a literary characteristic, however, it occupies a crucial place: it is not predicated of those who are depicted as God's opponents; on the contrary, it is predicated of those who are depicted as addressees of God's redeeming action, including his agent's action. The reader expects to see how God's redeeming action will be concretely accomplished in the ministries of John and Jesus.

## 2.2. References to Sin and Sinners in the Beginnings of the Ministries of John and Jesus in Luke 3–4

Since it is less common to see the beginnings of the ministries of John and Jesus as set in the same unbalanced parallel as the beginnings of their lives, it will be beneficial to reproduce here the disposition of the text that illustrates the parallel arrangement of Luke 3–4.[33]

*Table 3:* John-Jesus parallel in Luke 3–4

| 3:2b | 'Commission' | 3:21–22 | 'Commission' |
|---|---|---|---|
| 3:2c | Son of Zachariah | 3:23–28 | Son of Joseph; genealogy |
| 3:2d | In the desert | 4:1–13 | In the desert; temptation |
| 3:3–20 | Ministry | 4:14–44 | Ministry |
| 3a | Scene of ministry | 14f,44 | Scene of ministry |
| 4–6 | Fulfills Isaian Prophecy | 18f,21 | Fulfills Isaian Prophecy |
| 7–19 | Words (Deeds implied) | 14–44 | Words and Deeds |
| 18 | εὐηγγελίζετο τὸν λαόν | 43 | εὐαγγελίσασθαί ... τὴν βασιλείαν τοῦ θεοῦ |
| 20 | ἐν φυλακῇ | 44 | ἦν κηρύσσων ... Ἰουδαίας |

The ideal reader of Luke's work has already been trained to set the portrayals of John and Jesus in comparison. This skill, firmly established by the structural arrangement of Luke 1–2, will continue to be utilized in the task of maximizing the effects Luke 3–4 is to have on the reader.

---

[33] As already pointed out in §1.5, we follow here the disposition proposed by Ó FEARGHAIL, *The Introduction*, 30.

## 2.2.1. Ministry of John the Baptist (3:1–20)

The dramatic opening phrase – "in the fifteenth year of the rein of Emperor Tiberius" (3:1a) – signals a new phase in the story.[34] The final clause of the opening sentence – "the word of God came to John son of Zechariah in the wilderness" (3:2b) – identifies John as the leading character of this new opening in the unfolding of God's plan. The intertextual echoes[35] cast John in the role of an OT prophet. John now stands ready to fulfill the prophetic mission announced in 1:16–17 and 1:76–77. Luke will summarize John's ministry, explaining its significance with the help of a direct scriptural voice (3:4–6); he will show John performing his ministry (3:7–18); finally, he will report how John's ministry comes to an end (3:19–29).

The summary characterization of John's mission in 3:3 brings the notion of sin into the center of narrative attention. John is proclaiming "a baptism of repentance for the forgiveness of sins." John's addressees, inasmuch as in need of repentance, are indirectly characterized as sinful. The forgiveness of sins, that is, the liberation from the state of sinfulness, is depicted as an expected goal of repentance.

The narrator's recourse to scriptural citation in 3:4–6 allows the authoritative voice of the Scripture to reaffirm John's preparatory role in the unfolding of God's redemptive initiative: John's ministry is part of a larger salvific plan with a universal scope ("all flesh shall see the salvation of God").[36] However, when it comes to the detailed working out of the various components of John's ministry, the narrator lets the character John describe it in direct speech. It will be from John's point of view that the relationship between the notions of ritual, repentance, judgment, and forgiveness of sins will be now elaborated in his responses to those who come to him in the desert.

John's is a future oriented ministry. He is preparing the people for God's imminent final judgment. This judgment is mentioned at the beginning of

---

[34] For other functions performed by this phrase, and in fact the entire elaborate six-part synchronism 3:1–2a, see J. A. DARR, *Herod the Fox.* Audience Criticism and Lukan Characterization (JSNT.S 163; Sheffield 1998) 139. See also D. P. MOESSNER, "'Listening Posts' Along the Way: 'Synchronisms' as Metaleptic Prompts to the 'Continuity of the Narrative' in Polybius' Histories and in Luke's Gospel-Acts. A Tribute to David E. Aune", *New Testament and Early Christian Literature in the Greco-Roman Context.* Studies in Honor of David E. Aune (ed. J. FOTOPOULOS) (NT.S 122; Leiden 2006) 129–150, especially 143–145.

[35] Formulas similar to 3:2b introduce either the entire career of a prophet or initiate a new episode in that career in Mic 1:1; Joel 1:1; Jon 1:1; Zech 1:1; Jer 1:2; Ezek 1:3; 1 Kgdms 15:10; 2 Kgdms 7:4.

[36] The "new exodus" announcement in Isa 40:3–5 follows on the mention of the undoing of Jerusalem's sin (Isa 40:2 λέλυται αὐτῆς ἡ ἁμαρτία) in view of the completion of her humiliation (ταπείνωσις). Isa 40:3–5 is then connected to the themes of forgiveness and repentance both in its original Isaianic setting and its Lukan framing.

John's speech ("wrath to come" in 3:7; "ax at the root" and "fire" in 3:9). And it is depicted again at the end of his address, but this time with identification of the coming messiah as the executor of God's judgment (baptizing "with Holy Spirit and fire" in 3:16; separating grain from chaff, and burning the chaff with "unquenchable fire" in 3:17). The interpretation of this text, however, presents certain difficulties. The interpreters disagree as to the precise meaning of the "Holy Spirit and fire" baptism – whether there is to be one spirit-and-fire baptism or rather baptism by fire and baptism by spirit. They also dispute the agent of winnowing – whether the separation of grain and chaff is done by John the Baptist or by the coming "stronger one".

When it comes to the "Holy Spirit and fire" baptism, J. D. G. Dunn represents a view according to which both the spirit and the fire apply to both the repentant and the unrepentant, bringing about the purification of the former group and the destruction of the latter.[37] Apocalyptic Judaism was familiar with the image of the eschatological fiery stream (Dan 7:10; *1 En.* 67.13; *4 Ezra* 13.10–11), with fire denoting both destruction and purification (Isa 31:9; Amos 7:4; Zech 13:9; Mal 3:2–3), or fire as an instrument of judgment destroying the wicked but sparing the righteous (*T. Isaac* 5.21–25; *T. Ab* 13.11–14); also the association of Spirit with cleansing was well established (Ezek 36:25–27; Isa 4:4; 1QS III, 6–9; IV, 21–22).[38] It would then not be unnatural to hear, with Dunn, an expectation of a fire-like Spirit performing an act that at the same time destroys the wicked and brings blessing to the repentant. What counsels against this interpretation, however, is the present context. Luke has just associated the image of fire with the notion of destruction in 3:9, and he will do it again in 3:17. When we allow the weight of this association to bear on our interpretation of the "Spirit and fire" baptism, the final destruction of the unrepentant continues to appear as brought about by the baptism of fire. Its counterpart, the Holy Spirit baptism, becomes synonymous with final salvation.

From the metaphor of baptizing with the Holy Spirit and fire, John the Baptist shifts to a series of images set in the agricultural world. He describes the work of the messiah as the clearing of the threshing floor (διακαθᾶραι

---

[37] J. D. G. DUNN, *Baptism in the Holy Spirit. A Re-examination of the New Testament Teaching on the Gift of the Spirit in Relation to Pentecostalism Today* (London ²2010) 11, states: "the most probable interpretation is that Spirit-and fire together describe the one purgative act of messianic judgment which both repentant and unrepentant would experience, the former as a blessing, the latter as destruction." Similarly M. B. TURNER, "Holy Spirit", *Dictionary of Jesus and the Gospels* (ed. J. B. GREEN – S. McKNIGHT) (Downers Grove, IL 1992) 344, who says "[...] syntactically 'Holy Spirit and fire' is probably a hendiadys (i.e., one deluge consisting of Spirit and fire; not a baptism of Spirit for the righteous and one of fire for the wicked)."

[38] See TURNER, "Holy Spirit", 344; J. D. G. Dunn, "Sprit-and-Fire Baptism", *NT* 14 (1972) 87–91.

τὴν ἅλωνα). This could be understood in two ways. If ἅλων is understood as the space in which the threshing and winnowing take place, the messiah's task would be simply to clear that space by transporting the grain and the chaff to their final destinations, to the granary and the unquenchable fire respectively.[39] In this view, John the Baptist has done the winnowing; the messiah is to perform the storing. The second possible interpretation is to take ἅλων as a figurative way of referring to the threshed grain still lying on the threshing floor. The messiah's task would be now to winnow (cleanse) what has been threshed, and then to store it. In this view, it is the messiah who does both the separation (winnowing) and the subsequent destruction of the chaff and storing of the grain. The latter view is to be preferred. John cannot speak of himself as performing the task of winnowing simply because the baptism he administers does not constitute the final ground of separation between the repentant and unrepentant. To avoid the fire (3:9,16,17) and the destruction that it connotes, fruits of repentance are necessary. Baptism is not enough.[40] Repentance must be further manifested by an upright ethical conduct.[41] It is on the basis of the ethically conceived fruits of repentance that

---

[39] So R. L. WEBB, "The Activity of John the Baptist's Expected Figure At the Threshing Floor (Matthew 3.12 = Luke 3.17)", *JSNT* 43 (1991) 103–111. Webb's argument rests heavily on his claim that πτύον must be understood as a shovel with which one stores the grain, and not as a winnowing fan (θρῖναξ) with which one winnows. *Hesychii Alexandrini Lexicon* (ed. K. ALPERS – H. ERBSE – A. KLEINLOGEL) (Sammlung Griechischer und Lateinischer Grammatiker 11/3; Berlin – New York 2005) III, 208, however, defines πτύον precisely as a winnowing fan, identical with θρῖναξ. See U. LUZ, *Matthew 1–7*. A Commentary (tr. J. E. CROUCH) (Hermeneia; Minneapolis, MN 2007) 138.

[40] The imagery of cleansing operative in the ritual of baptism makes it suitable for signifying not just ritual but also moral purification. OT texts such as Isa 1:15–17 or Ps 51:4–5,9 use the language of cleansing, a "metaphor of morality" as Neusner calls it [J. NEUSNER, *The Idea of Purity in Ancient Judaism*. The Haskell Lectures, 1972–1973; With a Critique and a Commentary by Mary Douglas (SJLA 1; Leiden 1973) 11], in the sense of removal of moral guilt. It is important to keep in mind the metaphorical character of these expressions. As KLAWANS, *Impurity and Sin in Ancient Judaism*, 36 correctly notes, in these passages it is not said that the defiling force of sin could be removed by washing. Rather, "the real key to understanding these passages is this: The hope expressed is that full atonement from sin could prove to be as easy a matter as purification from ritual impurity" (*ibid.* 36). As Klawans further notes, even ritual washing is not always immediately effective: in Lev 15:5 after ritual purification one remains impure until evening (see *ibid.* 23). On various types of immersion practiced among the Second Temple Jews, see the chapter "Immersion and Purity" in J. E. TAYLOR, *The Immerser*. John the Baptist Within Second Temple Judaism (Studying the Historical Jesus; Grand Rapids, MI 1997) 49–100.

[41] Ancient Judaism often stressed the necessity of an upright ethical conduct for the effectiveness of rituals. For Philo, the right inward state of the worshipper is the condition of God's acceptance of the sacrifice. See *Spec.* 1.191, 203–04, 275, 283–84; 2.35. Similarly, for 1QS III, 6–9, proper inner dispositions are necessary for the washing of body to be effective. Finally, in Josephus' view, John's baptism purified those who had first purified

one can, "flee from the wrath to come" (3:7) and be saved in the final judgment.[42] The separation of the grain from the chaff will be done in view of the
fruits of repentance. The winnowing and the separation it connotes cannot be
seen as already accomplished in the ministry of John the Baptist.

If "the baptism of repentance for the forgiveness of sins" (3:3) summarizes
John's preaching, the reader is now ready to see that the forgiveness of sins is
not something that occurs at baptism, since baptism is not enough to save one
from the wrath to come. The forgiveness must be rather seen as something
God grants in response to the fruits of repentance. Forgiveness is equivalent
to being acquitted from the punishment earned by sin, i.e., to being spared
from the destruction allotted in the final judgment.[43] Reversely, being forgiv-
en amounts to the allocation of salvation in the judgment to come.[44] Baptism

---

their souls. See *Ant.* 18.117. See also *Sibylline Oracles* 4.162–70 where the combined acts
of abandoning evil deeds, washing the body, praying for forgiveness, and praising God are
meant to elicit God's forgiveness. The washing of the body does not purify the heart; it
rather is a sign of repentance that elicits God's forgiveness.

[42] The rhetorical situation in which Luke places John is that of a prophet calling for repentance. The effectiveness of his preaching hinges on the realization that repentance is
still possible, that is, that the final separation has not yet taken place. If John had been
speaking to the group of his close disciples, he would have stressed the fact that they had
already been selected, and now their selection simply awaits the divine sanctioning. In
such a case, he would not be calling for repentance but for perseverance in view of the
approaching divine sanctioning of his disciples' blessed status. His rhetorical situation
would not be that of the prophet of repentance, but rather of a reassuring teacher. See the
discussion of such a possibility presented in the attempt to reconstruct the original functions of the judgment discourses of the historical John the Baptist and the historical Jesus
in M. WOLTER, "'Gericht' und 'Heil' bei Jesus von Nazareth und Johannes dem Täufer.
Semantische und pragmatische Beobachtungen", *Der historische Jesus*. Tendenzen und
Perspektiven der gegenwärtigen Forschung (ed. J. SCHRÖTER – R. BRUCKER) (BZNW 114;
Berlin – New York 2002) 382–385.

[43] As associated with the image of judgment, the idea of forgiveness of sins is expressed
here by the so-called forensic metaphor. See KLAUCK, "Heil ohne Heilung? Zu Metaphorik
und Hermeneutik der Rede von Sünde und Vergebung im Neuen Testament", 32–34, for
the discussion of the forensic paradigm of forgiveness, that is, the use of the language of
judgment, conviction, amnesty, and renouncement of punishment in reference to sin and
forgiveness.

[44] WOLTER, "'Gericht' und 'Heil' bei Jesus von Nazareth und Johannes dem Täufer",
367–368, critically appropriating the work of E. BRANDENBURGER, "Gerichtskonzeptionen
im Urchristentum und ihre Voraussetzungen. Eine Problemstudie", *Studien zur Geschichte
und Theologie des Urchristentum* (SBAB 15; Stuttgart 1993) 289–338, and K. MÜLLER,
"Gott als Richter und die Erscheinungsweisen seiner Gerichte in den Schriften des Frühjudentums. Methodische und grundsätzliche Vorüberlegungen zu einer sachgemäßen Einschätzung", *Weltgericht und Weltvollendung*. Zukunftsbilder im Neuen Testament (ed. H.-
J. KLAUCK) (QD 150; Freiburg 1994) 23–53, groups various ancient Jewish images of
judgment into two categories: the judgment of destruction and the forensically oriented
process before the judge. The former is connected with the expectation of the final destruc-

is then best understood as a prophetic sign of hoped for forgiveness to be realized in the final judgment in view of the fruits of repentance.[45] In the future oriented ministry of John, the forgiveness of sins is a future event.

In the preaching of John the Baptist, the path towards the *release* from sins (εἰς ἄφεσιν ἁμαρτιῶν) is initiated by the ritual of baptism, marked by correct ethical conduct and crowned by God's act of sparing the so-converted sinner from the fiery destruction. What the *sins* are is shown indirectly through the depiction of those who come to John in the desert. Behind three vignettes of John's interactions with the crowds, the tax collectors, and the soldiers (3:10–11,12–13,14), the reader finds an indirect description of sins these groups are likely to commit. Thus indifference to those who lack the essentials of food and clothing stands out as the primary fault the crowds are encouraged to rectify. John's exhortation to the tax collectors[46] in 3:13

---

tion of God's enemies (Zech 14; *As. Mos.* 10.1–10; 1QM XII, 3–16); the latter centers on the notion of allocation of condemnation and salvation to the sinners and the righteous respectively (*1 En.* 62). Both types of judgment are essentially salvific. It would be wrong to postulate any kind of contradiction between the images of God as savior and the images of God as judge. In reality, "der Richter handelt als Retter und umgekehrt; das Richten und das Retten Gottes sind 'Korrelate' ein und desselben Handelns Gottes."

[45] The fact that forgiveness of sins is to be perceived not as something realized already in the ritual of baptism but rather as a future event coinciding with God's final judgment, has been stressed by commentators. MARSHALL, *The Gospel of Luke*, 135, writes: "As a prophetic sign of what was to come, John's baptism was an effective anticipation of this future cleansing and forgiveness." Similarly, DILLON, "The Benedictus in Micro- and Macrocontext", 478, following KAUT, *Befreier und befreites Volk*, 67, observes that for Luke, "the preposition εἰς in the formula εἰς ἄφεσιν ἁμαρτιῶν expresses the 'pointing-forward' effect of John's proclamation – '*toward* the forgiveness of sins' – rather than any saving effect of what John was doing." The future aspect of forgiveness is reflected in the following comments about conversion as condition of forgiveness: "Lukas läßt Umkehr in der Verkündigung des Täufers als zu erfüllende Bedingung für eine mögliche Abwaschung der Sünden im Gericht erscheinen" [BÖHLEMANN, *Jesus und der Täufer*, 101], and "Der Gen. μετανοίας [...] qualifiziert die 'Eintauchung' als Bestandteil eines unwiederholbaren und darum eschatischen Umkehrgeschehens, das zur Vergebung der Sünden und damit zur Rettung im andringenden Zorngericht führt" [WOLTER, *Das Lukasevangelium*, 15]. For an opposing view see C. G. MÜLLER, *Mehr als ein Prophet*. Die Charakterzeichnung Johannes des Täufers im lukanischen Erzählwerk (HBS 31; Freiburg 2001) 165.

[46] Since tax collectors of the synoptic tradition did not collect direct state taxes but indirect taxes (tariffs, tolls, etc.), and since the right to collect the tolls was farmed out to individual contractors, J. R. DONAHUE, "Tax Collectors and Sinners. An Attempt at Identification", *CBQ* 33 (1971) 54, proposes to call them *toll collectors*. Similarly F. HERRENBRÜCK, *Jesus und die Zöllner*. Historische und neutestamentlich-exegetische Untersuchungen (WUNT 2.R 41; Tübingen 1990) 225, speaks of them as *Abgabenpächter*. B. D. CHILTON, "The Purity of the Kingdom as Conveyed in Jesus' Meals", *Society of Biblical Literature 1992 Seminar Papers* (ed. E. H. LOVERING) (SBL.SPS 31; Atlanta, GA 1992) 479, while commenting on Herrenbrück's suggestion, proposes to translate it as *revenue-*

– "collect no more than the amount prescribed for you" – points to extortion as their typical sin.[47] Soldiers are to temper their greed. What they are indirectly accused of is violence and false accusations.[48] The common denominator of the actions indirectly characterized as sinful is that they are violations of the rules of human relationships flowing from the nation's covenant with God (Lev 19). Such notion of sin conforms to the reader's pre-existing beliefs about sin and sinners.[49]

The prominence of the theme of sinfulness in the presentation of the ministry of John the Baptist is further highlighted by the manner in which this ministry is brought to an end. In 3:19–20 we find out that Herod is reproved by John on account of Herodias and "all the evil things he had done," to those actions being added the shutting of John in prison. John is ministering to sinners, and John is imprisoned by a sinner to whom he attempts to minister.

The compositional form of Luke 3–4, where the beginnings of the ministries of John and Jesus are set in an unbalanced parallel, prompts the reader to expect an elaboration of the theme of sinfulness in the corresponding description of Jesus' initial words and deeds.

### 2.2.2. Jesus' Commission, Genealogy, and Testing (3:21–4:13)

As "the word of God came to John" (3:2) so the direct voice of God accompanied by the bodily form of the Holy Spirit come to Jesus (3:21–22). Jesus' divine sonship is reaffirmed. It happens precisely at the moment when Jesus' submission to the baptism of repentance raises the question of Jesus' relation to repentant Israel. The prior narrative gives no grounds for assuming a need for repentance on the part of Jesus. God's complete approval of Jesus in 3:22 confirms that conclusion. In effect, Jesus' relation to repentant Israel is marked with a tension. Jesus is associated with all the people (ἅπαντα τὸν λαόν) and yet is set apart from them. He joins them in undergoing the same baptism; he is set apart by his unique affirmation as God's beloved son. Je-

---

*contractors.* We shall retain the traditional name "tax collector" while keeping in mind the distinct character of their profession.

[47] DONAHUE, "Tax Collectors and Sinners", 58, makes an important observation about Lk 3:12–13: "Not only does this text support the charge of dishonesty against the toll collectors, but it suggests that the *telōnai* are here minor functionaries in the toll farming system, rather than prime contractors. The word *diatassō* (3:13) is used often in the Lucan writings for orders a subordinate follows in performing some assigned duty and conveys the subordinate quality of the *telōnai* of this pericope."

[48] L. BRINK, *Soldiers in Luke-Acts* (WUNT 2.R 362; Tübingen 2014) 79, concludes her study of the representation of soldiers in ancient novels and satires by saying that "the most prevalent stereotype of a soldier on assignment away from his legion is that of the terrorizing brute."

[49] See the discussion of the implied reader's pre-existing beliefs about sin and sinners in §1.4.

sus' genealogy (3:23–38) draws the reader deeper into the same tension of being on the side of the people and yet set apart from them. The list of Jesus' paternal ancestors confirms his belonging to humanity as such, but it also, by invoking the sonship of Adam, the first man, points to the special status of the beloved son, Jesus.[50] This beloved son proves his allegiance to God through the series of temptations (4:1–13). An echo of Israel's desert experience of temptations and failures (Deut 6–8) contributes to the portrayal of Jesus as the one who undoes the rebelliousness of the people of Israel. The same dialectic of being part of the people (here, in virtue of undergoing the same temptations) and set apart from the people (here, in virtue of not failing the test) contains now an indirect reference to the sinlessness of Jesus and the sinfulness of the people. How the sinless one will interact with the sinful ones is the question that the inauguration of Jesus' ministry will begin to answer.

### 2.2.3. Jesus' Ministry (4:14–44)

The preliminary narrative of Luke 1–4 culminates with the description of Jesus' ministry by word and deed (4:14–44). Jesus' proclamation stands at the center of his Nazareth visit; his miraculous activity dominates his stay in Capernaum. What comes at the very beginning is Jesus' use of Isaiah. It is through the OT prophecy that Jesus conveys an authoritative understanding of his ministry in general and his stance vis-à-vis sinners in particular.

Jesus' Isaianic self-presentation is significant not just by what it takes from Isaiah but also by what it omits. What Jesus reads out loud is a conflation of 61:1a,b,d; 58:6d; 61:2a. Conspicuously missing is Isa 61:2b, "and the day of vengeance of our God." Surprisingly added is Isa 58:6d, "to send forth the oppressed in release." Thus the negative image of God's vengeance seems to be substituted by an added emphasis on release (κηρύξαι … ἄφεσιν and ἀποστεῖλαι ἐν ἀφέσει). Jesus' mission is directed to the poor, the captives, the blind, and the oppressed. It involves bringing good news to the poor and recovery of sight to the blind. But in relation to both the captives and the oppressed it involves a ministry of release (ἄφεσις). The double reference to release, a noun already used twice to convey the notion of forgiveness ("release") of sins (1:77; 3:3), invites the reader to include a reference to for-

---

[50] O'Toole's argumentation further illuminates this point: "'Of God' most directly refers to Adam as son of God; however, Adam is not the son of God as the other individuals in this genealogy are sons of their given fathers. We do not have here a Lukan presentation of Jesus as the New Adam. On the other hand, since we are dealing with Jesus' genealogy, which surprisingly is tracked back to God, Luke might intend that his reader understand 'of God' in terms of what he has written in Luke 1:35; 2:49 and 3:22 (cf. v. 23). The implication would be that 'of God' in the genealogy reminds the reader of its import in these three passages, that is, Jesus' unique relationship with God." R. F. O'TOOLE, *Luke's Presentation of Jesus. A Christology* (SubBi 25; Rome 2004) 171.

giveness of sins in the activity of releasing the captives and the oppressed. Echoes of Jubilary theology perceivable in the concept of the acceptable year (ἐνιαυτὸς δεκτός), reflect back on the category of the captives,[51] and encourage the reading of their release in terms of the jubilarian release of the imprisoned debtors. Thus the release of debts, a common metaphorical expression for the forgiveness of sins, further confirms an implicit inclusion of forgiveness of sins in Jesus' general ministry of release.[52]

---

[51] R. F. O'TOOLE, "Jesus as the Christ in Luke 4,16–30", *Bib* 76 (1995) 512–513, asserts that even though not many agree that Luke is speaking literally of the Jubilee, "most would grant that themes associated with the jubilee year appear in Luke 4:16–30." Noting how Jubilee themes rather than more literal Jubilee legislation are employed in the texts such as *Jub.* 1.21–25; *Psalms of Solomon* 11; or Dan 9:24–27, GREEN, *The Gospel of Luke*, 212, n. 33, makes a sound observation: "It seems more prudent, then, to speak of 4:18–19 as encouraging our reading of Jesus' mission against the backdrop of the theme of eschatological jubilee, but not our concluding that Luke thus develops or is controlled by a theology of Jubilee."

High prominence of the Jubilee theology in Luke is postulated by R. SLOAN, *The Favorable Year of the Lord. A Study of Jubilary Theology in the Gospel of Luke* (Austin, TX 1977). He assigns to it the function of "a paradigmatic, Old Testament *Vorbild* of the present/future eschatological salvation of God that has been inaugurated by and will be consummated through Jesus the Christ" (*ibid.* 166). See also S. H. RINGE, *Jesus, Liberation, and the Biblical Jubilee* (Overtures to Biblical Theology 19; Philadelphia 1985) 16–90. A literal understanding of the reference to a Jubilee Year is assumed in Strobel's discussion of the chronology of Jesus' visit to Nazareth. See A. STROBEL, "Die Ausrufung des Jubeljahres in der Nazarethpredigt Jesu. Zur Apokaliptischen Tradition Lc 4,16–30", *Jesus in Nazareth* (ed. W. ELTESTER) (BZNW 40; Berlin 1972) 38–50. Jesus' words and deeds are read against the backdrop of the eschatological Jubilee in J. A. SANDERS, "Sins, Debts, and Jubilee Release", *Luke and Scripture. The Function of Sacred Tradition in Luke-Acts* (ed. C. A. EVANS – J. A. SANDERS) (Minneapolis, MN 1993) 84–92; K. SUN-JONG, "Lecture de la parabole du fils retrouvé à la lumière du Jubilé", *NT* 53 (2011) 211–221.

[52] Such jubilary liberation of the captives from their sins is described in the Qumran *Melchizedek* document (11Q13). The passage draws on a Jubilee text (Lev 25:13) and Sabbatical year text (Deut 15:2) to paint a vision of eschatological release (דרור in Lev 25:10 and שמטה in Deut 15:1–2, but interestingly, ἄφεσις in the LXX translation of both texts). The release is enacted by Melchizedek. It is a release from iniquities: ויקרא להמה דרור לעזוב להמה] משא [כול עוונותיהמה; "and liberty shall be proclaimed to them, to free them from [the debt of] all their iniquities;" 11Q13 II, 6 [text and translation from F. GARCÍA MARTÍNEZ – J. C. TIGCHELAAR – A. S. VAN DER WOUDE, "11 QMelchizedek", *Qumran Cave 11.II: 11Q2–18, 11Q20–31* (DJD 23; Oxford 1998) 221–233]. Isa 61:1–2 is not explicitly cited, but as J. S. BERGSMA, *The Jubilee from Leviticus to Qumran. A History of Interpretation* (VT.S 115; Leiden 2007) 282, demonstrates, it "clearly lies behind the *pesher* of lines 4–6." See also M. MILLER, "The Function of Isa 61:1–2 in 11Q Melchizedek", *JBL* 88 (1969) 467–469. J. A. SANDERS, "From Isaiah 61 to Luke 4", *Luke and Scripture. The Function of Sacred Tradition in Luke-Acts* (ed. C. A. EVANS – J. A. SANDERS) (Minneapolis, MN 1993) 46–69, notes an important difference between 11QMelch and Luke. While in 11QMelch, those to be released "are the in-group or Essenes, Jesus' citation of the gracious acts of Elijah and Elisha toward the Sydonian widow

The compositionally sustained dynamic of comparison between John and Jesus materializes now in a simple question: if John ministered to sinners by calling them to repentance, how is Jesus' ministry to them similar or different from John's? The Lukan summary of John's preaching in 3:3 made it clear that his was a ministry directed to the forgiveness of sins (εἰς ἄφεσιν ἁμαρτιῶν). In Jesus' inaugural sermon, references to forgiveness of sins are present, but only implicitly. They are imbedded, so to speak, in Jesus' general ministry of release. Thus the notion of forgiveness of sins, with its concomitant understandings of sin, sinners, and conversion, must be understood only in and through a larger project foregrounded in that scene, namely, that of proclaiming the good news of release to the poor, the captives, the blind, and the oppressed. The following points of contrast with John's preaching highlight the specificity of Jesus' mission to the poor in general and to those captive to sin in particular:

a) John points to the future; Jesus brings fulfillment "today" (4:21).
b) John speaks of release from sins in the approaching fiery judgment; Jesus proclaims the year of favor, suppressing the reference to God's vengeance in his Isaianic quote.
c) John points towards the coming one who will punish the unconverted; Jesus comes with a message of release to the imprisoned and oppressed.
d) John demands fruits of repentance; Jesus speaks of the fruits of his own ministry of release.

The contours of the larger project of Jesus frame the issue of forgiveness of sins in a new way. The specific working out of this new way of handling sin and sinners will begin with the calling of the first sinner in Lk 5:1–11. However, before Jesus meets the first sinner, he enacts the Nazareth program in the immediately following sequence of episodes at Capernaum (4:31–44). There, the first captive to be released is a man possessed by an unclean demon (4:33). Subsequently, Jesus heals Simon's mother-in-law by setting her free from a high fever (4:38–39). Finally, at the end of his day in Capernaum, Jesus performs numerous healings and exorcisms (4:40–41). Thus demonic possession and physical illness stand as the primary forces by confronting which Jesus demonstrates his power to bring release.[53] This demonstration of

---

and the Syrian leper shows that [...] the words meaning poor, captive, blind, and oppressed do not apply exclusively to any in-group but to those to whom God wishes them to apply" (*ibid.* 62).

[53] G. E. RICE, "Luke 4:31–44: Release For the Captives", *AUSS* 20 (1982) 23–28, sees illness as an instrument of Satan and, consequently, treats healings and exorcisms as acts of release from Satan's power. Rice bases his argument on the fact that Jesus rebuked (ἐπετίμησεν) both the demon (4:35) and the fever (4:39). But the parallelism of expressions used here for the healing and the exorcism is not meant to suggest that illness and

Jesus' power of release further highlights the same points of contrast we have already noted between John's and Jesus' ministries. Jesus' program has a larger scope than that of John's ministry or, for that matter, than the kind of messianic program John's ministry would prompt the reader to expect. Jesus does not limit himself to announcing the hoped for forgiveness of sins for those who have produced the fruits of repentance. He brings release "today" and from various oppressive forces. That is not to say that the problem of sin is dismissed. It is framed in a new way.

## 2.3. The Theme of Sinfulness and the Likely Effects of Luke 1–4

Clearly, the preliminary narrative of Lk 1:5–4:44 aims at introducing the protagonist, Jesus, both in terms of who he is and what he is to accomplish. The wealth of information provided in Luke 1–4 forms an impressive portrayal of Jesus' person and mission. Jesus is described as king (1:27,32–33; 2:4; 3:31), messiah (2:11,26; 3:15–16; 4:41), anointed prophet (4:18), comparable to other prophets (4:24–27), savior (2:11), Son of God (1:35; 3:22; 4:3,9,41), and teacher (2:46–47; 4:15,31,32). He enjoys all the necessary endorsements of the heavenly figures (1:30–33,35; 2:10–12), including the heavenly Father (3:22), to whom he proves completely loyal in the midst of diabolic temptations (4:1–13). His mission will be universal (2:30–32; 3:6, and more subtly 3:23–38; 4:25–27), although it will not be universally accepted (2:34–35; 4:29).[54] Such titles and themes, including the paradigmatic reactions of acceptance and rejection, will be picked up and developed by the narrative to follow. In this sense Luke 1–4 truly foreshadows and anticipates all the major developments of the narrative of Luke-Acts. But the cumulative power of

---

demonic possession stem from the same satanic power. Rather, this parallelism serves to demonstrate that the same powerful word of Jesus (4:32,36) causes a release from both types of evil, the illness and the satanic possession. Cf. WOLTER, *Das Lukasevangelium*, 204.

[54] This list does not exhaust the themes present in Luke 1–4. Ó FEARGHAIL, *The Introduction*, 150, while listing well-known themes such as "the Spirit, salvation, joy, repentance, the fulfillment of the promise, the kingdom of God, the divine 'must,' Israel and its divided response, the Gentiles and their paraenetic use in warning Israel, the poor, the temple" notes that other themes such as "prayer (cf. 1,10; 2,36–38; 3,21), peace (cf. 1,79; 2,14–29), compassion (cf. 4,33–36.38–41), social justice (cf. 3,10–14), Jerusalem (cf. 1,5–2,52; 4,12), and the way (cf. 4,30) are also found in these chapters." What is not found is the relationship between Jesus and his disciples, something that will begin in the narrative proper and continue as an organizational principle of that narrative. But note that it is mentioned in Luke's proemium in the reference to "eyewitnesses and ministers of the word." See *ibid.* 152, n. 229.

different traits of Jesus scattered throughout Luke 1–4, and the anticipatory potential of literary and theological themes developed in Luke 1–4, do not exhaust the effects Luke 1–4 has on the reader. As we attend to sequences and compositional structures by which Luke controls his presentation of the themes and characteristics of Jesus, an additional effect is revealed. The reader is not just informed about Jesus. The reader is maneuvered into perceiving Jesus as the authoritative source of information. Let us briefly retrace the narrative strategy responsible for this effect.

Jesus is a static character, but his characterization is remarkably dynamic. In Luke 1–4, other than the growth from childhood to adulthood, Jesus does not develop. But the reader's acquaintance with him constantly does.[55] As we have seen, by the end of Luke 2, God's eschatological intervention is firmly tied to his agent Jesus. The story of God's action becomes the story of God's agent.[56] In Luke 3–4, the reader's perception of the contours of Jesus' mission (a functional equivalent of God's eschatological intervention) is formed in and through the comparison with John. The parallelism between John and Jesus culminates and intensifies with the parallelism between their respective ministries. It is an unbalanced parallel. What Jesus does both corresponds and differs from what John is doing. But there is more at stake here. The discrepancy between John and Jesus extends to the discrepancy between John's expectation of Jesus' mission and the actual realization of this expectation. There is no linear continuity between John's and Jesus' ministries.[57] John

---

[55] I am paraphrasing here Sternberg's elegant conclusions reached at the end of his analysis of the effects the temporal ordering of Homer's presentation of Odysseus has on the reader. Sternberg notes how Homer's presentation gradually progresses "from a stock-response to an idealized portrait of a conventional hero to a highly complex, subtly balanced valuation of a unique character." Sternberg concludes: "Odysseus is a static character, but his characterization is remarkably dynamic. He does not develop in the course of the action, but the reader's acquaintance with him incessantly does." STERNBERG, *Expositional Modes*, 128.

[56] As M. B. COLERIDGE, *The Birth of the Lukan Narrative*. Narrative as Christology in Luke 1–2 (JSNT.S 88; Sheffield 1993) 203–204, aptly observes, "as the initiative passes to Jesus, the OT citations and echoes dwindle to almost nothing, and the language becomes less heavily semitized. As Jesus comes to a language of his own, the language of the past becomes more muted."

[57] Against NAVE, *Repentance in Luke-Acts*, who notices only elements of continuity between the ministries of John and Jesus. See *ibid.* 166,169,174–5. It appears that for Nave it is the same concept of repentance that comes to light in the preaching of John the Baptist and Jesus. A similar outlook dominates in MÉNDEZ-MORATALLA, *The Paradigm*. Méndez-Moratalla contends that underneath various conversion stories in Luke there is a Lukan paradigm of conversion. None of the stories is paradigmatic, but "there is a certain number of elements present in most conversion stories. Each individual element of the pattern is not a sufficient description of the process, so that it is in its totality and interdependence that these elements are to be considered" (217). As he analyzes the stories, Méndez-Moratalla sees the elements of *the same paradigm* in the ministry of John the Baptist (3:1–

points to Jesus (3:16–17); there is no doubt about that. But the expectations he has, such as that of an immediate judgment, are largely frustrated.[58] Not even John is capable of adequately describing the mission of Jesus. The normative interpretation of Jesus' mission can come only from Jesus. The comparative strategy of Luke 1–4 not only sharpens our understanding of various titles given to Jesus, but also effects the realization that Jesus is the only one capable of revealing the true meaning of those titles.[59]

The way the references to sinfulness function within Luke 1–4 conforms to and further illuminates this dynamic. The theme of sinfulness was first revealed in Gabriel's announcement of John's birth as a condition to be addressed by the divine eschatological intervention. Forgiveness of sins was prophetically proclaimed by Zechariah to be an outcome of John's and Jesus' ministries. Sinners were finally addressed by John and promised to be addressed by Jesus. At the surface level of the text, the theme of sinfulness was prominent in the description of the mission of John the Baptist. The notion of sinfulness received there its initial shape: it was firmly established by its references to eschatology, repentance, ritual and ethical conduct, and divine forgiveness. To recover the place of sinfulness in the ministry of Jesus, our comparative look at Jesus' mission had to penetrate underneath the text, into the indirect references imbedded in Jesus' larger project of release. But in the act of presenting the shape of Jesus' mission, as the person of Jesus comes to the fore as the only one capable of authoritatively interpreting his own life (and the divine intervention which it embodies), sinfulness no longer appears simply as a problem to be addressed. The center of attention is Jesus, the mysterious agent of God who addressed sinfulness on his own terms. To use the heuristic notions of the plot of resolution and the plot of revelation,[60] sinfulness is no longer simply a problem in need of resolution, as it had appeared at the beginning of the story. As the story of God's action slowly becomes the story of God's agent, the resolution of the problem of sinfulness is

---

17) and the ministry of Jesus (5:27–32; 7:36–50; 15:11–32; 19:1–10; 23:39–43, the non-conversion of a ruler in 18:18–30).

[58] The tension between John's expectations and Jesus' actual ministry will be confirmed later in 7:18–20, when John sends two of his disciples to interrogate Jesus.

[59] COLERIDGE, *The Birth*, 187–213, contends that this effect is first realized in Lk 2:41–52, in the scene that records the very first words of Jesus. The twelve-year-old Jesus interprets his otherwise puzzling behavior in light of his unique relation to his heavenly Father. For the first time Jesus appears as an interpreter of his own person. See a similar conclusion in J. -N. ALETTI, *Le Jésus de Luc* (Jésus et Jésus-Christ 98; Paris 2010) 73: "À partir de maintenant, en effet, c'est Jésus qui va principalement développer la christologie." Regarding the scene in Nazareth, Aletti echoes the same conclusion when he describes Jesus as taking on the role of "l'unique hermenéute". See J.-N. ALETTI, *L'art de raconter Jésus Christ*. L'écriture narrative de l'évangile de Luc (Parole de Dieu; Paris 1989) 42.

[60] For more on these notions, see MARGUERAT – BOURQUIN, *How to Read Bible Stories*, 56–57; CHATMAN, *Story and Discourse*, 48.

placed at the service of revealing the one meant to solve it. As the theme of sinfulness becomes reframed, the act of reframing forcefully manifests the intriguing authority of its author. This dynamic both reveals and confirms that the theme of sinfulness is deployed in a way that structures the reader's recognition of Jesus' point of view as authoritative. What the reader understands about sinners is that he or she must discover and assimilate Jesus' perception of them. One cautionary note, however, must accompany this conclusion.

At the end of chapter 2 and twice in chapter 4, Luke presents scenes in which misunderstanding of Jesus figures prominently. Mary and Joseph "did not understand what he said to them" (2:50). Jesus' fellow Nazarenes, while astounded by his teaching, did not move beyond their preconceived perception of Jesus as the son of Joseph (4:22). The citizens of Capernaum tried to prevent him from leaving (4:42), demonstrating that they too failed to understand what his mission involved.[61] This is surprising given both the privileged information Mary had received and the fact that, unlike their counterparts in Nazareth, the citizens of Capernaum did accept Jesus. Jesus' explanation – he points to a necessity (δεῖ) in both 2:49 and 4:43 – reveals as much as it conceals[62] both to the characters in the story and to the reader. Jesus explains his actions by a reference to the necessity that only he knows and enacts.[63] The finitude of human knowledge about Jesus emerges here with new power and nuance. Mary's repeated reaction of grappling with the significance of the events[64] could be said to model an attitude which the reader is now invited to

---

[61] The importance of the theme of misunderstanding is highlighted by a logical progression discernible in its development: misunderstanding comes first from Jesus' parents, then from his extended family and neighbors in Nazareth, and finally from a larger group represented by the people of Capernaum. For an attempt to deal with the theme of misunderstanding within the entire Gospel, see B. C. FREIN, "The Literary and Theological Significance of Misunderstanding in the Gospel of Luke", *Bib* 74 (1993) 328–348.

[62] See COLERIDGE, *The Birth*, 217–218; D. GERBER, *"Il vous est né un Sauveur."* La construction du sens sotériologique de la venue de Jésus en Luc-Actes (Genève 2008) 97. The same revealing-concealing dynamic seems to be at the heart of what Sternberg calls the distance between the truth and the whole truth. See the chapter "Between the Truth and the Whole Truth" in M. STERNBERG, *The Poetics of Biblical Narrative*. Ideological Literature and the Drama of Reading (ISBL; Bloomington, IN 1987) 230–263.

[63] C. H. COSGROVE, "The Divine ΔΕΙ in Luke-Acts. Investigations into the Lukan Understanding of God's Providence", *NT* 26 (1984) 168–190, warns against downplaying the human side of the fulfillment of God's plan. "Jesus is no passive pawn of divine necessity in Luke's Gospel; he is the executor of that necessity. He initiates the temptation event by going out into the wilderness, in contrast to the Markan Jesus who is 'driven' there by the Spirit. He provokes the clash at Nazareth with all its typical overtones for the Lukan scheme" (*ibid.* 180). Jesus appears as the strategist of the divine purpose.

[64] She reasoned (διελογίζετο) 1:29; she treasured (συνετήρει) and pondered (συμ-βάλλουσα) 2:19; she treasured (διετήρει) 2:51.

adopt. The reader must keep pondering. This is more than just curiosity. This is an active struggle with incomprehension, a struggle carefully orchestrated by Jesus. We have already observed how Luke establishes Jesus' view as the only one capable of interpreting God's intervention. Now we see how Jesus' authority is both expressed and exercised in his handling of his normative view: he reveals as well as conceals, warning against any premature success in our discovery and assimilation of his view, including his view of sin and sinners.

In the unfolding of Luke 1–4, the gap between Jesus' normative view and the human ability to grasp it is not completely unexpected. In a way, it extends and modifies the basic tension inherent in the interaction between God's redemptive initiative and the human response it provokes. Beginning with the announcements of John's and Jesus' births, God's plan has met with various degrees of human readiness to collaborate. Like any withholding of information, this gap, too, will stimulate the reader's interest in the story. But for the characters in the narrated world it presents a more fundamental challenge: they must decide whether they will submit to the authority of the one who now appears to control their access to the whole truth. This challenge foreshadows the theme in the story of Jesus that is about to begin: Jesus' relationship with his disciples.

It seems instructive at this point to compare briefly the results of our analysis of Luke 1–4 with the results Mark Coleridge obtained in his narrative study of Luke 1–2. For Coleridge, "the two seminal questions generating the Lukan infancy narrative are these: how does God visit his people, and how is one to recognize his visitation?"[65] The former question represents theology, the latter epistemology. The divine visitation (the theological side of the infancy narrative) operates according to the promise-fulfillment dynamic. The human recognition (the epistemological side of the infancy narrative) is constructed along the faith-interpretation dynamic: "faith in the promises and interpretation of the signs of fulfillment."[66] Both theology (God's visitation) and epistemology (human recognition) converge in Lk 2:41–52, "where in the last episode Jesus becomes interpreter of the embryonic sign of fulfillment which he himself is."[67] Thus both fulfillment of God's promise and the interpretation of that fulfillment are performed by the person of Jesus. Lukan Christology is born.

Our study of Luke 1–4 in general and Luke 1–2 in particular agrees with Coleridge that the interplay of God's visitation and the human reception of that visitation generates the infancy narrative. To put it differently, the Lukan infancy narrative repeatedly demonstrates that God's visitation constitutes a

---

[65] COLERIDGE, *The Birth*, 23.

[66] COLERIDGE, *The Birth*, 23.

[67] COLERIDGE, *The Birth*, 24.

challenge to the human ability to recognize and accept it. In fact, the two seminal questions of which Coleridge speaks – how God visits and how it is recognized – can be reduced to one: what is the right way of recognizing God's visitation? (Recognition of God's visitation implies the recognition of *how* this visitation happens). This question reveals, as it intends to bridge, the gap between God's visitation and the human ability to grasp it. Inasmuch as Coleridge's study points to the tension between God's visitation and the human recognition of that visitation, it captures the basic engine of the Lukan plot. Coleridge, however, seems to obscure this truth when he speaks of the convergence of theology and epistemology in Lk 2:41–52. While our study agrees with Coleridge that, in the person of Jesus, God's action and the interpretation of that action converge, we find it necessary to stress that the convergence of theology and epistemology, of which Coleridge speaks in this context, is not complete. The challenge of epistemology continues in the form of the gap between Jesus' interpretation of himself (as agent of God's visitation) and the characters' and the reader's ability to grasp that interpretation.[68] The two constitutive components, God's visitation and human recognition, do not converge. They are rather reconfigured. As God's visitation becomes subsumed under Christology (Jesus as the one who fulfills the promises and interprets the fulfillment), human recognition continues its quest. In this sense, what is born at the end of the infancy narrative is not just Christology but ecclesiology: the reader's need to turn to Jesus, the faithful interpreter of God's visitation, is established.

To recapitulate, Luke's narration prompts a triple dynamic effect: the reader moves from (1) growing in the knowledge of God's agent, Jesus, through many revelatory statements about him, to (2) the realization that Jesus is the only one capable of authoritative interpretation of himself, to (3) becoming subjected to Jesus' didactic of piecemeal revelation of the truth about his redemptive mission. The reader's understanding of sinfulness becomes shaped by this triple dynamic. The reader moves from (1) perceiving the sinfulness as a condition to be addressed by God's eschatological intervention, to (2) realizing that the sinfulness can be properly perceived only from the perspective of God's eschatological agent. The story about to unfold in Lk 5:1–6:11 will be punctuated with references to sinfulness. It will provide the reader with plenty of opportunities to decipher and appropriate Jesus' view of sin.

---

[68] Coleridge is very much aware of that gap, see *The Birth*, 218, 231.

Chapter 3

# The Calling of Simon Peter (5:1–11)

Our interest in Lk 5:1–6:11, the first cycle of episodes within the narrative proper of Luke, has been triggered by the realization that the story narrated in these episodes contains multiple references to the characteristic of sinfulness. These references are both direct and indirect, the latter being not infrequently ambiguous. If, as we assume, the proper assessment of the role of sinners in Luke implies not just an examination of the pericopae containing the word sinner or its cognates but also the study of all the strategies by which the text evokes for the reader the trait of sinfulness even in the absence of its textual referent, then Lk 5:1–6:11 constitutes a promising field for examining the complexity of the Lukan portrayal of sinners. Having traced the emergence of the reader's perception of sinfulness effected by the unfolding of the preliminary narrative of Luke 1–4, we are now ready to conduct a close reading of Lk 5:1–6:11 with a view to assessing its presentation of sinners.

Our reading will be guided by the basic question: what is it that the text communicates to its reader by a frequent recourse to the characteristic of sinfulness and, intriguingly, by the ambiguity that often surrounds its correct predication? Naturally, this cannot be separated from the question of the overall meaning of Lk 5:1–6:11. The hermeneutic circle, which directs the progress of our understanding of the text, upholds the part and the whole in a mutually interpretive relationship: just as our understanding of the role of the references to sinfulness is illuminated by our comprehension of the overall narrative effects Lk 5:1–6:11 is likely to have on the reader, so our understanding of the principal effects of Lk 5:1–6:11 is sharpened by our better grasp of the function Luke ascribes to the references to sinfulness.

Faithful to our methodological presuppositions, we will move sequentially through the text of every single pericope contained in Lk 5:1–6:11. Our analysis will aim to disclose and assess all the textual strategies that prompt the reader to infer the characteristic of sinfulness, even in the absence of its direct textual referent. At the end of each pericope, and then again at the end of the entire cycle, we will ask about the relationship between the maximal realization of the strategies by which Luke evokes for the reader the notions of sin and sinners and the overall goals of his narration. Informed by our study of Luke 1–4, we begin our investigation of Lk 5:1–6:11 aware that the protagonist, Jesus, is not just an agent of God's redemptive intervention but also its authoritative interpreter prone to challenging others to struggle with their incomprehension of his normative point of view.

The reader has seen the preview of Jesus' ministry of word and deed in Lk 4:14–44. Now the first cycle of his activity begins. The first scene will bring together Jesus' words and deeds skillfully employed to forge a relationship of discipleship between Jesus and his first followers. This relationship will be sustained and developed through the rest of Luke-Acts. That the first disciple will characterize himself as a sinful man will bear on the understanding of discipleship to be advanced in the story to come. But Simon's self-characterization will first of all contribute to illustrating and advancing that which has already been announced, namely, Jesus' project of release, including the release from sin.

Our analysis of Lk 5:1–11 will be divided into three sections reflecting the three major divisions by which the dramatic tensions and movements structure and consolidate the pericope. Thus verses 1–3 will be considered together. By naming the place and introducing the personages, they create the set up of the story. Verses 4–7, describing the miraculous catch, are bound by the complication-resolution relationship. Jesus' command in 5:4 to go fishing at mid-day creates a dramatic tension: as Peter, a professional fisherman, knows, one does not fish during the day.[1] The tension becomes resolved with the miraculous catch described in 5:6–7. Verses 8–11 describe the reaction to the catch. The dramatic movement from a lack to an abundance of fish has been accomplished. What governs the progression of the plot now is a question of the identity of the one who has performed the miracle. In 5:8–11, Simon's request, Jesus' answer, and then Simon and his companions' final reactions reveal the new levels of knowledge the characters have gained at this point of the story.

---

[1] Cf. John 21:3. On the Lake of Galilee night fishing was usually better than day fishing; fresh fish could be quickly sold in the morning. See R. E. BROWN, *The Gospel According to John (XIII–XXI)*. Introduction, Translation, and Notes (AncB 29A; New York 1970) 1069. GREEN, *Luke*, 232 following D. BIVIN, "The Miraculous Catch: Reflections on the Research of Mendel Nun", *Jerusalem Perspectives* 5/2 (1992) 7–10 suggests the use of 'trammel nets' "made of linen, visible to fish during the day and so used at night, requiring two to four men to deploy, and needing washing each morning."

## 3.1. The Initial Situation (5:1–3)

A new episode in the life of Jesus is announced by the ἐγένετο+καί+finite verb[2] style of the opening verse. That Jesus is presented on the lakeshore preaching the word of God (ὁ λόγος τοῦ θεοῦ) easily harmonizes in the mind of the reader with the necessity to evangelize announced by Jesus in 4:43 (εὐαγγελίσασθαί με δεῖ τὴν βασιλείαν τοῦ θεοῦ). Without any indications to the contrary, the reader must assume that Jesus himself chose the lakeshore location out of the same divine necessity (δεῖ)[3] that motivated him to leave Capernaum (4:42–43). The genitive *of God*, whether taken as subjective (the word from God) or objective (the word about God), places the ministry of Jesus in a strictly theocentric perspective.

Unlike Jesus the protagonist, Simon is introduced indirectly. First there is the description of the scenery in which he will be encountered. The reader is presented with a lakeshore on which Jesus addresses the crowd of his listeners. Next, the reader discovers two boats and the group of fishermen washing their nets. Finally, as Jesus enters one of the boats, the narrator informs us that this boat belongs to Simon. In retrospect, it becomes clear that Simon must belong to the group of fishermen washing their nets on the shore and that, among the boats Jesus first spotted, one belonged to Simon. Two elements of Simon's characterization stand out. First of all, by introducing Simon's boat through the perception of Jesus (5:2a Jesus "saw two boats"[4]), that is, by using a *represented* point of view[5] of Jesus, the narrator hints at the

---

[2] Cf. Lk 5:12,17; 8:1,22; 9:28,51; 14:1; 17:11; 19:15; 24:4,15; Acts 5:7; 9:19. See the discussion of various types among the Lukan uses of καὶ ἐγένετο or ἐγένετο δέ in É. DELEBECQUE, "La vivante formule ΚΑΙ ΕΓΕΝΕΤΟ", *Études grecques sur l'Évangile de Luc* (Paris 1976) 123–165.

[3] See the discussion of the role of δεῖ in the context of Luke's notion of salvation-history in FITZMYER, *Luke*, I, 179–192.

[4] The importance of this action is conveyed by the fact that, syntactically, it is the real apodosis (καὶ εἶδεν...) of the opening sentence of the account; καὶ αὐτὸς ἦν ἑστὼς παρὰ τὴν λίμνην Γεννησαρέτ needs to be regarded as a circumstantial clause; see SCHÜRMANN, *Lukasevangelium*, I, 267, n. 30; MARSHALL, *The Gospel of Luke*, 201. Furthermore, DELEBECQUE, "La vivante formule ΚΑΙ ΕΓΕΝΕΤΟ", 142, observes that "L'instant d'un pareil choix, qui engage l'avenir des hommes, est d'une rare gravité. Ce n'est pas le moment pour Luc d'employer un καὶ ἰδού qui a un je ne sais quoi de trop simple, naïf, familier, pour convenir à l'occasion. Alors il bannit ἰδού au bénéfice du vrai verbe, le solennel εἶδεν, réservé pour les moments décisifs où vibre à la fois chez lui le cœur et l'esprit."

[5] Following D. MARGUERAT, "Le point de vue dans le récit: Matthieu, Jean et les autres", *Studien zu Matthäus und Johannes / Études sur Matthieu et Jean. Festschrift für Jean Zumstein zu seinem 65. Geburtstag* (ed. A. DETTWILER – U. POPLUTZ) (AThANT 97; Zürich 2009) 91–107, who in turn follows A. RABATEL, "Fondus enchaînés énonciatifs. Scénographie énonciative et point de vue", *Poétique* 126 (2001) 151–173, we distinguish

fact that it is Jesus and not Simon who initiates the chain of events leading to an encounter between the two of them. Secondly, when Simon is identified as one of the fishermen, he takes upon himself a number of characteristics proper to that profession.[6] A few pieces of information can be gleaned from the story in this regard. Since he owns a boat, Peter is not a poor fisherman.[7] Certain fishing techniques involved two boats and therefore partners.[8] It is not surprising then that Peter is seen in the company of other fishermen and that there are more boats than just one on the scene. Finally, the fact that the fishermen are washing, and not repairing,[9] their nets might function as a subtle indication that they caught nothing.[10]

When Jesus enters the boat of Simon, it seems to be simply a matter of logistics: it creates a convenient distance needed to address the crowd without being pressed by it. But since there are two boats on the shore, the choice of Simon's boat is more than just incidental. As with the glance of Jesus in verse 1, so here too the narrator indicates that Simon is sought out by Jesus for reasons that will soon become clearer. At the same time, Jesus' use of Simon's boat in 5:3, while justifying narratively the upcoming interaction between Jesus and Simon, characterizes Jesus as a resourceful preacher, not to be confounded by inhibiting circumstances (he "was standing beside the lake" and "the crowd was pressing in on him"). It also demonstrates a certain level of

---

three types of point of view: represented, recounted, and asserted. "Le PDV [point de vue] représenté est celui à partir duquel les perceptions sont véhiculées, de même que les pensées associées à ces perceptions. [... ] Le PDV raconté [...] c'est le PDV à partir duquel les événements sont abordés, mais sans qu'un verbe de perception vienne le signaler par un débrayage énonciatif ; le narrateur se contente d'empathiser par le récit sur un acteur de la scéne (je rappélle que le procédé d'empathie consiste pour le narrateur à faire partager au lecteur les sentiments ou émotions qui habitent un personnage). [...] Le PDV asserté transparaît dans le cadre des paroles et des valeurs qu'elles expriment. [...] Le PDV raconté est le type le plus effacé de représentation du PDV: le récit présente les événements d'aprés la perspective choisie (narrateur ou personnage), mais sans le signaler par le débrayage énonciatif que constitue un verb de perception. [...] À l' autre extrémité de la représentation, c'est-à-dire sur le mode le plus expressif, on trouve le PDV asserté. [...] Dans les textes narratifs, on le rencontre à chaque fois qu'un personnage parle ou que le narrateur donne son avis" (*ibid.* 101–102).

[6] For historical background regarding Palestinian fishing, see E. F. F. BISHOP, "Jesus and the Lake", *CBQ* 13 (1951) 398–414, particularly the section "How Men Fished and Fish" 400–403; W. H. WUELLNER, *The Meaning of the 'Fishers of Men'* (The New Testament Library; Philadelphia 1967) 26–63.

[7] Typically, the poorer fishermen who did not have a boat used a casting net. They operated it during the daytime standing in the shallow water near the shore. See MARSHALL, *The Gospel of Luke*, 202.

[8] BISHOP, "Jesus and the Lake", 401.

[9] See Mark 1:19.

[10] G. ROSSÉ, *Il Vangelo di Luca.* Commento esegetico e teologico (Collana scritturistica di Città Nuova; Roma 1992) 172.

authority, which Jesus already enjoys in Simon's eyes. Jesus' request to put out a little way from the shore (5:3) meets no verbal reaction from Simon. That Simon complies is not even mentioned; it is simply assumed. The seated posture of Jesus accords with his authority to teach.[11]

The crowd's attraction to Jesus is not new. The crowds looked for Jesus in 4:42, attempting to prevent his departure. They did not understand the demands of his mission then. The crowd's role continues to be somewhat ambivalent in that their pressing in on Jesus threatens to hinder his proclamation of God's word. But even this adverse aspect of the crowd's attraction to Jesus is calculated into the narrative's progression: it offers Jesus the chance to use Simon's boat. Ultimately, the presence of the crowd at the beginning of the story gives the first illustration of the power of God's word to attract listeners, that is, to catch them. The catch of fish and Jesus' prophecy about catching people alive (ζωγρέω) will function in relation to the opening scene with the crowd. The disappearance of the crowd from the rest of the story highlights the story's focus on Simon and his companions.

The narrator does not specify whether Simon, having put out a little way from the shore, remains in the boat with Jesus, or whether he goes back to his companions to continue to wash the nets with them.[12] It seems that in either case Simon is near enough to hear the teaching of Jesus. After all, when Jesus, having finished speaking to the crowd, asks him to put out into the deep water, we get the impression that Simon is near enough for Jesus to make that request. Simon himself then has been among the listeners of the word of God (5:1). He is also a firsthand witness of how the word of God attracts the crowd of listeners. The characterization of Simon with its secular, fishing related features, moves slowly into the realm of religious qualities.

## 3.2. The Miraculous Catch (5:4–7)

Jesus' command to put out into the deep and to lower the nets for a catch (Lk 5:4) puts the narrative spotlight on Simon. As the crowd recedes from the scene, Simon becomes the main recipient of Jesus' attention. Not only because it is to Simon that Jesus directs his words, but also because these words put Simon to the test.

The reader has already seen Jesus' prophetic powers manifested in Jesus' recognition of people's lack of faith in 4:23–27 and in his mastery over demons in 4:33–37. But now Jesus does something more. Before he manifests

---

[11] Cf. Lk 4:20.

[12] According to Y. MATHIEU, *La figure de Pierre dans l'oeuvre de Luc (Évangile et Actes des Apôtres).* Une approche synchronique (Études bibliques. Nouvelle série, 052; Gabalda 2004) 69, Simon stays in the boat.

his powers, he wants to elicit Simon's faith. Thus Simon's active participation is needed for Jesus' power to be manifested. Or to be more exact, Jesus decides to make his ministry depend on the collaboration of Simon. To teach the crowd Jesus needed Simon's boat. To teach Simon about his prophetic identity Jesus needs more than Simon's boat, he needs Simon's act of faith. Jesus progressively increases the measure of involvement on the part of his future Apostle.

Naturally, by asking Simon to perform a daytime catch Jesus creates a tension with which the reader is already very familiar. The preliminary narrative of Luke 1–4 has impressed awareness on the reader of the gap between Jesus' authoritative point of view[13] and the human ability to grasp it. The reader is then capable of detecting the emergence of that very tension in the command Jesus now directs to Simon. What makes this particular instance of tension even more dramatic is the fact that Jesus is not talking about God, a field in which he could be assumed to have more expertise than Simon. Jesus' command relates to mid-day fishing.

Simon has good reasons to see Jesus' command as a negative challenge to his own self-worth and self-respect as a fisherman: an experienced fisherman is told by a non-fisherman to catch fish at the time when it is not normally done, and with the crew that has just experienced failure at the more opportune period for fishing.[14] Simon's response in verse 5a ("we have worked hard all night and caught nothing") brings the challenging character of Jesus' command to the fore. In the end, however, he contrasts Jesus' command with

---

[13] As M. A. POWELL, "The Religious Leaders in Luke: A Literary-Critical Study", *JBL* 109 (1990) 100 puts it: "Jesus, of course, always evinces the evaluative point of view of God." Or to phrase it in somewhat modified Bakhtinian terms, Jesus represents an "aestheticized absolute consciousness." Cf., J. A. BARNET, *Not the Righteous but Sinners*. M. M. Bakhtin's Theory of Aesthetics and the Problem of Reader-Character Interaction in Matthew's Gospel (JSNT.S 246; London 2003) 67–75.

[14] According to the findings of cultural anthropology, public (outside of family) social interaction among members of the first-century Mediterranean world was dominated by a mutual attempt to acquire honor from one's social equal. Since honor, like all the other goods, was thought to be in limited supply, gaining honor meant depriving somebody else of honor. See B. J. MALINA – J. H. NEYREY, "Honor and Shame in Luke-Acts: Pivotal Values of the Mediterranean World", *The Social World of Luke-Acts*. Models for Interpretation (ed. J. H. NEYREY) (Peabody, MA 1993) 25–65. Social interaction, which functioned as a contest for honor, followed a form of challenge-riposte exchange. The exchange began when the source of the challenge sent a message by which he attempted to enter the social space of another, either for positive reasons, "to gain a share in that space or to gain a cooperative, mutually beneficial foothold," or negatively, "to dislodge another from his or her social space" (*ibid.* 30). Is Simon then entering a challenge-riposte exchange with Jesus? Is this interaction a contest for honor? The dialogue between Jesus and Simon appears to be headed in this direction. Nevertheless, challenge-riposte exchange can function only between the socially equal. When Simon calls Jesus *Master*, he addresses him with a title that establishes inequality and dismisses challenge-riposte encoding for their interaction.

his own experience in fishing only to emphasize that his final decision is based not on his own experience but rather on his recognition of the status of Jesus and of the power of Jesus' word.

Simon calls Jesus ἐπιστάτης, literally the one who is set over, the Master.[15] As a title addressed to Jesus, it will be later found almost exclusively on the lips of Jesus' disciples,[16] marking both Jesus' status as the group leader and their status as his followers. However, at this initial point in Jesus' relationship with his disciple-to-be, if any religious overtones are to be ascribed to this title they must be found in the connection Simon makes between Jesus as a Master and the authority of his word. In agreeing to Jesus' request, Simon bases his yes on the word of Jesus: "at your word (ἐπὶ δὲ τῷ ῥήματί σου) I will lower the nets."[17] The use of ἐπί with the dative case indicates what is the basis and the ground, that is, the reason for Simon's decision.[18] Simon acts because of Jesus' word (ῥήμα). Jesus who speaks the word of God (λόγος τοῦ θεοῦ; 5:1) is now recognized as the Master whose word (ῥήμα) can be trusted.[19] Simon, who found himself among those who listened to Jesus' proclamation of the word of God, now places his trust in Jesus' command. Simon is a disciple who listens to the word of Jesus and who acts

---

[15] Cf. LSJ, 659; BDAG, 381.

[16] Lk 8:24,45; 9:33,49; 17:13. According to O. GLOMBITZA, "Die Titel διδάσκαλος und ἐπιστάτης für Jesus bei Lukas", ZNW 49 (1958) 277, "Lukas diesen Titel benutzte, weil er für ihn Träger eines Amtes, Man mit ἐξουσία bedeutete; und er benutzt ihn gerade dann, wenn er Jesus als den darstellt, der zu Offenbarung seiner ἐξουσία herausgefordert ist."

[17] When in agreeing to lower the nets Simon omits the part "for a catch," it is not a sign of incomplete agreement with the command of Jesus ("let down your nets *for a catch*"). Cf. T. WIARDA, *Peter in the Gospels*. Pattern, Personality and Relationship (WUNT 2.R 127; Tübingen 2000) 101, n. 106. Contra J. DELORME, "Luc 5,1–11: analyse structurale et histoire de la redaction", NTS 18 (1972) 336.

[18] For the use of ἐπί to denote grounds for reactions, see M. ZERWICK, *Biblical Greek Illustrated by Examples* (English Edition Adapted from the Fourth Latin Edition by J. SMITH) (SPIB 114; Rome 1963) §126; BDF, §235,2. For other examples in Luke-Acts, see Lk 1:14,29,47; 2:20,47; 4:22,32; 5:9; 9:43; 15:7; 20:26; Acts 4:21; 26:6. As J. C. POLICH, *The Call of the First Disciples*. A Literary and Redactional Study of Luke 5:1–11 (Diss. Fordham University; New York 1991) 161, contends, "in so far as the dative case indicates the grounds for Peter's subsequent action, ἐπὶ τῷ ῥήματί σου must be translated, 'on the strength of' (e.g., Luke 2:20), for only on the basis of Jesus' commanding word does Peter, in faith, lower the nets." For J. L. NOLLAND, *Luke 1–9:20* (WBC 35a; Dallas, TX 1989) 222, "'at your word' points to the intrinsic authority of Jesus' words." Similarly, GREEN, *The Gospel of Luke*, 232.

[19] It is true that Luke uses here ῥήμα and not λόγος as in 5:1 or 4:32,36. But since in Lukan usage ῥήμα θεοῦ (3:2) and λόγος τοῦ θεοῦ (5:1) can be seen as synonyms, Simon's reference to the word (ῥήμα) of Jesus, as opposed to the λόγος of Jesus, should not be seen as meant to exclude the implicit reference to the authority of Jesus' word (ἐξουσία; 4:32,36). Contra WOLTER, *Das Lukasevangelium*, 213.

on it.[20] If Jesus is recognized as a Master it is because of his religious status as a speaker of God's word.

Luke presents Jesus' word as if it were an active agent eliciting manifold reactions from the listeners. Some are amazed because of Jesus' gracious words (ἐπὶ τοῖς λόγοις τῆς χάριτος; 4:22); others are astounded because of his teaching (ἐπὶ τῇ διδαχῇ αὐτοῦ; 4:32). Simon moves beyond these reactions in that he decides to act against his professional experience on account of Jesus' word (ἐπὶ δὲ τῷ ῥήματί σου). In this he resembles Mary, for whom the words of God's messenger (κατὰ τὸ ῥῆμά σου, 1:38) determine the course of action. It is this resemblance to Mary, the only character thus far to be explicitly characterized as a believer,[21] that permits speaking of Simon's obedience to Jesus' command as an act of faith. By agreeing to lower the nets for a catch Simon expresses his faith in the realizability of the result intended by Jesus' command. He believes that the words of Jesus – "lower your nets *for a catch*" – will be fulfilled.[22]

But if Simon's decision is an act of faith how are we to understand his comment about having fished all night without catching anything? Is it an expression of doubt which diminishes the quality of his faith, or, on the contrary, a respectful objection which, while contrasting Simon's fisherman experience with Jesus' command, highlights the greatness of his faith, and the greatness of the miracle? In other words, is Simon a model of faith as some commentators suggest?[23] Or is his faith mixed with skepticism and thus not yet an ideal faith?[24] Again, the reader who has witnessed a similar scene in which an initial objection is followed by obedient submission to the divine request in 1:34–38 will tend to interpret Simon's response as a genuine act of faith.[25] Of course, the exemplary character of Simon's obedience at this point does not negate the possibility of further growth.[26] In fact, the climax of Si-

---

[20] Cf. Lk 6:46–49.

[21] Elizabeth categorizes Mary's assent to God's message as an act of faith in 1:45. Mary's characterization as a believer is all the more significant in that it stands in contrast to the unbelief of Zechariah (1:20).

[22] Cf. Lk 1:45: "Blessed is she who believed that what was spoken to her by the Lord would be fulfilled."

[23] For ROSSÉ, *Luca*, 173, this act of faith "è il primo autentico atto di fede presentato nel ministero pubblico." MARSHALL, *The Gospel of Luke*, 203 speaks of an attitude of obedience.

[24] So WIARDA, *Peter in the Gospels*, 101.

[25] According to L. T. JOHNSON, *The Gospel of Luke* (SP 3; Collegeville, MN 1991) 90, the careful reader will detect in Peter's objection and acquiescence not only an echo of Mary's objection (1:34) and subsequent acceptance of the word of the Lord (1:38) but also the lesson pronounced by the angel regarding the barrenness and miraculous fertility of Elizabeth: "nothing is impossible for God" (1:37).

[26] For BOVON, *Luke 1*, 170, Simon "is beginning to articulate his faith." For MATHIEU, *La figure de Pierre*, 71, we can speak of "une grande foi qui ne cesse de progresser."

mon's faith will be seen at the end of the episode. But it does not mean that at this point Simon's confidence in Jesus is far from complete.[27] It is complete in the measure of the revelation of Jesus' identity Simon has so far received. The familiar gap between Jesus' normative point of view and the human ability to grasp it is bridged here by an act of faith. The miracle of the catch will soon confirm that Jesus' word is trustworthy.

Having drawn the reader in verses 4–5 into the dialogue and thus into the points of view of Jesus and Simon, the narrator shifts in verses 6–7 to a neutral, recounted point of view, from which he describes the abundant catch. The personage of Simon blends into the group of fishermen. He is now seen as one of those who, overwhelmed with plenty of fish, struggle with nets at the point of breaking and with boats at the point of sinking. The narrative has a different pace now. Previously, it kept pace with that of the story in verses 4–5. Now the time of the narrative is shorter than the time of the story. The time-consuming actions of catching fish, pulling in the nets, asking for help, and filling two boats with fish, are related in just two verses. This will all change in verse 8.

## 3.3. The Reactions (5:8–11)

The narration takes a new direction here. First of all, the narrator describes Simon by a double name, Simon Peter,[28] possibly a subtle indication of the fact that a new quality is emerging in Simon. Secondly, the narrator employs the represented point of view of Simon, that is, through the verb of perception

---

[27] Against WIARDA, *Peter in the Gospels*, 101. According to him "the skeptical attitude communicated in vs. 5 stands in contrast to and thus highlights the awe and humility which are shown to overwhelm Peter following the miracle." Instead of seeing here a transition from skepticism to faith, we consider it more appropriate to speak of a growth of Simon's faith in accordance with the measure of the divine revelation he has received.

[28] For SCHÜRMANN, *Lukasevangelium*, I, 269, the double name functions as a proleptic indication of his future office. Similarly G. SCHNEIDER, *Das Evangelium nach Lukas. Kapitel 1–10* (ÖTNT 3/1; Gütersloher – Würzburg 1977) 125: "Der Name weist auf das Amt des Simon und hat hier die Funktion, auf den Ursprung der Beauftragung durch Jesus (V 10b.c: «von jetzt an») hinzuweisen." W. DIETRICH, *Das Petrusbild der Lukanischen Schriften* (BWANT 94; Stuttgart 1972) 45, n. 66, disagrees saying that the name Peter "bei Lukas die Gleichsetzung mit dem «Amtsnamen» nicht erträgt." He points to Lk 22:31 and Lk 24:34 and asks whether the name "Peter" should not be then expected here "da es in diesen Stellen um in der Zukunft liegende «Amts»-Funktionen geht?" Dietriech might be right in saying that there is no equivalency between the use of the name "Peter" and the reference to the future office. But to see how the narrative creates a link between the scene of the calling of Simon in 5:1–11 and the naming of the apostles in 6:12–16 it is enough to proleptically connect the double name in Lk 5:8 with Jesus' naming of his first apostle by that name in 6:14, and not necessarily with every other occurrence of the name "Peter."

(ἰδών), he invites the reader to share in Simon's experience.[29] Finally, by switching to the asserted point of view, the narrator lets Simon describe his experience in direct speech. All the elements of the narrative strategy, the slowing down of narrative time, the double name given to Simon, the progressive alignment of the narration's point of view with that of Simon, alert the reader to the importance of what takes place. Both the gestures ("he fell down at Jesus' knees")[30] and the words ("Go away from me, Lord, for I am a sinful man"), and finally even the narrator's explanation ("for he was seized with astonishment" 5:9a), indicate that the characterization of Simon reaches its climax:[31] as Simon recognizes Jesus as Lord, he recognizes himself as a sinner. In the end, the aesthetic appeal of the visual dimension of this scene – the vividness with which Luke paints before the reader first the abundance of the catch and now Simon's reaction to it is meant to engage the reader's imagination[32] – further impresses on the reader the double content of Simon's

---

[29] Regarding the effects of the narration conducted from the point of view of one of the characters, see the observation made by R. A. CULPEPPER, *Anatomy of the Fourth Gospel. A Study in Literary Design* (Foundations and Facets. New Testament; Philadelphia 1983) 20: "A narrator may also give inside views of some characters but not of others, thereby creating a difference in the reader's sense of distance from the various characters."

[30] The construction προσπίπτειν τοῖς γόνασιν is quite classical; see references in BDAG, 884 and in A. PLUMMER, *A Critical and Exegetical Commentary on the Gospel According to S. Luke* (London 1896) 144. Typically, it desccribes a gesture of supplication, as in Euripides, *Orest.* 1332 ["ἱκέτης γὰρ Ἑλένης γόνασι προσπεσὼν βοᾷ"] or Josephus, *Ant.* 19.234. It is construed as a gesture of reverence in Plutarch, *Adv. Col.* 17 (*Mor.* 1117b).

[31] Even the spatial movement of the second boat toward Simon's boat in verse 7 brings together all the personages around Simon, allowing him again to be a spokesperson for the whole group. For more on the function of space in the narrative, see DELORME, "Luc 5,1–11", 338–341.

[32] The visual dimension of literary art was thematized in ancient literary and rhetorical theory under the category of ἐνάργεια/illustratio/depictio, [see H. LAUSBERG, *Handbook of Literary Rhetoric. A Foundation for Literary Study* (tr. M. T. BLISS – A. JANSEN – D. E. ORTON) (ed. D. E. ORTON – R. D ANDERSON) (Leiden – Boston – Köln 1998) § 810–819; R. WEBB, *Ekphrasis, Imagination and Persuasion in Ancient Rhetorical Theory and Practice* (Farnham, UK 2009), in particular the chapter titled "*Enargeia*: Making Absent Things Present," *ibid.* 87–106; J. M. F. HEATH, "Absent Presences of Paul and Christ: *Enargeia* in 1 Thessalonians 1–3", *JSNT* 32 (2009) 8–12]. The display of ἐνάργεια was valued by rhetors [see Quintilian, *Inst.* VIII 3,62: "Magna virtus res de quibus loquimur clare atque ut cerni videantur enuntiare. Non enim satis efficit neque, ut debet, plene dominatur oratio si usque ad aures valet, atque ea sibi iudex de quibus cognoscit narrari credit, non exprimi et oculis mentis ostendi" (It is a great gift to be able to set forth the facts on which we are speaking clearly and vividly. For oratory fails of its full effect, and does not assert itself as it should, if its appeal is merely to the hearing, and if the judge merely feels that the facts on which he has to give his decision are being narrated to him, and not displayed in their living truth to the eyes of the mind); text and translation from *The Institutio Oratoria of Quintilian* (ed. H. E. BUTLER) (LCL; London – New York 1922) III, 244–245]

recognition. Simon now knows Jesus to be the Lord just as he knows himself to be a sinner.

Some commentators are reluctant to ascribe definitive content to Simon's recognition of Jesus as the Lord and of himself as a sinner. Discussing the former, Nolland simply states: "Luke offers no clear picture of the development of Christological awareness. His concern here is more to set forth an experience of the numinous as present in Jesus and his deeds."[33] To support this claim, Nolland points to OT theophanies[34] as a model against which Simon's reactions to the miracle are to be understood. Green seems to move in a similar direction when he explains Simon's admission of sinfulness as the recognition of "the vast difference between Jesus and himself" causing Simon to recoil in "the terror experienced in the presence of the revelation of the Holy One (cf. Exod 3:5–6; Isa 6:1ff.)."[35] Green's conclusion follows on his observation that there is no basis in the text for any determinate meaning of Simon's sinfulness.[36] Both Nolland and Green are correct in interpreting the scene as an epiphany of the Holy One with a corresponding reaction of reverential fear on the part of Simon. The question is, however, whether their conclusions exhaust the effects this scene is likely to have on the reader. Could Luke's narration permit a more detailed understanding of Simon's recognition of Jesus as the Lord and of himself as a sinner, beyond a reverential fear before a largely undetermined representative of holy power? To answer this question let us first take note of the Lukan characterization of Jesus.

---

and expected from historians [see Lucian, *Hist. Conscr.* 51: "τοιοῦτο δή τι καὶ τὸ τοῦ συγγραφέως ἔργον — εἰς καλὸν διαθέσθαι τὰ πεπραγμένα καὶ εἰς δύναμιν ἐναργέστατα ἐπιδεῖξαι αὐτά. καὶ ὅταν τις ἀκροώμενος οἴηται μετὰ ταῦτα ὁρᾶν τὰ λεγόμενα καὶ μετὰ τοῦτο ἐπαινῇ, τότε δὴ τότε ἀπηκρίβωται καὶ τὸν οἰκεῖον ἔπαινον ἀπείληφε τὸ ἔργον τῷ τῆς ἱστορίας Φειδίᾳ" (The task of the historian too is something like this – to arrange events with a view to beauty and to display them very vividly with a view to power. And when a person listening to them thinks that he sees what is being spoken of and thereafter offers praise, then indeed the task of the Phidias of history has been completed with precision and has received the praise proper to it); text and translation from M. D. MACLEOD (ed.), *Luciani Opera.* III. Libelli 44–68 (SCBO; Oxford 1980) 315–316].

[33] NOLLAND, *Luke*, I, 222–223.

[34] Isa 6:1–8; Ezek 1:1–2:3; cf. NOLLAND, *Luke*, I, 222. Though one could argue that the biblical model of the divine commissioning of an ancient religious hero such as Isaiah (Isa 6) points to a rather high Christology (Jesus' functional equivalency to God), and permits a more profound anthropology (literal understanding of sinfulness as in Isa 6:5,7).

[35] GREEN, *The Gospel of Luke*, 234, following W. GRIMM, "θαμβέω, θάμβος", *EDNT*, II, 129.

[36] GREEN, *The Gospel of Luke*, 234, though with a cautionary remark that "this interpretation leaves room for the development of a more definitive understanding of 'sinner.'"

First of all, Jesus is acknowledged no longer as Master but as Lord. There are reasons to see in this appellation more than just a polite title.[37] Gestures (falling down at the knees of Jesus),[38] and words ("Go away from me, Lord, for I am a sinful man"),[39] serve to depict Jesus as the focal point of the epiphany. Furthermore, Luke, who rarely intervenes with his authorial comments, here combines showing (5:8) and telling (5:9–10a) with the result that Simon's interior reaction, expressed externally by words and gestures, is explained by the intervening narratorial voice as a state of being overwhelmed with astonishment (θάμβος). Astonishment, a typical reaction of the recipient of God's revelation,[40] signals to the reader that an epiphany has taken place. At the same time, the astonishment has as its object the catch of fish (5:9), that is, an action that manifests the prophetic power of Jesus' word. The fisherman's perception of the holiness of Jesus moves toward the recognition of the divine efficacy of Jesus' prophetic word. The reader who, guided by the narrative voice, knows that Jesus speaks the word of God, recognizes in the abundance of fish the actualization of God's word accepted by Simon with faith (ἐπὶ δὲ τῷ ῥήματί σου, 5:5b). The final outcome – the prophetic word of Jesus about Simon in verse 10b – will further confirm that the logic of the entire account aims at portraying Jesus as a prophet who catches people with the word of God: Jesus' word catches people (5:1–3); on the basis of Jesus' prophetic word Simon catches fish (5:6–7); Jesus' prophetic word incorporates Simon in the ministry of catching people (5:10b–11).[41] The miraculous catch is a symbolic representation of the power of the word of God to catch people, with Jesus as the prophet who manifests that power. Simon's new

---

[37] For GREEN, *The Gospel of Luke*, 233, the title κύριος demonstrates that Simon recognizes in Jesus "the agency of God." Similarly DIETRICH, *Das Petrusbild*, 49, for whom Simon's reaction "kennzeichnet die Einsicht, es in Jesus mit einem göttlichen Kyrios zu tun zu haben." FITZMYER, *Luke*, I, 568, disagrees; for him κύριος is a form of polite address, found in the Greek text in an unemphatic final position. For BOCK, *Luke*, I, 459, it is more than a polite title, but how much of Jesus' sovereignty is intended is not clear.

[38] See a similar reaction of Ezekiel in front of a theophany in 1:28: "When I saw it, I fell on my face, and I heard the voice of someone speaking" (NRSV).

[39] As ROWE, *Early Narrative Christology*, 87, bluntly states: "This self-characterization [of Simon Peter as a sinner] simply does not make any sense on the supposition that κύριε is a polite address – the categories are all wrong, and the exclamatory force is missed."

[40] G. HOLZ, "Zur christologischen Relevanz des Furchtmotivs im Lukasevangelium", *Biblica* 90 (2009) 484–505, analyzes the theme of fear expressed through such synonyms as φόβος, ἔκστασις, θάμβος, πτοέω, ἐκπλήσσομαι, and in some cases θαυμάζω. Holz argues that the theme of fear is an indispensable part of the Lukan presentation of the revelation of the glory of God in the life of Jesus and that Luke's use of this theme echoes the revelation theology of the book of Exodus.

[41] See GREEN, *The Gospel of Luke*, 233: "success in fishing, under Jesus' authority, is a prophetic symbol for the mission in which Peter and the others will participate, while Jesus himself, in his word and miraculous deed, is himself engaged in 'catching.'"

awareness of Jesus – reflected by his passage from the use of the title *Master* to the use of the title *Lord* – does not stop at the natural fear of the Holy but aims toward recognition of the divine efficacy of Jesus' word.

Secondly, in Lukan usage so far, μὴ φοβοῦ has developed a theological connotation: it has appeared in connection with God's will or God's deeds.[42] As angels had done before while announcing the new stage in the realization of God's salvific plan to Zechariah (1:13), Mary (1:30), and the shepherds (2:10), so now Jesus reveals Simon's participation in the unfolding of salvation. In the case of Zechariah, Mary, and the shepherds, the presence of otherworldly beings served to authenticate God's message. Jesus' presence is enough to announce the divinely sanctioned plan to Simon.[43] Jesus appears then as more than just a manifestation of God's power. He announces and prophetically enacts God's plan.

When it comes to Simon's admission of sinfulness, at least three features of Luke's narration allow for a deeper determination of its meaning. First of all, Jesus' calling of Simon, a self-confessed sinner, fits into Jesus' activity of release (ἄφεσις) announced in his inaugural speech in Nazareth (4:18).[44] We have seen how Jesus' program implies a ministry of release from the captivity of sin. Simon is not released here from fear only. There is a strong literary connection by which the words of Simon, "Go away from me" (ἔξελθε ἀπ' ἐμοῦ) must be interpreted against the words of Jesus directed to an unclean demon in 4:35: "Come out of him" (ἔξελθε ἀπ' αὐτοῦ). The use of ἐξέρχομαι + ἀπό in both scenes suggests that the same distance that separates Jesus from an unclean demon is now asserted to obtain also between Simon's sinfulness and Jesus.[45] Simon then is depicted as someone who understands the seriousness of his sinfulness well enough to acknowledge that in front of the holiness of Jesus he remains as alienated as the unclean spirits. While Jesus creates and asserts the distance between himself and an unclean spirit, he cancels the distance between himself and Simon the sinner. Jesus does not deny Simon's identification as a sinner. Rather, by encouraging Simon not to fear and by proclaiming Simon's participation in his own mission, Jesus denies and negates the distance that separates him from Simon's sinful-

---

[42] DIETRICH, *Das Petrusbild*, 47.

[43] See DIETRICH, *Das Petrusbild*, 47.

[44] G. E. RICE, "Luke's Thematic Use of the Call to Discipleship", *AUSS* 19 (1981) 54–55, argues that the motif of release, announced by Jesus' proclamation of Isaiah in Nazareth, constitutes the main narrative connection between the episodes that follow: it is developed as release from (1) Satan's power (4:31–44), (2) the power of sin (5:1–32), and (3) cultic traditions (5:33–6:11). Accordingly, Peter's confession of his sinfulness is the climax and the central point of the pericope in Lk 5:1–11. See *ibid.* 56.

[45] "Though the immediate context contains no exorcism implications, the genitive ἀπ' ἐμοῦ highlights the same contrariety as that between Jesus and the unclean spirits." POLICH, *The Call of the First Disciples*, 176.

ness. Simon is released from the alienation of sin. Being released from the alienation of sin amounts to being forgiven.[46]

Secondly, Simon's reaction is not so much about fear of the Holy as it is about the recognition of an unmerited gift. The miraculous catch epiphany is not threatening or menacing in the way the divine epiphanies typical of natural religion are. There is no terrifying vision taking place on the lake; rather, the epiphany has to be perceived (ἰδών, 5:8) in and through the natural phenomenon of the abundance of fish. Simon has already placed his faith in Jesus' command to lower the nets for a catch (5:4–5). Now his faith is rewarded beyond his expectation: one boat was not enough to receive the gift, another boat was needed – clearly a sign of how unanticipated the catch was. The gift surpasses what Simon's faith might have prompted him to expect. Simon's look (ἰδών) penetrates through the gift and recognizes the divine giver (κύριος). The motif of faith needed to initiate the miracle and then needed again to perceive the author of the miracle, as well as the motif of unmerited gift, form the contextual frame for the admission of sinfulness. Simon Peter acknowledges sinfulness not because the divinity threatens him but because he receives an unmerited gift and recognizes the giver.[47]

Thirdly, in light of the various reactions to the ministry of Jesus described thus far in the narrative, the reaction of Simon stands out, not only because he identifies himself as a sinner, but also because in identifying himself as a sinner he approaches Jesus in the correct way. Simon is the first one during the public ministry of Jesus to go beyond the temptation to manipulate the divinity for his own advantage. Previously, the crowds, who were amazed (θαυμάζω, 4:22; ἐκπλήσσω, 4:32; θάμβος, 4:36) with Jesus' teaching or his miracles, attempted to control Jesus by either killing him (4:29) or keeping him for themselves (4:42). Simon, overwhelmed with astonishment (θάμβος) at the miracle of the catch, does not try to keep Jesus from going away, but

---

[46] R. C. TANNEHILL, *The Narrative Unity of Luke-Acts*. A Literary Interpretation. Volume One: The Gospel According to Luke (Philadelphia 1986) 204 compares the call of Simon with the story of Levi's call (5:27–28) and concludes that "both of these call stories are stories of sinners called to a new future as followers of Jesus." For Tannehill, Simon not only confesses his sinfulness but also receives forgiveness: "Jesus' call of a sinful man to share his life and work is equivalent to a declaration of forgiveness" (*ibid.* 204). On the correlation between forgiveness of sins and the prophetic identity of Jesus in light of the historical early Jewish understanding of prophetic mediation of forgiveness, see T. HÄGERLAND, *Jesus and the Forgiveness of Sins*. An Aspect of His Prophetic Mission (MSSNTS 159; Cambridge 2011) 142–166.

[47] Some elements of the same dynamic will be visible in Acts 2, where Peter steps into his role of the catcher of people: the gathering of the multitude (πλῆθος Acts 2:6 as πλῆθος of fish in Lk 5:6), amazement (2:12), recognition of the gift of Jesus' power, wonders, and signs done among the people (ἐν μέσῳ ὑμῶν 2:22), the recognition of sin (τοῦτον … προσπήξαντες ἀνείλατε 2:23), and the joining of Jesus' community in 2:41.

acknowledges Jesus' freedom to depart (5:8).[48] Simon's reaction then is meant to exhibit more than just a reverential fear before the Holy. It is designed to be a model of a proper attitude toward Jesus. Simon's self-confessed sinfulness functions as a crucial element of that model.

In the end, the narrative prior to 5:1–11 has prepared the reader to expect Jesus' ministry to sinners. That Simon's sinfulness is not specified – no concrete sin is named or alluded to – does not mean that it should be neutralized and dissolved into mere creaturely unworthiness. By characterizing Simon as sinner, Luke places him among those indirectly characterized as sinners whom the reader has already encountered. They were first seen gathered around John the Baptist (3:10–14). There they were indirectly accused of violating the rules of human relationships flowing from the nation's covenant with God. Their sinfulness conformed to the reader's pre-existing beliefs about what made one sinful. There is no reason to think that Simon's characterization as sinner would have to depart from the realm of the possible referential content established by the prior narrative. That Simon's sinfulness remains unspecified is rather to be seen as a mark of its representative character,[49] or perhaps even of its universal appeal.

In 5:10b the narrator shifts one more time to the asserted point of view and allows Jesus to announce the new identity of Simon: from now on Simon will be catching people alive. A new beginning (ἀπὸ τοῦ νῦν),[50] a correlate to Simon's new perception of himself and of Jesus, is prophetically announced. When Simon, joined by his companions, leaves everything behind and follows Jesus (verse 11), the reader knows that Simon has placed his faith again in the prophetic word of the Lord, and that in leaving everything behind Simon has acted out that faith. Simon's new identity is that of the follower and, at the same time, coworker of Jesus.[51] Interestingly, Jesus does not issue a

---

[48] Interestingly, Simon does not break the bond with Jesus. Rather, his request for Jesus to depart puts the moment of rupture back within the bond of relation. The relation is sustained by his recognition of Jesus as the Lord and by his physical movement toward Jesus.

[49] PESONEN, *Luke, the Friend of Sinners*, 91, is correct in noticing that Peter's unspecified sinfulness differs from the concrete sinfulness of "tax collectors and sinners," and that thanks to this difference Luke "is working from the theological acceptance of general sinfulness towards recommending his special sinners to his audience." However, to claim that "Peter's sinfulness is purely theological," in the sense that it has no moral underpinning, is to introduce distinctions more at home in the modern than in the first-century mentality.

[50] The phrase is used throughout Luke-Acts to mark a new phase in the unfolding of God's salvific plan. It is used in reference to concrete individuals such as Mary (Lk 1:48), Jesus (Lk 22:18,69), and Paul (Acts 18:6), and once in reference to the followers of Jesus in Lk 12:52. See further discussion in POLICH, *The Call of the First Disciples*, 192–194.

[51] M. HENGEL, *The Charismatic Leader and His Followers* (tr. J. C. G. GREIG) (Edinburgh 1981) 50ff points out that rabbinic disciples were not called to abandon everything and follow their teacher's itinerant life. We do not know to what degree Luke and his audience shared the cultural expectations created by the rabbinic model of a teacher-disciple

call to follow him, but the reaction of Simon and his companions to the prophetic announcement of Jesus makes clear that the prophetic announcement
functions as a call. Jesus then does what the God of the Old Testament did
when he called individual prophets.[52] Jesus' authority, spoken of in 4:32,36,
is now dramatically illustrated. That the followers of Jesus leave everything
behind serves to illustrate the radical novelty that their attachment to Jesus
creates in their lives. A new quality emerges also in Jesus' life. He is no
longer only a teacher and healer. He begins to form a group of coworkers and
followers, proleptically setting in motion the future mission of the Church.[53]

Importantly, and at the risk of being redundant, it is not just the mere fact
of issuing the call (or an equivalent of that call) on the part of Jesus and the
accepting of it on the part of Peter that invites the reader to conclude that the
forgiveness of sins has taken place. It is rather the entire configuration of
theological understandings formed by the story so far that favors such a conclusion. First of all, Jesus' ministry has taken the form of a ministry of release. In light of the Nazareth manifesto, the release from sins is an expected
component of the general ministry of release. Secondly, Peter's awareness of
sin has been expressed with the help of a spatial metaphor ("Go away from
me"). The reality of discipleship, that is, the cancelling out of the presumed
distance that separates the sinner from the divine presence must be seen as
remission of (alienating) sin. Our understanding of the calling of Levi (5:27–
28) will owe much to the link now forged between the acceptance of the call
to discipleship and the status of being reconciled with God.

## 3.4. The Theme of Sinfulness and the Likely Effects of Lk 5:1–11

The prominence that the story of the calling of Peter acquires is best seen in
the multiple functions the story performs at the various levels of theological
discourse: the story engages themes that are theocentric, Christological, anthropological and ecclesiological. The pericope remains theocentric in that it
has its starting point in the proclamation of God's word and the events de-

---

relationship. But even in Greek tradition in many of the philosopher-disciple relationships
there was a greater emphasis on the attachment to the teaching than to the teacher. (HEN-
GEL, *Leader*, 32). Read against this cultural background, the Peter-Jesus relationship appears to be all the more radical.

[52] See Amos 7:15; Jer 1:5–10.

[53] D. J. SCHOLZ, *Luke 5:1–11*. The Call and Commission of Simon Peter (Diss. Marquette University; Milwaukee, WI 1997) 5, considers it to be the main point of the story:
"Luke 5,1–11 is a critical episode in the story of Luke-Acts because it begins a process of
informing the implied reader of the Gentile mission and inclusion in the early church, one
of the text's governing norms and values."

scribed constitute the unfolding of God's plan. The pericope advances the Christology of the macro-narrative in that it depicts Jesus as a skillful strategist of the missionary enterprise: Jesus is not just calling but also involving followers in his own mission, attracting them by the example of his own "catching," setting them free *from* a sinful past and *for* the new life in his company. The passage at hand enfleshes Lukan religious anthropology in that it incorporates the confession of sinfulness into the presentation of the dynamics of faith. The pericope's ecclesiological import rests on the fact that the formation of the first circle of disciples is depicted as the fruit of deeper Christological awareness (recognition of Jesus' identity) accompanied by inner transformation (recognition of one's own sinfulness). This, briefly, summarizes its various effects. But the way that Luke arranges the various components of the story creates not just a multiplicity of effects but also a hierarchy among them.

First of all, the way Luke characterizes Simon, his companions, and Jesus, makes clear that the story is ultimately about Jesus. Let us briefly recapture this dynamic effect of pointing towards Jesus.

The activities of the fishing companions of Simon, such as washing nets (5:2), catching fish (5:6–7), being astonished with the catch (5:9), leaving everything behind and following Jesus (5:11), are shared with Simon. As a group they are addressed by Jesus only once, in the command addressed first in the singular to Simon, "put out into the deep water," and then in the plural to all of them with Simon: "and let down your nets for a catch" (5:4). Simon acts as their spokesperson when he replies in the first person plural "we have worked all night long but have caught nothing," and he assumes the role of their leader when he adds "but I will let down the nets" –an activity that will involve an engagement of the whole crew. The only two business partners of Simon to be singled out from that group are John and James. Their names are mentioned and their relation to Simon is described by a different term (κοιν-ωνός, 5:10) than the one used for the rest of the crew (μέτοχος, 5:7). The fact that the names of John and James are not given at the beginning of the story but only at the end, that is, in connection with their astonishment at the manifestation of Jesus' power, indicates that their importance as characters is limited to that of sharing and replicating the reactions of Simon. They have no independent role in this story.

In contrast with the fishing companions, Simon comes out as a vivid character.[54] First of all, his characterization comes from multiple sources: it is

---

[54] That part of that vividness reflects something of Peter's actual historical character is argued by WIARDA, *Peter in the Gospels*. Wiarda has identified within various characterizations of Peter contained in the gospels a recurring trait briefly defined as a pattern of reversal: in many episodes in all four Gospels Peter's well-intentioned move meets with failure, correction, or rebuke (Mark 8:31–33; 9:5–7; 14:29–30; 14:54,66–72; Matt 14:28–31; Lk 5:8–11; John 13:6–7; 13:8; 13:9–10; 18:10–11; 21:15b–16a; 21:16b–17a). There is

conducted by the narrator, by Jesus, and through Simon's own direct speech. It is done at the level of words and the level of actions. There is a notable progression in the characterization as it moves from traits connected with Simon's trade to those pertaining to his religious identity. In its core, the characterization of Simon reflects his itinerary of faith: from providing material support for Jesus (use of Simon's boat) and thus finding himself among those reached by the proclamation of God's word; through putting trust in Jesus' word at the cost of acting against Simon's own professional experience; to seeing in Jesus the Lord at whose word Simon receives an unmerited gift and sees himself as without merits. At the end, he puts his trust again in Jesus' words and acts out Jesus' pronouncement of his new identity. Being more than a plot functionary, Simon possesses traits that give him a certain distinctive profile. The reader identifies easily with Simon's objections, his faith, or his honest self-evaluation. But even these traits – his secular profession, his emotionally charged expressiveness, his honesty – are all calculated into his itinerary of faith, and thus ultimately point to Jesus.

Thus the reader discovers that even though the main tensions in the story might revolve around Simon, they are orchestrated and executed by Jesus. Jesus is depicted as the one in charge of all the events: he has staged the encounter, he puts Simon to the test, his word causes the catch, he reveals his prophetic powers to Simon, he attracts the crowds with the word of God, and he attracts followers with the word of prophecy.[55] Unlike Simon, Jesus does not undergo interior transformation. His character undergoes no major development. He simply causes his identity to be revealed. At the crucial junctures of the narrative, in verses 4–5, 8, and 10b, the narrator withdraws into the background allowing Jesus to present himself through his own words or through the reaction of Simon, which Jesus both provokes and corrects. Thus

---

only one instance of the reversal pattern in Luke: to Peter's expression of unworthiness in verse 8, Jesus responds with correction and assurance in verse 10b. The multiple attestation of this pattern, the embarrassing qualities of Peter's portrayal that it conveys, and the discontinuity between the portrayal of Peter the disciple and the role and image associated with Peter as an apostle in the early Church, suggest that "the reversal motif and the trait-clusters which make up a significant part of Peter's characterization in the Gospels do reflect something of his actual character and experience" (*ibid.* 226).

[55] MATHIEU, *La figure de Pierre*, 67, is correct in noticing that through the use of Simon's point of view in verse 8 the reader is invited to identify with Simon's reactions to the miracle. Contra Mathieu, however, the identification with Simon does not signify that the story is ultimately about the apostolic mission of Peter and not about the epiphany of Jesus. It is true that the epiphany *through the miraculous catch of fish* is at the service of the apostolic commissioning of Simon, but the apostolic commissioning functions as the *revelation* of Jesus' power to commit his followers to a mission. The reader's siding with Simon still means discovering with Simon who Jesus is and doing with Simon what Jesus commands. In this sense the story continues to be governed by interest in the identity of Jesus, that is, in his epiphany.

Jesus, who appears as a resourceful preacher, skillful teacher, and Lord of creation, is depicted above all as a prophet whose word now catches and forms the nascent Church. In this sense Jesus is the original missionary, and his actions are the paradigm of the missionary strategy.[56] In the end, the story is about Jesus. It points to him by confirming and expanding the cumulative knowledge the reader has about Jesus' identity. But there is more to this story than just an accumulation of traits by which Jesus can be described.

Our study of Luke 1–4 has revealed a triple dynamic effect: the reader moves from (1) growing in the knowledge of God's agent, Jesus, through many revelatory statements about him, to (2) the realization that Jesus is the only one capable of an authoritative interpretation of himself, to (3) becoming subjected to Jesus' didactic strategy of a piecemeal revelation of the truth about his redemptive mission. Our initial decision to divide Lk 5:1–11 into three sections (1–3, 4–7, 8–11) was based on the simple fact that the middle part of the story recounts a miraculous catch by which the situation of the lack of fish is remedied. A need is met. Our close reading, however, clearly shows that a deeper need and a more fundamental tension are being handled by means of a miracle story. As expected on the basis of our reading of Luke 1–4, the need at work here is the need to recognize and to submit to Jesus' normative point of view expressed in verse 4 by way of a command to lower the nets. The tension holds here between the truthfulness of Jesus' view (Jesus prophetically knows the catch will be successful) and its apparent absurdity in the eyes of Simon. Simon does what the reader of Luke 1–4 has been told must be done: he recognizes Jesus' authority and submits to it in spite of reasonable objections. Simon models for the reader the realization of the effects prompted by the preliminary narrative of Luke 1–4.

Secondly, regarding the way the text of Luke 1–4 structures the reader's understanding of sinfulness, we noted that the reader moves from (1) perceiving sinfulness as a condition to be addressed by God's eschatological intervention, to (2) realizing that sinfulness can be properly perceived only from the perspective of God's eschatological agent. Simon again models[57] for us the realization that sinfulness can be properly understood only on Jesus' terms. Having asserted a distance between himself and Jesus on account of his own sinfulness, Simon ultimately submits to Jesus' call, indirectly recognizing Jesus' authority to cross and eliminate the alienation caused in Simon's mind by his sin. If Simon's empty boat is filled with fish and if his sin is forgiven, it is because he is ready to give up his understanding of how fish-

---

[56] The focus on Jesus' identity does not diminish the role of Peter but rather strengthens it in that Peter will subsequently be depicted as the imitator and executor of the missionary strategy set in motion by Jesus. Thus the authority of Peter as the primary "eyewitness" of the story of Jesus is reinforced by his role as the primary imitator of Jesus.

[57] Simon's uniqueness in terms of his ecclesiological position (the primary eyewitness) highlights the universality of his anthropological profile (a self-confessed sinner).

ing is to be done and how sinfulness is to be handled. In both cases he surrenders to Jesus' authoritative view.

Jesus' Nazareth program referred to sinfulness only in an implicit way. As Jesus begins his Galilean ministry, the reference to sinfulness is not just simply made explicit, it is also centrally staged – it coincides with the climax in the corresponding occurrences of Simon Peter's transformation and Jesus' revelation. Conversely, any interpretation that renders Simon's sinfulness as mere creaturely unworthiness obscures the dramatic nature of Simon's transformation and constricts the shape of Jesus' ministry. The content of Simon's sinfulness, that is, the nature of Peter's sin, is unspecified. It could be a proleptic reference to the future denial of Jesus by Peter. However, inasmuch as it refers to Simon's present condition, the potential content of his sinfulness must fall within the range of the reader's pre-existing beliefs about what makes one sinful. The narration at this point does not alter the reader's understanding of what makes one sinful; it does, however, change the reader's perception of how one is released from sin. The conspicuous lack of any call to moral reform understood as a condition of future forgiveness – something just seen in the preaching of John the Baptist – presents Jesus as one who enacts the release from sin in virtue of his own words and gestures. Both the manifestation of and the release from sinfulness are positioned in a Christological frame.[58]

---

[58] POLICH, *The Call of the First Disciples*, 180, might refer to the same Christological framing of the manifestation of and the release from sinfulness when he states that "[...] the same elective grace which enables Simon's self-understanding as sinner empowers his response as 'catcher.'"

Chapter 4

# The Healing of a Leper (5:12–16)

There are no references to sinfulness in Lk 5:12–16.[1] That, of course, does not mean that the story of the healing of a leper has no bearing on the reader's understanding of sinfulness. In the Lukan narrative, both the sick and sinners have been designated as addressees of Jesus' activity. The Nazareth speech, where Isaiah 61:1–2 and 58:6 are quoted as being fulfilled, has already presented acts of healings, such as recovery of sight to the blind, and acts of forgiveness of sins, evoked by jubilarian themes, as essential aspects of Jesus' ministry of release.[2] Jesus' ministry to Peter, the sinful man, and to the leper, the sick man, is not unexpected. Soon (5:17–26) Jesus will both perform healing and declare forgiveness of sins for the same individual, sick and sinful. Jesus combines healings and forgiveness as aspects of his ministry of release. The study of sinfulness must account for the function of that connection.

Our analysis of Lk 5:12–16 will be divided into three sections reflecting the three major dramatic movements within the pericope. Verse 12a functions as a short exposition: the protagonist, Jesus, and his physical location are identified. Verses 12b–13 are bound together by a complication-resolution relationship. A miraculous healing performed by Jesus solves the complication triggered by the leper's need for cleansing. Verses 14–16 constitute the third dramatic segment. It is initiated by Jesus' command to the healed man to show himself to the priest. On the one hand, Jesus' command aims to fulfill the need for the legally expected authentication of the miracle. On the other hand, it forms the first link in the chain of subsequent reactions: the authentication of the miracle triggers the spread of the news about Jesus (v. 15a); the resulting attraction of the crowds to Jesus (v. 15b) is countered by Jesus' withdrawal into prayerful solitude (v. 16).

---

[1] Which is not to say that there are no possible equivocations between leprosy or ritual impurity and sin. Part of our task will be to prove that references to sinfulness are, in fact, absent.

[2] B. WITHERINGTON, III, "Salvation and Health in Christian Antiquity. The Soteriology of Luke-Acts in Its First Century Setting", *Witness to the Gospel. The Theology of Acts* (ed. H. I. MARSHALL – D. PETERSON) (Grand Rapids, MI 1998) 151.

## 4.1. The Setting (5:12a)

A Septuagint-style formula (καὶ ἐγένετο ἐν τῷ + infinitive + accusative subject)[3] introduces a new episode in the story of Jesus. He is in one of the cities (ἐν μιᾷ τῶν πόλεων). The name of the city is not given. The time elapsed since the previous scene on the lake (5:1–11) is not mentioned either. Yet, the brief identification of location as "one of the cities" is very telling. First of all, it is connected with 4:43 where Jesus reveals his imperative to preach the good news of the kingdom of God to other cities also (καὶ ταῖς ἑτέραις πόλεσιν). His presence in one of the cities is then fully congruent with the program expounded in 4:43. Secondly, the fact that the city remains unnamed – it is simply "one of the cities" – creates an impression that as readers we are now witnessing one of many events that would have occurred since Jesus and his disciples had left the Lake of Gennesaret in 5:11. We are given a selected example of Jesus' activity.[4] The reader's impression of being brought into the midst of Jesus' ongoing activity, together with the information about the spread of Jesus' fame in 4:37, allows the reader to conclude that Jesus might be entering the city as someone already well known.

The presence of the disciples – in 5:11 they left everything and followed Jesus (ἠκολούθησαν αὐτῷ) – must be assumed.[5] The fact that they are not mentioned means that their function as catchers of men (5:10) is not immediately realized. Apparently, they must first simply follow Jesus. The reader now joins them inasmuch as he or she is permitted to follow, just like the disciples, an episode in Jesus' life.

## 4.2. The Healing (5:12b–13)

From the information about Jesus' presence in the city, which the narrator reports briefly and in a subordinate temporal clause, our attention shifts to a surprising announcement of the presence[6] of a man covered with leprosy (καὶ

---

[3] See Gen 19:29; Josh 15:18; Judg 1:14; cf. WOLTER, *Das Lukasevangelium*, 216.

[4] WOLTER, *Das Lukasevangelium*, 216; BOVON, *Luke 1*, 174.

[5] W. ECKEY, *Das Lukasevangelium*. Unter Berücksichtigung seiner Parallelen (Neukirchen-Vluyn [2]2006) I, 247.

[6] SCHNEIDER, *Lukas*, I, 130 contends that it is Jesus who comes to the leper, the leper simply being there from the beginning. This claim assumes that since Jesus is presented as the one who comes to the city, the leper must already be there. But the text does not preclude another possible explanation. The leper, just like Jesus, could be a visitor to the city. Perhaps, he is drawn to the city precisely by the fact that Jesus can be found there.

ἰδοὺ ἀνὴρ πλήρης λέπρας).[7] The interjection ἰδού, a marker of strong emphasis,[8] throws into relief a new personage in the story. In fact, it throws into relief the only characteristic this man possesses at this point: he is a leper. Literally, he is "full of leprosy" (πλήρης λέπρας),[9] and therefore in need. It is this man's need, the nature of which we must consider, that now calls for resolution, giving rise to a dramatic tension.

The Greek word λέπρα refers to a range of skin ailments of various degrees of seriousness.[10] That said, across ancient medical and religious texts, *lepra* is often presented not only as a bodily disease but also as a marker of ritual impurity.[11] In the Jewish tradition, the story of the healing of Naaman (2 Kgs 5:1–19) concentrates on the former, while Lev 13–14 on the latter aspect of *lepra*. When it comes to the cultic impurity produced by leprosy, just as bodily impurity in general (bodily discharges, corpse related impurity), it was thought to be impermanent and contagious and thus separate from so-called moral impurity, that is, from the kind of defilement produced by certain evil deeds (sexual sins, idolatry and bloodshed).[12] Other important

---

[7] Grammatically, "ἀνὴρ πλήρης λέπρας" functions as the apodosis of the opening sentence. The finite form of εἶναι after ἰδού is elided. See BDF, §128,7. Cf. WOLTER, *Das Lukasevangelium*, 217.

[8] BDAG, 468. Introduced by ἰδού, the main clause could be, somewhat colloquially, rendered as: "and, see, right there, a man covered with leprosy."

[9] That the man is full of leprosy (πλήρης λέπρας), and not just leprous, heightens the difficulty Jesus will have to resolve. See GREEN, *The Gospel of Luke*, 236. For U. BUSSE, *Die Wunder des Propheten Jesus. Die Rezeption, Komposition und Interpretation der Wundertradition im Evangelium des Lukas* (FzB 24; Würzburg ²1979) 110, Luke differentiates here between the man (ἀνήρ) and his illness (πλήρης λέπρας).

[10] BDAG, 592, lists psoriasis, lupus, ringworm, and favus, among probable conditions designated by *lepra* and advises, in the absence of more precise data, to use the more general term "serious skin disease". In the biblical idiom, *lepra* translates the Hebrew צרעת, a term which in Lev 13–14 denotes a number of skin anomalies. According to FITZMYER, *Luke*, I, 573–574, what is known today as leprosy (Hansen's disease, caused by *mycobacterium leprae*) was known in antiquity but by a different name. So neither λέπρα nor צרעת would actually refer to leprosy as known in modern times. For more on the biomedical explanation, see H. AVALOS, *Illness and Health Care in the Ancient Near East. The Role of the Temple in Greece, Mesopotamia, and Israel* (HSM 54; Atlanta, GA 1995) 311–315.

[11] See the discussion of *lepra* in relation to ancient constructions of the body and illness, in P. SHELLBERG, *From Cleansed Lepers to Cleansed Hearts. The Developing Meaning of Katharizo in Luke-Acts* (Diss. Marquette University; Milwaukee, WI 2012) 54–97, and in particular Shellberg's summary statement: "From within ancient medical and religious texts, *lepra* emerges as something of an ambiguous affliction, its varied presentations ranging along what might be best described as a cultic purity – bodily disease continuum" (*ibid.* 16).

[12] T. KAZEN, *Jesus and Purity Halakhah. Was Jesus Indifferent to Impurity?* (CB.NT 38; Stockholm 2002) 203–204, groups the impurity terminology found in the Hebrew Bible into three categories: 1) classification of animals into clean and unclean (Lev 11); 2)

aspects of leprosy can be discerned. Leprosy is a punishment for sin in Num 12:9–10; 2 Chr 26:16–21; and 2 Kgs 5:19–27.[13] According to 2 Kgs 5:7 only God can cure it. Lepers are compared to the dead in Job 18:13; 2 Kgs 5:7; Josephus *Ant.* 3.264.[14] However, since the Law contained provisions for authenticating the healing of leprosy, the recovery of health was possible.

Having identified the man as full of *lepra*, the narrator aligns the perspective from which the events are narrated with that of the leprous man. He does it in three steps. First by using the verb of perception: the man sees Jesus (ἰδὼν δὲ τὸν Ἰησοῦν).[15] Secondly, by describing the gesture evocative of

the system of bodily transferable impurity (Lev 12–15; Num 19); 3) laws concerning certain sexual sins and idolatry which were regarded as polluting (Lev 18–20; Num 35). Leprosy belongs to the second category. The so-called moral impurity constitutes the third category. It is the status of the third category that is being debated by scholars. KLAWANS, *Impurity and Sin in Ancient Judaism*, 26–31, argues that the use of the language of impurity for the gravely immoral acts of the third category should be seen as literal and not simply metaphorical. He contends that although the three grave sins of the *Holiness Code* (Lev 17–26), that is, sexual sins, idolatry and bloodshed, do not make sinners ritually impure in the sense of a impermanent and contagious impurity, the impurity they cause is felt as real, factual defilement. H. MACCOBY, *Ritual and Morality.* The Ritual Purity System and its Place in Judaism (Cambridge 1999) 201, disagrees. He claims the defilement of the land caused by immoral deeds is just an image. KAZEN, *Jesus and Purity Halakhah*, 206, simply states that it is not always obvious where to draw the line between literal and metaphorical. His final remark, though, is illuminating: "While Klawans is to be believed that ancient Jews did not generally confuse the system of bodily impurity (Lev 12–15) and that of defiling immorality (*Holiness Code*), this was not due to their application of categories such as literal and metaphorical, but because of the clearcut instructions about consequences and purifications which differed between the two systems" (*ibid.* 206–207). See also S. HABER, *"They Shall Purify Themselves."* Essays on Purity in Early Judaism (ed. A. REINHARTZ) (SBL Early Judaism and Its Literature 24; Atlanta, GA 2008) 9–71, who offers three bibliographical essays, which summarize the development of scholarly understandings of ritual and moral impurity in the Hebrew Bible, Second Temple Judaism, and the Dead Sea Scrolls. Scholars such as Mary Douglas, Jacob Neusner, Jacob Milgrom, Jonathan Klawans, and Hannah Harrington are discussed. For a more recent treatment of the moral and ritual impurity in Qumran, see G. HOLTZ, "Purity Conceptions in the Dead Sea Scrolls: 'Ritual-Physical' and 'Moral' Purity in a Diachronic Perspective", *Purity and the Forming of Religious Traditions in the Ancient Mediterranean World and Ancient Judaism* (ed. C. FREVEL – C. NIHAN) (Leiden 2013) 519–536.

[13] See also H. HARRINGTON, *The Purity Texts* (Companion to the Qumran Scrolls 5; London 2004), who dedicates a chapter to the view of leprosy in the Qumran community (*ibid.* 86–93); and there describes the moral failings often assumed as its cause (*ibid.* 91–92). Interestingly, in the Priestly presentation of Lev 13–14, leprosy carries no religious or moral guilt; it is not associated with any kind of sin. See J. S. BADEN – C. R. MOSS, "The Origin and Interpretation of ṣāraʻt in Leviticus 13–14", *JBL* 130 (2011) 643–653.

[14] For more on social ramifications of leprosy, see K. SEYBOLD – U. MUELLER, *Sickness and Healing* (Biblical Encounters Series; Nashville, TN 1981) 139.

[15] This is the *represented* point of view of the leper. See the discussion of represented, recounted, and asserted point of view in §3.1.

the leper's attitude towards Jesus: the leper bows with his face to the ground, or literally, falls on his face (πεσὼν ἐπὶ πρόσωπον). And finally, resorting to direct speech, the narrator withdraws completely, allowing the leper to assert his point of view in the most expressive way, namely, in his own words.[16] These narrative techniques not only invite the reader's participation in the leper's perception of Jesus; they are also mutually interpretive. The gestures reveal and the words further clarify how the leper views Jesus. Naturally, who the leper is – someone capable of recognizing Jesus' power to heal – becomes disclosed as well.

The leper pleads with Jesus (ἐδεήθη αὐτοῦ). His wish is to be made clean. It becomes clear that the dramatic tension revolves around the leper's need for healing.[17] That said, the leper's petition is formulated not as a plea but as a statement that, while implying the situation of a need, communicates recognition of Jesus' capacity to heal and expresses submission to Jesus' will. In other words, while at one level the plot simply moves a step forward – before the problem is solved, it is articulated – at another level it moves a step deeper by reconfirming and reestablishing for the reader the need for two foundational attitudes: the recognition of Jesus' authority and submission to that authority. The leper's plea manifests both. His statement – "Lord, if you choose, you can make me clean" – does not question Jesus' power to heal. It recognizes it. Unlike the citizens of Capernaum who, while recognizing Jesus' healing powers, tried to have Jesus work according to their schemes (4:42), the leper asserts the will of Jesus as the only factor determining his healing. He does not manipulate Jesus' will; he submits to it. The title "Lord" (κύριε) carries with it the weight of the unique authority that the leper recognizes in Jesus.[18]

---

[16] This is an *asserted* point of view.

[17] The verb καθαρίζω can convey both the notion of cultic purification and the notion of healing. In LXX 4 Kgdms 5:14 Naaman's flesh became like that of a little child. He was cured (ἐκαθαρίσθη). The verb καθαρίζω conveys here primarily the notion of health restoration. In Lev 13:6,7,13, on the other hand, it is used to denote the pronouncement of ritual cleanness. Since in the case of lepers the pronouncement of the ritual cleanness was reserved to priests, the leper's request in Lk 5:12 is best seen as a request for healing. He is not asking to be pronounced clean; he is asking to be made clean, that is, to be healed. As it will be revealed in verse 14, the healing will necessitate the need for a separate procedure of ritual confirmation of purity. See also A. WEISSENRIEDER, *Images of Illness in the Gospel of Luke. Insights of Ancient Medical Texts* (WUNT 2.R 164; Tübingen 2003) 152, for the discussion of the use of καθαρίζω to characterize the healing of *lepra* in the Corpus Hippocraticum (*De morbis* IV, 17/48; *Epidemiae* IV,1; *De ulceribus* 2.17).

[18] The combination of the title Lord with the gesture of falling is not necessarily restricted to God as its addressee. See 1 Kgs 1:23–4; 18:7; cf. WOLTER, *Das Lukasevangelium*, 217. That, of course, is not to say that on the lips of the leper the "Lord" is just a polite address. Commentators point to "something more" than just a polite *Sir* being conveyed by *kyrie*. See BOCK, *Luke*, I, 473; NOLLAND, *Luke*, I, 227. For W. RADL, *Das Evan-*

Jesus' reaction described in 5:13 parallels the request of the leper in that it too consists of words and gestures. What is more, Jesus' words clearly echo the words of the leper.[19] Thus Jesus indirectly confirms an important characteristic ascribed to him by the leper: Jesus' power over leprosy is not a matter of being or not being able to cure; it is only a matter of willing. Jesus is not presented as intercessor or mediator;[20] he commands with his own authority.[21] Naturally, Jesus' own authority is not to be understood as something opposed to or independent from God's authority. The fact that Jesus' desire expressed in the first person active verb ("I do choose") is combined with a command in the second person passive ("be made clean!") hints at God as the true agent of healing (divine passive) without, however, negating Jesus' role as the one who commands the actualization of divine agency in the miracle of healing. Here God does what Jesus wills.

Jesus could have healed the leper with words alone, as he did in curing Simon's mother in law (4:39).[22] Instead, he employs a gesture that, in the case of leprosy, acquires a special significance. It is to be recalled that when the leper approached Jesus, he fell on his face. Unlike Peter who fell down at Jesus' knees (5:8), presumably touching Jesus, the leper kept a distance, precisely not to touch him. Now Jesus stretches out his hand and touches the man.[23] The physical contact with a man *full* of leprosy suggests that Jesus

---

*gelium nach Lukas.* Kommentar. Erster Teil: 1,1–9,50 (Freiburg im Breisgau 2003) 308, the leper ascribes divine power to Jesus, because, in general, there is oneness of will and ability only in God (Wis 12:18: πάρεστιν γάρ σοι ὅταν θέλῃς τὸ δύνασθαι; Job 42:2; Lk 1:37). To be correct, the leper does not assume an unrestricted unity of will and power in Jesus, but only the unity of will and power *to heal*. Still, the unique authority the leper recognizes in Jesus could be said to refer to Jesus as a bearer of God's power to heal.

[19] Lk 5:12: if you *choose*, you can *make* me *clean* (ἐὰν θέλῃς δύνασαί με καθαρίσαι). Lk 5:13: I do *choose*, *be made clean* (θέλω, καθαρίσθητι).

[20] C. A. EVANS, *Luke* (NIBC 3; Peabody, MA 1990) 87–88, notes how the leper does not ask Jesus to intercede for him, but simply assumes that it is within Jesus' power to heal him. ECKEY, *Das Lukasevangelium*, I, 250, notes also that Jesus surpasses Moses who interceded for the cleansing of Miriam (Num 12:13–15), and surpasses Elisha by whose mediation Naaman was cleansed in the Jordan (2 Kgs 5).

[21] SCHÜRMANN, *Lukasevangelium*, I, 276, contends that when Jesus says "I will" he speaks with unsurpassable divine sovereignty.

[22] But see also Lk 4:40 where the healing is accompanied by the gesture of laying hands on the sick.

[23] For some commentators, Jesus' gesture of stretching out the hand is meant to recall the soteriological meaning conveyed by this gesture in some passages in the LXX: Jesus would act in the manner of God in Exod 3:20; 15:12, or like Moses in Exod 4:4; 9:22–23; 14:16,21,26–27, or like Aaron in Exod 7:19; 8:1–2. See BOVON, *Luke 1*, 175; MARSHALL, *The Gospel of Luke*, 209; ROSSÉ, *Luca*, 177; RADL, *Lukas*, I, 309. WOLTER, *Das Lukasevangelium*, 217, however, is correct in noting that in Lk 5:13 the stretching out of the hand functions simply – like it does in Gen 8:9; 19:10; 22:10 – to introduce another act, namely, the touching of the leper.

touches the diseased skin. Luke mentions neither the risk of physical contagion, something his readers could perhaps expect in the case of a direct contact with infected skin,[24] nor the risk of incurring ritual impurity.[25] He focuses
instead on presenting the workings of the opposite force. It is neither the
sickness nor the impurity that enters Jesus; it is rather Jesus' healing power

---

[24] Aretaeus, whom most scholars date to the first or second century CE [see V. NUTTON,
"Medicine", *The Cambridge Ancient History*. The High Empire, A. D. 70–192 (ed. A. K.
BOWMAN – P. GARNSEY – D. RATHBONE) (Cambridge ²2008) XI, 951; S. M. OBER-
HELMAN, "On the Chronology and Pneumatism of Aretaios of Cappadocia", *ANRW* 2 37 2
(1994) 959], describing skin deformation caused by elephantiasis (ἐλέφας), remarks:
"When in such a state, who would not flee; – who would not turn from them, even if a
father, a son, or a brother? There is danger, also, from the communication of the ailment
[δέος καὶ ἀμφὶ μεταδόσιος τοῦ κακοῦ]. Many, therefore, have exposed their most beloved relatives in the wilderness, and on the mountains, some with the intention of admin-
istering to their hunger, but others not so, as wishing them to die" [Aretaeus, *Sign. diut.*
4.13.19; English translation taken from F. ADAMS, *The Extant Works of Aretaeus, The
Capadocian* (London 1856) 372; the Greek text from C. HUDE (ed.), *Corpus Medicorum
Grecorum II.* Aretaeus (Berlin ²1958) 89–90]. Aretaeus describes contagion caused not by
λέπρα but by ἐλέφας. Still, as S. R. HOLMAN, "Healing the Social Leper in Gregory of
Nyssa's and Gregory of Nazianzus's 'περὶ φιλοπτωχίας'", *HThR* 93 (1999) 287, argues,
skin diseases variously termed as λέπρα, λεύκη, ψώρα, or ἐλέφας are best understood as
falling under the same broad category insofar as ancient medical writers understood these
diseases to be caused by an imbalance of choleric humors, and inasmuch as they used various terms for what they themselves considered as the same disease in its different states.

[25] Ritual impurity being contagious, whoever touched a leper became impure. See Josephus, *Ag. Ap.* 1.281 who states that whoever touches a leper or lives under the same roof
with them should be esteemed unclean. See also a remark by KAZEN, *Jesus and Purity
Halakhah*, 116: "Physical contact and staying for some amount of time with a 'leper' in the
same house, was considered to render a person unclean in the first century CE. This much
can be said with confidence."

For S. GRASSO, *Luca* (Roma 1999) 164, the gesture of stretching out the hand and
touching the leper, other than evoking God's powerful acts (Exod 6:6; 7:5; 14:16; 15:12;
etc.), can be seen as an emphatic articulation of the transgression of the Law, which, according to Grasso, prohibits contact with lepers in Lev 5:3. Lev 5:3 indeed speaks of
touching human uncleanness and of guilt, but it does not connect the guilt to the touch but
rather to the failure to cleanse the impurity as soon as it occurs (see J. MILGROM, *Leviticus
1–16.* A New Translation with Introduction and Commentary [AncB 3; New York 1991]
310). Jesus then does not transgress the law by touching a leper. He simply incurs a bodily
impurity, which of itself was not considered sinful. Bodily impurity necessitated a temporary restriction with respect to contact with the sacred. GREEN, *The Gospel of Luke*, 237, n.
40, aptly observes that Leviticus 13 does not explicitly prohibit touching a leper; it imposes separation of lepers from others. According to E. P. SANDERS, *Jewish Law from Jesus to
the Mishnah* (Philadelphia 1990) 151, only two specific impurities were prohibited: contact
with the carcass of an impure animal and eating what dies of itself. See also P. FREDRIK-
SEN, "Did Jesus Oppose the Purity Laws?", *BR* 11/3 (1990) 20–25, 42–47 for a critique of
some historical reconstructions of Jesus which mistakenly conflate bodily impurity, sin,
and social status.

that drives the leprosy out.[26] The touch has an immediate (εὐθέως) effect. This effect is not just therapeutic. Jesus both heals and breaks through the barrier of separation that the sickness and ritual impurity created around the leper. Even before the leper is officially readmitted to society through a temple ritual that confirms his cleansing, he experiences the nearness and acceptance of the one who wills him to be clean.[27]

While communicating the results of the healing of the leprous man, Luke simply states that the leprosy left him (ἀπῆλθεν ἀπ' αὐτοῦ). The leprosy departs just like the demon at the end of the exorcism in Lk 4:35 (ἐξῆλθεν ἀπ' αὐτοῦ) or like the fever rebuked by Jesus in Lk 4:39 (ἀφῆκεν αὐτήν), or like the demons exorcised out of many in Lk 4:41 (ἐξήρχετο ... ἀπὸ πολλῶν). Some commentators take these descriptions to mean that Luke demonizes the sickness and presents the healing as an act of liberation from the power of the demons.[28] But this would mean that Luke, in the end, conflates exorcisms and healings. The fact that Luke divides Jesus' ministry into healings (4:40) and exorcisms (4:41) speaks against such a conflation. The similarity of phrases used to describe the effects of healings and exorcisms is rather to be understood as an expression of a certain affinity between various oppressive forces. For Luke, the devil and sickness are separate but related

---

[26] As NOLLAND, *Luke*, I, 229 puts it: "The uncleanness retreats before the touch and command of Jesus." A convincing theory as to how the illness retreats from the body is offered by SHELLBERG, *From Cleansed Lepers to Cleansed Hearts*. She analyzes (*ibid.* 76–80) the role of the spirit/wind (pneuma) in ancient medical theories, and points to the spirit's health-giving and life-giving effects. This allows her to conclude that the Lukan characterization of the leper as the man "full of *lepra*" evokes the characterization of Jesus as "full of the Holy Spirit" (Lk 4:1). Thus, when Jesus touches the leper, "the extension of Jesus' *pneuma hagiou* (sic!) corrects the imbalance of humours, such that the *lepra* leaves, or evacuates, the *lepra*-afflicted one" (*ibid.* 169). Shellberg's reasoning finds further confirmation in light of the ancient construct of human body as something porous, that is, open to the influence of outside spirits. See references to the Corpus Hippocraticum that confirm that the skin was construed as a porous structure in WEISSENRIEDER, *Images of Illness in the Gospel of Luke*, 218–220.

[27] J. J. PILCH, *Healing in the New Testament.* Insights from Medical and Mediterranean Anthropology (Minneapolis, MN 2000) 52, sees touching as "physically symbolizing an acceptance back into the community." G. B. FERNGREN, *Medicine and Health Care in Early Christianity* (Baltimore, MD 2009) 132, offers an important insight regarding the problem of the social exclusion of the sick: "In classical antiquity the household or family [...] provided the chief locus of health care. [...] It was not uncommon for the chronically ill to be shunned, either because they posed too great an economic burden on a family whose very survival was threatened or because the risk of contagion."

[28] So BUSSE, *Die Wunder*, 112. Similarly, R. PESCH, *Jesu ureigene Taten?* Ein Beitrag zur Wunderfrage (QD 52; Freiburg 1970) 103: "Die Lepra ist von Lukas wie eine dämonische Krankheit behandelt, die auf Jesu Berührung und Wort hin weicht."

realities.[29] As related, they act alike: they all depart when confronted by Jesus.

Finally, the "departure" of sickness recalls yet another oppressive force. As we have seen, Simon's petition for Jesus to depart (ἔξελθε ἀπ' ἐμοῦ; 5:8), served to depict separation caused by sin as a mirror image of the separation between Jesus and the evil spirits. The reader is led to view the healing of the leper as another victory in Jesus' continuing combat against the oppressive forces of Satan, sickness, and sin.

## 4.3. Jesus' Command and Reactions (5:14–16)

Jesus' negative command not to tell anyone is combined with a positive instruction to comply with the Mosaic Law.[30] The rhetorical force of this combination deserves attention. The conjunction ἀλλά contrasts the positive command with the preceding negative one forming a rhetorical figure of *correctio* (not x but y).[31] The point of Jesus' command is not that the man is to refrain from talking but that he is to go to the temple. The silence that Jesus imposes on the healed man intends to facilitate an immediate fulfillment of the legal obligation.[32] Jesus' knowledge of the Law as well as his concern for compliance with the Law are visible here.[33]

Jesus commands the healed man to show himself to the priest and to make an offering for his cleansing "for a testimony to them" (εἰς μαρτύριον αὐτοῖς). Commentators disagree on the kind of testimony intended here.[34] Is

---

[29] As BOVON, *Luke 1*, 175 puts it: "The realm of leprosy is thus not far from that of death and of the devil." Although, see KAZEN, *Jesus and Purity Halakhah*, 303–304, who points to the 4Q versions of *Damascus Document* (4Q266 6 I, 5–7; 4Q269 7 1–3; 4Q272 1 I, 1–3), which suggest that leprosy was thought to be caused by demonic powers.

[30] See Lev 14.

[31] See LAUSBERG, *Handbook of Literary Rhetoric*, § 785. Cf. WOLTER, *Das Lukasevangelium*, 218.

[32] GREEN, *The Gospel of Luke*, 238; GRASSO, *Luca*, 165.

[33] NOLLAND, *Luke*, I, 228. In addition to an emphasis on Jesus' faithfulness to the Law, MARSHALL, *The Gospel of Luke*, 209; SCHÜRMANN, *Lukasevangelium*, I, 277, and W. WIEFEL, *Das Evangelium nach Lukas* (ThHK 3; Berlin 1988) 117, speak of Jesus' desire to withdraw as a motive behind his injunction to silence. If the imposition of silence is to be connected with Jesus' withdrawal, as these commentators suggest, the connection should not be found in the intention of Jesus to withdraw, as if he imposed silence to avoid publicity and be able to withdraw into solitude. The connection is to be found in the way the three separate events are presented and therefore linked: Jesus imposes silence out of concern for the Law. The legal authentication of the miracle triggers the spread of the news about Jesus. Despite the publicity, Jesus withdraws.

[34] Two main lines of interpretations can be discerned, with some commentators adhering to both. A number of commentators consider the phrase "for testimony" to refer to

Jesus concerned here with the testimony to his own healing powers, or is he rather interested in the testimony to the ritual cleanness of the healed man, this latter testimony being a necessary condition for the readmission of the healed man into regular social life? As already noted, Jesus' command to give witness is embedded in the rhetorical figure of *correctio* (not x but y). The contrast between the negative and positive commands of *correctio* points to the right kind of giving witness. The man is to engage in the kind of witness demanded by the Law, and not in a simple spreading of the news to any passerby. Jesus' concern then is with the necessary legal action. Indeed, nothing in Jesus' words and gestures towards the leper suggests that Jesus is concerned with the spread of his own esteem. Rather, Jesus' attention is directed to the man in need. Jesus wills him to be made clean. The only thing needed to complete the healing is its authentication by the priest.[35] The reference to testimony is then most naturally understood as referring to that final stage of healing in which the performance of the ritual serves as the final attestation of the cure.[36] Jesus wants to have the man reintegrated into the social fabric.

In 5:15a Luke will recount the spread of the news about Jesus, presumably as a result of the healing of the leper. But this spreading is just a natural consequence of the miracle having been now officially authenticated. It is not something Jesus intends, or for that matter does not intend, when he tells the man to perform the rituals "for testimony to them." The intensity described in

---

something that is testified about Jesus. What is testified is Jesus' power to heal (KLEIN, *Das Lukasevangelium*, 231; BOCK, *Luke*, I, 477), God's messianic act in Jesus (MARSHALL, *The Gospel of Luke*, 210), presence of messianic times (BOCK, *Luke*, I, 477), God purifying his people in Jesus (MEYNET, *L'Évangile de Luc*, 244), or Jesus' faithfulness to the Law (J. ERNST, *Das Evangelium nach Lukas* [RNT 3; Regensburg [6]1993] 191). Further down this Christological line of thinking goes C. F. EVANS, *Saint Luke* (TPI New Testament Commentaries; London 1990), 295, who suggests that perhaps the end of purificatory sacrifice is announced here, and GRASSO, *Luca*, 165, who thinks the testimony is for the conversion and salvation of the leaders. FITZMYER, *Luke*, I, 575, and JOHNSON, *The Gospel of Luke*, 92, speak of two possible meanings. Like the above-mentioned commentators, they think that what receives testimony is Jesus' power to heal. As the second option they propose testimony to the fact that the man is clean. It is this second interpretation that is accepted by NOLLAND, *Luke*, I, 228; RADL, *Lukas*, I, 130; SCHÜRMANN, *Lukasevangelium*, I, 277; R. C. TANNEHILL, *Luke* (ANTC; Nashville, TN 1996) 103; and WOLTER, *Das Lukasevangelium*, 218. At the core of this second line of interpretation, the testimony refers to the public authentication of the healing by means of priestly ritual.

[35] FITZMYER, *Luke*, I, 575, notes that "the priest" refers to the one on duty in the Temple. WOLTER, *Das Lukasevangelium*, 218, contends that the plural form "to them" (εἰς αὐτοῖς) refers to priests as *constructio ad sensum*. See BDF §134,1.

[36] From the point of view of the form critical analysis of the pericope, this would fulfill the function of demonstrating the miracle's success. Luke has narrated similar demonstrations in 1:64 and 4:39. Cf. BOVON, *Luke 1*, 176; WOLTER, *Das Lukasevangelium*, 218.

5:15a – "so the news about him spread *even more*" – highlights the comparative growth of Jesus' fame in relation to Lk 4:37.[37]

Having drawn the reader into the dialogue in verses 12b–14 and thus into the points of view of Jesus and the leper, the narrator shifts in verses 15–16 to a neutral, recounted point of view. The narrative has a different tempo now. Previously, it kept pace with that of the story in 12b–14. Now the time of the narrative is shorter than the time of the story. The spread of the news about Jesus, the movement of the crowds, and the opposite movement of Jesus are durative actions[38] now condensed into three brief sentences. Some commentators want to see these actions as iterative.[39] Crowds would repeatedly gather, and Jesus would repeatedly interrupt his work to pray. It is assumed that Jesus actually gives to the crowds what they seek – to hear him and to be healed – and only then goes off to solitary places.[40] While an iterative aspect of the movement of the crowd toward Jesus and the movement of Jesus away from the crowd is possible, the interpretation given to this repetition, namely, that Jesus actually ministers to them before withdrawing from them, seems to resist an image of Jesus as someone who could actually ignore the needy crowds. Jesus has already said no to the crowds in 4:42–43. And the fact that he avoids them now does not mean that he is not going to be ready to teach and heal them in the next scene. Jesus is not driven by the crowd's expectations. He follows a different agenda. The fact that Jesus avoids the crowds in order to commune with his Father highlights his autonomy in this regard.

There is a clash then between Jesus' ministry to the needy leper on the one hand, and Jesus' withdrawal from the needy crowds on the other. To the reader, this clash recalls a familiar tension between Jesus' authoritative point of view and the characters' limited ability to grasp it. Jesus does not explain his decision to the crowds. Neither does the narrator explain Jesus' motivation to the reader. Jesus acts with an autonomy that remains opaque to the reader. The image of Jesus at prayer reminds the reader that Jesus' autonomous decisions are fully aligned with God's perspective.[41]

---

[37] WOLTER, *Das Lukasevangelium*, 218.

[38] The imperfect forms διήρχετο, συνήρχοντο, ἦν [ὑποχωρῶν] express a durative meaning.

[39] TANNEHILL, *Luke*, 104.

[40] For RADL, *Lukas*, I, 310–311, Jesus does not run away from the task of preaching and healing. The care for people stands next to solitariness. On such reading, verse 16 says that Jesus first dedicates himself to the crowds and then goes off to solitary places. For SCHÜRMANN, *Lukasevangelium*, I, 278; MARSHALL, *The Gospel of Luke*, 210; WOLTER, *Das Lukasevangelium*, 218, Jesus never meets the crowds. He avoids them.

[41] Commentators offer other possible interpretations of the reference to Jesus' solitary prayer. For KLEIN, *Das Lukasevangelium*, 214, Jesus' need for prayer demonstrates that his healing power comes from God. For MEYNET, *L'Évangile de Luc*, 245, it indicates where the source of his word is to be found and whose reign it is that he proclaims. BUSSE, *Die Wunder*, 105, thinks Jesus prays because he needs strength for the upcoming confron-

# 4.4. The Theme of Sinfulness and the Likely Effects of Lk 5:12–16

This simple scene, in which a powerful Jesus rewards a needy leper, and in which neither Jesus nor the leper develops as characters, is used by Luke to introduce a new development in the reader's relationship with Jesus. It has to do with the reinforcement and refinement of the reader's understanding of Jesus' status vis-à-vis the oppressive force of disease. Whatever the contagious nature one might ascribe to leprosy, it does not affect Jesus. Touching a leper does not make Jesus ill. Jesus appears to possess a purifying power that drives the sickness away.

This special status of Jesus acquires an additional significance in light of the Lukan deployment of the references to sinfulness. The first thing to note is that Luke does not mix morality and sickness. Although leprosy was often thought to result from sin, there are no grounds in the text to assume that when the leper stands before Jesus he does so as a sinner. In fact, Jesus' prior mention of Elisha's healing of Naaman – where leprosy is connected neither with moral fault nor with punishment for sin – suggests to the reader that in 5:12 Jesus, like Elisha before him, meets someone who is simply a leper and not a sinner punished with leprosy. Jesus' reference to the Mosaic prescription in 5:14 does not refer to sin either. It does, by implication, point to the legal prescription in which issues of cultic purity figure prominently, but even that implication makes of the leprosy a sign of ritual impurity, not a mark of moral shortcomings.[42] That said, Luke presents as parallel the reactions of sinful Peter in 5:8 (he saw, he fell down, he confessed his sinfulness) and the leper in 5:12 (he saw, he fell down on his face, he indirectly confessed his illness),[43] and thus the issues of sinfulness and alienating disease, as reflected in these reactions, become related and mutually illuminating.

---

tation. Similarly RADL, *Lukas*, I, 310–311. According to THEOBALD, "Die Anfange der Kirche", 94–95, prayer prepares for the exercise of saving activity in the following scene.

[42] Which is not to say that ritual and moral impurity are not related. See "Impurity, Ritual, and Emotion: A Psycho-Biological Approach" in T. KAZEN, *Issues of Impurity in Early Judaism* (CB.NT 45; Winona Lake, IN 2010) 13–40, where the underlying cognitive-emotional experiences of disgust, fear, and sense of justice are seen as a common denominator in the categories of moral and ritual impurity. Furthermore, the ritual dimension is not independent from the cultural dimension and a certain ethos that the cultural dimension implies. See C. FREVEL – C. NIHAN, "Introduction", *Purity and the Forming of Religious Traditions in the Ancient Mediterranean World and Ancient Judaism* (ed. C. FREVEL – C. NIHAN) (Leiden 2013) 21.

[43] RADL, *Lukas*, I, 311 notes the parallel between ἀνὴρ ἁμαρτωλός in 5:8 and ἀνὴρ πλήρης λέπρας in 5:12, their respective awareness of separation from Jesus and the reaction of falling down. MEYNET, *L'Évangile de Luc*, 246–247, notes how the gesture of the leper mirrors the gesture of Peter. We can add that they both refuse to control Jesus' mi-

We have seen how, having asserted a distance between himself and Jesus on account of his own sinfulness in 5:8, Simon ultimately submits to Jesus' call, indirectly recognizing Jesus' authority to cross and eliminate the alienation caused in Simon's mind by his sin. Without calling for a moral reform with a view to future forgiveness, Jesus enacts forgiveness with his own words and gestures here and now. In a very similar way now, without waiting for official recognition on the part of the temple authorities, Jesus touches the leper, driving away the sickness in virtue of his own words and gestures. Jesus' handling of both sin and leprosy reinforces in the reader a conviction that Jesus possesses a status which allows him to eliminate the alienation of sin and sickness – an alienation asserted by Peter in 5:8, and implied by the leprous status of the man described in 5:12.

Our study of Luke 1–4 has identified a triple dynamic effect prompted by the preliminary narrative: the reader moves from (1) growing in the knowledge of God's agent, Jesus, through many revelatory statements about him, to (2) the realization that Jesus is the only one capable of authoritative interpretation of himself, to (3) becoming subjected to Jesus' didactic of piecemeal revelation of the truth about his redemptive mission. In Lk 5:1–11, Simon Peter's progress in his recognition of Jesus and his concomitant submission to Jesus' authority modeled for the reader the realization of this dynamic effect. This modeling included Simon's submission to Jesus' view of sinfulness: by his adherence to Jesus, Simon recognizes Jesus' authority to cross and eliminate the alienation caused in Simon's mind by his sin. Compared with the Calling of Simon, the scene of the Healing of a Leper is less complex. There is no *growth* in faith narrated in 5:12–16. Faith in Jesus' power to heal is simply enacted. The growth and complexity emerge instead in the reader's perception of Jesus. The reader's understanding of Jesus' power to bring release is expanded. Jesus is not just resistant to the contagion of sin and sickness; he is capable of driving these oppressive and alienating forces away in virtue of his own words and gestures. As to the complexity, it enters the reader's understanding of Jesus' relationship to the needy crowds. Jesus' prayerful withdrawal from the incoming crowds in 5:15–16 seems surprising. He helps the leper in need, but he is not driven by the needs of people. As a character in the story, Jesus remains mysterious. His reasons are not fully transparent to the reader. They are anchored in God's plan, as the picture of Jesus in prayer makes clear, but the reader must, somewhat like the crowds, submit to Jesus' decision about what will be revealed, and how.

---

raculous powers. Peter does not keep Jesus for the sake of benefiting from additional miracles; the leper stresses Jesus' free choice in bringing about the cleansing.

Chapter 5

# The Healing of the Paralytic (5:17–26)

In the next two scenes – 5:17–26 and 5:27–39 – Luke will sustain the reader's relationship with the protagonist Jesus by concentrating on Jesus' ministry to sinners. What was implicit in Jesus' encounter with sinful Peter will be made explicit in 5:17–26, namely, Jesus' authority to release from sin.

The story narrated in 5:17–26 begins with a short exposition in verse 17. We see Jesus engaged in the activity of teaching, with the Pharisees and the teachers of the Law as his audience. The dramatic tension, hinted at in 5:17 by the mention of Jesus' power to heal, surfaces in verse 18 with the appearance of the paralyzed man. His sickness sets up an expectation of healing. The healing, however, does not happen immediately. Two obstacles delay it.[1] First, the crowd blocks access to Jesus (5:19). Secondly, Jesus' surprising declaration of forgiveness triggers a dispute with the Pharisees and the teachers of the Law (5:20–24). It is while responding to their challenge that Jesus finally heals the man. That the man becomes healed is described in verse 25; the final reaction of all those gathered is depicted in verse 26.

Considering how the above-mentioned obstacles to the healing both sustain and structure the flow of the story, our analysis of this pericope will advance in four steps corresponding to the story's four dramatic segments. We shall analyze the initial setting (5:17), the overcoming of the first obstacle (5:18–19), emergence and resolution of the second obstacle (5:20–24), and finally the results of the healing (5:25–26).

## 5.1. The Setting (5:17)

The scene opening – καὶ ἐγένετο formula followed by the indication of time, ἐν μιᾷ τῶν ἡμερῶν ("on one of those days") – produces an effect similar to the one observed at the opening of the previous pericope. We are again witnessing a selected incident from the ongoing activity of Jesus. Out of the many happenings involving Jesus, we are given access to a single event. A careful reader detects how his or her access to the protagonist Jesus is both controlled and guided.

---

[1] GREEN, *The Gospel of Luke*, 239.

From the time indication the story shifts directly to the description of the protagonist, Jesus. Jesus' location is not identified. It is only by hearing about the roof in 5:19, that the reader will place Jesus inside a house. Jesus appears in a familiar way: just like in 4:15,31 and 5:3, he is engaged in teaching. What is new is the type of audience that now gathers around Jesus. There are the Pharisees and the teachers of the Law sitting around. They have come from every village of Galilee and Judea and from Jerusalem. Coincidentally, every village of Galilee and Judea is now exposed to the teaching of Jesus.

Luke does not explain who the Pharisees and the teachers of the Law are. Still, by grouping the Pharisees and the teachers of the Law together and making them represent not just Jerusalem but every village[2] of Galilee and Judea, he manages to project some important characteristics of that composite group: they seem influential enough to be able to draw representatives from every village;[3] their present gathering has the appearance of an official delegation formed to face Jesus;[4] finally, that the Pharisees come together with the teachers of the Law hints at their common concern for the Law.[5]

---

[2] BOVON, *Luke 1*, 178–179, suggests that it might be a sign of contempt that Luke situates the enemy party in the villages. Certainly, as WOLTER, *Das Lukasevangelium*, 221, notes, there is a contrast between Jesus' activity in the cities (4:29,31,43; 5:12) and the presentation of the Pharisees and scribes as a village movement.

[3] See, however, A. J., SALDARINI, *Pharisees, Scribes and Sadducees in Palestinian Society. A Sociological Approach* (Wilmington, DE 1988) 181, who states that historically "it is doubtful that the Pharisees were the community leaders in Galilean agricultural villages."

[4] C. BROCCARDO, *La Fede Emarginata*. Analisi narrativa di Luca 4–9 (Studi e ricerche; Assisi 2006) 32; GREEN, *The Gospel of Luke*, 240.

[5] This concern corresponds to what J. NEUSNER, "The Rabbinic Traditions about the Pharisees before 70 CE: An Overview", *In Quest of the Historical Pharisees* (ed. J. NEUSNER – B. D. CHILTON) (Waco, TX 2007) 311, proposes as a conclusion of his study, namely, that "for the rabbinic traditions about the Pharisees, the three chief issues of sectarian consequence are ritual purity, agricultural taboos, and Sabbath and festival behavior."

On Luke's overall portrayal of the Pharisees, see R. L. BRAWLEY, *Luke-Acts and the Jews.* Conflict, Apology, and Conciliation (SBL.MS 33; Atlanta, GA 1987) 84–106; J. T. CARROLL, "Luke's Portrayal of the Pharisees", *CBQ* 50 (1988) 604–621; J. A. DARR, *On Character Building.* The Reader and the Rhetoric of Characterization in Luke-Acts (Literary Currents in Biblical Interpretation; Louisville, KY 1992) 85–126; D. B. GOWLER, *Host, Guest, Enemy, and Friend.* Portraits of the Pharisees in Luke and Acts (Emory Studies in Early Christianity 2; New York 1991); J. D. KINGSBURY, *Conflict in Luke.* Jesus, Authorities, Disciples (Minneapolis, MN 1991) 21–28, 86–107; J. D. KINGSBURY, "The Pharisees in Luke-Acts", *The Four Gospels.* Festschrift Frans Neirynck (ed. F. VAN SEGBROECK – C. M. TUCKETT) (BEThL 100; Louvain 1992) II, 1497–1512; A.-J. LEVINE, "Luke's Pharisees" *In Quest of the Historical Pharisees* (ed. J. NEUSNER – B. D. CHILTON) (Waco, TX 2007) 113–130, 445–446; POWELL, "The Religious Leaders in Luke: A Literary-Critical Study"; J. T. SANDERS, "The Pharisees in Luke-Acts", *The Living Text.* Essays in Honor of Ernest W. Saunders (ed. D. GROH – R. JEWETT) (Lanham, MD 1985) 141–188; J. A. ZIESLER, "Luke and the Pharisees", *NTS* 25 (1979) 146–157.

This brief presentation of the audience contains seeds of possible dramatic tension. If Jesus is teaching (διδάσκων) in the presence of the teachers of the Law (νομοδιδάσκαλοι),[6] are not the two bearers of the authority to teach, Jesus and the Pharisaic party,[7] destined to compete? This possibility might be hinted at, but it is not realized immediately. Instead, the primary anticipation of what is to happen is formed at the end of the exposition contained in 5:17. The reader is informed that the power of the Lord was with Jesus[8] to heal (ἰᾶσθαι).[9] This brief statement, occupying the final, emphatic position in the sentence, sets the expectation of a healing miracle. The appearance of a paralytic announced in the very next sentence will confirm the correctness of that expectation.

The mention of the Lord's power (δύναμις κυρίου) to heal reaffirms the characterization of Jesus as the one acting on behalf of God. Earlier elements of that characterization are now brought together in the mind of the reader and reinforced. Since John the Baptist was to go in the *spirit* and *power* (ἐν πνεύματι καὶ δυνάμει) of Elijah (1:17), and since Jesus' conception was accomplished through the Holy *Spirit* (πνεῦμα ἅγιον) and the *power* of the Most High (δύναμις ὑψίστου) (1:35), the presence of the *power* of the Lord (δύναμις κυρίου) becomes connected with Jesus' experience of the Spirit of

---

[6] As the commentators frequently note, the teachers of the Law mentioned in 5:17 are a synonym of the scribes (γραμματεῖς) from 5:21. See FITZMYER, *Luke,* I, 581; M.-J. LA-GRANGE, *Évangile selon Saint Luc* (EtB; Paris 1948) 165; MARSHALL, *The Gospel of Luke,* 212; NOLLAND, *Luke,* I, 233. BUSSE, *Die Wunder,* 119, suggests the name "teachers of the Law" is used so that the Hellenistic audience of Luke would not misinterpret the scribes (γραμματεῖς) thinking of them as simple writers.

[7] See, BROCCARDO, *La Fede Emarginata,* 33; GREEN, *The Gospel of Luke,* 240.

[8] Literally, "with him to heal" (εἰς τὸ ἰᾶσθαι αὐτόν). Grammatically, however, αὐτόν could be either the object or the subject of the infinitive. What advises against considering αὐτόν as the object of the infinitive ("to heal *him*") is the fact that αὐτόν has no clear referent. As yet, no one to be healed has been mentioned in the story. See, however, ROWE, *Early Narrative Christology,* 97, n. 54, who entertains a slight possibility of αὐτόν functioning as a proleptic pronoun whose referent is finally announced in 5:18 by καὶ ἰδοὺ ... ἄνθρωπον.

[9] On the meaning of ἰάομαι see L. WELLS, *The Greek Language of Healing from Homer to New Testament Times* (BZNW 83; Berlin – New York 1998), 100–101, who, having traced the literary evidence surrounding the Greek god of healing, Asklepios, in four differing asklepeia of Epidauros, Athens, Kos and Pergamon, affirms the consistent meaning and contextual use of words such as σώζω, ἰάομαι, and ὑγιαίνω. "The verb σώζω continues to mean the rescuing from the possibility of imminent death on particular occasions, ἰάομαι continues to denote (successful) medical treatment, and is the verb used to describe the intervention of the god and miraculous healing, while the verb ὑγιαίνω continues to imply a restoration to a previous state of (good) health."

the Lord (3:22; 4:1,14,18–19).[10] Endowed with the Lord's power and the Lord's Spirit, Jesus' activity is placed in a theocentric perspective.

## 5.2. The Obstacle of the Crowd (5:18–19)

The plot steers in the direction of a healing miracle. With the appearance of the paralytic[11] in 5:17, Jesus' power to heal meets its potential beneficiary. The narrator clearly establishes this potentiality, or narrative expectation, by leaving aside the religious elite gathered around Jesus and focusing on the man in need of healing. First, the interjection ἰδού fixes the reader's attention on the action of some men who carry their paralyzed companion on a bed. Secondly, the emphatic force of ἰδού is coupled with the syntactical passage from the subordinate temporal clause contained in 5:17 to the apodosis initiated by καὶ ἰδού.[12] The event announced by the initial καὶ ἐγένετο is finally named. Thirdly, the movement of the man unable to move contrasts with the static image of the audience seated around Jesus in 5:17.[13] It is around the need to move the paralytic toward Jesus that the micro-plot of 5:17–18 now develops.

The narrator does not just describe the movement of the men carrying their companion. He lets us perceive their inner resolution. The men are intent (ἐζήτουν)[14] on bringing in their companion and placing him in front of Jesus.

---

[10] Connection between the power of the Lord and the Spirit of the Lord is noted, among others, by GREEN, *The Gospel of Luke*, 240; L. SABOURIN, *L'Évangile de Luc*. Introduction et commentaire (Roma 1985) 141. NOLLAND, *Luke*, I, 234, states that, with the reference to the power of the Lord, Luke continues "to clarify what it means for Jesus to have become through the descent of the Spirit the repository of the power of God."

[11] KLEIN, *Das Lukasevangelium*, 219, n. 30, contends that the use of παραλελυμένος, unlike παραλυτικός used in Mark 2:3, indicates that the man was not born paralyzed. BUSSE, *Die Wunder*, 120, thinks the same. WOLTER, *Das Lukasevangelium*, 221, disagrees, noting that Luke simply uses here a more common medical expression.

[12] WOLTER, *Das Lukasevangelium*, 220.

[13] L. BASSET, "La culpabilité, paralysie du cœur. Réinterprétation du récit de la guérison du paralysé (Lc 5/17–26) ", *ETR* 71 (1996) 334, points to the contrast between the mobility of all who had come to Jesus from around Galilee and Judea and the immobility of the one paralyzed. We stress a reversed contrast detectable between the movement of the paralytic carried by his companions and the immobility of the audience gathered around Jesus.

[14] The verb ζητέω is capable of expressing ideas such as looking for, seeking, investigating, demanding, or striving for. See BDAG, 428. It is the notion of seeking, in the sense of trying to obtain, that best fits the context of verse 18. Two aorist infinitives (εἰσενεγκεῖν, θεῖναι) name that which is being sought. Still, when the reader discovers in verse 19 a concrete illustration of the effort involved in seeking the desired goal, the meaning of the verb ζητέω intensifies. The notion of seeking is enriched with another idea the

At the same time, however, because of the crowd they are unable to simply bring him in. This tension is quickly resolved. Going up to the roof, they lower the sick man with his bed through the tiles.[15] The repetition of participial forms – they were carrying (φέροντες), they could not find the way (μὴ εὑρόντες), they were going up (ἀναβάντες) – describes the undeterred progression of the men's efforts to reach their goal, but also places in sharp relief the first final aorist form that announces the completion of their task. They lowered (καθῆκαν) the paralytic in the middle in front of Jesus. The obstacle of the crowd has been overcome. The paralytic is now in front of Jesus (ἔμπροσθεν τοῦ Ἰησοῦ), precisely where his companions first sought to place him.[16]

## 5.3. Jesus' Dispute with the Pharisees and Teachers of the Law (5:20–24)

Everything is ready for the healing miracle. The paralytic has been placed in the center of the space, and thus in the center of attention of all those gathered. More importantly, however, he has been placed in front of Jesus, thus demanding Jesus' attention. As expected, Jesus responds to the situation, which, on the surface, appears to disrupt his teaching activity. At this crucial moment, the narrator withdraws, allowing Jesus to assert his authoritative view. It is accomplished in two steps. First by referring to the perception of Jesus ("seeing their faith") and then by switching to Jesus' direct speech: "Friend,[17] your sins are forgiven[18] you." The resulting effect of surprise is patent.[19] Jesus does not heal the man; instead, he announces forgiveness of

---

verb ζητέω is capable of expressing, namely, to "devote serious effort to realize one's desire or objective" (*ibid.*). In retrospect, the men do more than just seek; they strive to bring their companion to Jesus.

[15] Such a procedure was not completely unknown in antiquity as Josephus, *Ant.* 14.459, shows. See other examples in H.-J. KLAUCK, "Die Frage der Sündenvergebung in der Perikope von der Heilung des Gelähmten (Mk 2,1–12 parr)", *BZ* 25 (1981) 225, n. 8.

[16] See Lk 5:18: ἐζήτουν ... θεῖναι [αὐτὸν] ἐνώπιον αὐτοῦ.

[17] In address, the vocative ἄνθρωπε can mean "friend." See BDAG, 82. But it can also have the opposite meaning: "in the voc. freq. in a contemptuous sense" (LSJ, 141). It is this latter meaning that C. F. EVANS, *Saint Luke*, 301 postulates, suggesting that it "may be used here to imply that the patient was indeed a sinner." But the words of forgiveness spoken by Jesus are not an expression of contempt or rebuke. Quite the contrary, they are words of good news. The address "friend" fits the context.

[18] The perfect tense ἀφέωνται conveys the lasting result of forgiveness. It is rendered by the present tense "are forgiven". See BDF, §342.

[19] See GRASSO, *Luca*, 168.

his sins. This time it is not the crowd but Jesus who frustrates the expectation of an immediate cure of the paralyzed man.

This is the first explicit reference to Jesus' act of forgiving sins. Formulated in the perfect passive tense (ἀφέωνται),[20] the declaration of forgiveness points to God as the agent of forgiveness (divine passive) and stresses the resulting state of freedom from sin. The relation between Jesus' word and God's agency will be discussed below. For now let us take note of Jesus' decision to represent the workings of forgiveness by the use of the verb ἀφίημι. First of all, in his programmatic sermon in Nazareth, Jesus described his mission as directed to the poor, the captives, the blind, and the oppressed. Twice, in relation to the captives and the oppressed, he defined his mission as a ministry of release (ἄφεσις). The double reference to release, a noun that had already been used twice to convey the notion of forgiveness ("release") of sins (1:77; 3:3), pointed to forgiveness of sins as an integral part of Jesus' ministry of releasing the captives and the oppressed. The forgiveness of the paralytic's sins constitutes now a direct enactment of the Nazareth program of release. Secondly, the verbal idea conveyed by the use of ἀφίημι in 5:20 is that of sins being dismissed, sent away.[21] The sins can be said to depart just like other oppressive forces did when confronted by Jesus in 4:35,39,41; 5:13. But there is more to the construal of sinfulness in 5:20 than just the notion of the remittal of sins. In view of Jesus' program of releasing the captives and letting the oppressed go free (4:18), sinfulness appears as a state of captivity and oppression from which the forgiven sinner is set free. That it is physical paralysis that afflicts the sinner becomes very telling. As sinfulness is metaphorically represented as a state of bondage, physical paralysis assumes the function of an eloquent symbolic representation of the oppression and captivity brought about by sin.

The paralyzed man is not explicitly called a sinner. Yet, the words of forgiveness addressed to him constitute an indirect reference to his sinfulness. In the eyes of Jesus, and so in the reader's mind, he is a sinner, albeit a sinner whose sins have now been forgiven. Jesus thus both reveals and remits the sinfulness of the paralyzed man. Interestingly, Jesus does it "seeing their faith," that is, the faith of the paralytic and his companions.[22] He sees it either by the external gestures of overcoming difficulties or by the same prophetic ability by which he will soon perceive the questioning of the scribes and the Pharisees. Thus Jesus combines forgiveness of sins with faith in his own person. The connection between forgiveness of sins and faith is not surprising.

---

[20] The perfect passive form ἀφέωνται is based on the Doric-Ionic-Arcadian perfect form ἕωμαι instead of the Attic εἶμαι. See BDF, §97,3.

[21] BDAG, 156–157.

[22] The paralytic is logically included among those whose faith (τὴν πίστιν αὐτῶν) Jesus recognizes. See BOVON, *Luke 1*, 181.

Just as Peter's faith in Jesus' word brought about a chain of events culminating in new life in Jesus' company, an equivalent of forgiveness for the self-confessed sinner, so the faith of the paralytic and his friends leads to more than a physical healing: it brings about the forgiveness of sins. Forgiveness and faith are connected for the second time.

Finally, forgiveness of sins is predicated of someone who is both sinful and sick. We have noted how Jesus combines exorcisms, healings, and forgiveness as aspects of his ministry of release. We have also observed how Luke's depiction of the oppressive forces of Satan, sin, and sickness represents them as related without however collapsing the differences between them. Luke's characterization of the paralytic as someone both sick and sinful now advances the reader's understanding of the relation between sin and sickness.

Sin and sickness are distinct. Jesus' words of forgiveness do not constitute the expected act of healing.[23] Even though it was not uncommon within the Jewish worldview to attribute physical illness to sin,[24] paralysis is not presented as a punishment for sin. If it were, the sick man would have been healed immediately at the words of forgiveness and not at the later word of healing.[25] Nor is Jesus' declaration of forgiveness just a preparatory spiritual stage in the process leading to physical healing. When the healing finally takes place, it will be performed to authenticate the claim to forgiveness. The healing will be at the service of forgiveness, not the other way around. That said, the function of healing is not therefore limited to demonstrating Jesus' authority to forgive. Both the healing and forgiveness are manifestations of the same ministry of release,[26] just as both sin and paralysis constitute forces that oppress humans. The fact that Jesus chooses first to forgive the sins of the paralytic does not mean that forgiveness is all he intends to do. It rather suggests that forgiveness of sins is a more immediate need.[27] In the end, both acts, the forgiveness of the paralytic's sins and the healing of his sickness, will be subordinated to yet another narrative interest. The paralytic's quest for well-being will yield to the question about the identity of Jesus.

---

[23] N. GELDENHUYS, *Commentary on the Gospel of Luke* (NICNT; Grand Rapids, MI 1954) 188, thinks that in this particular case sin did lie at the root of paralysis. Similarly SCHÜRMANN, *Das Lukasevangelium*, I, 282, thinks the sickness is conditioned by sin. For GREEN, *The Gospel of Luke*, 241, pronouncement of forgiveness is the healing moment.

[24] Exod 5:3; 1 Sam 5:6–12; 2 Kgs 15:5; Prov 3:7–8; 3 Macc 2:21–22; *Let. Aris.* 233; *T. Reu.* 1.7–8; see M. L. BROWN, *Israel's Divine Healer* (Grand Rapids, MI 1995) 101–105; 133–137; 239–242.

[25] WOLTER, *Das Lukasevangelium*, 222.

[26] Even though healing and forgiveness are separate acts, they are different aspects of one divine saving act. So SELLNER, *Das Heil Gottes*, 190.

[27] Forgiveness in place of expected healing implies soteriological hierarchy of needs. See SELLNER, *Das Heil Gottes*, 183.

The questions about the identity of Jesus that Luke puts on the lips of the scribes and the Pharisees – "who is this who is speaking blasphemes? Who can forgive sins but God alone?"[28] – mark a shift in the unfolding of the plot. The resolution plot, the dynamics of which push the story towards the expected healing of the paralyzed man, becomes secondary to the plot of revelation that now begins to govern the unfolding of events. The declaration of forgiveness triggers reactions that center not on the possibility of subsequent healing, but on the identity of the expectant healer.

The reaction of the scribes and the Pharisees, provoked by Jesus' unexpected declaration of forgiveness, is significant not only because it instantiates the theme of conflict between Jesus and the religious leaders of Israel, but also because of how it frames the main issue of the conflict. While Jesus' declaration of forgiveness has been formulated without the agent of forgiveness being specified – "your sins are forgiven you" – that is, presumably with God as the implied agent of forgiveness, the Pharisees and the scribes understand Jesus to declare himself capable of forgiving sins. In their minds, he blasphemes,[29] claiming for himself what God alone (μόνος ὁ θεός)[30] can do. Jesus threatens the uniqueness of Israel's God. The scribes and the Pharisees interpret Jesus' words of forgiveness in the strongest possible sense. For them Jesus does not just announce that someone has been forgiven by God, as for instance Nathan once announced to David. In their mind, Jesus enacts divine forgiveness.[31] A touch of Lukan irony could be seen in the fact that

---

[28] As J. N. BAILEY, "Looking for Luke's Fingerprints: Identifying Evidence of Redactional Activity In 'The Healing of the Paralytic' (Luke 5:17–26)", RestQ 48 (2006) 154, observes, "Luke's use of the masculine interrogative pronoun τίς, the masculine demonstrative pronoun οὗτος, and the masculine relative pronoun ὅς, all referring to Jesus, places the emphasis on Jesus rather than on his statement."

[29] In ancient Judaism "wird Gott gelästert, wenn ein Mensch ihn schmäht, seinen Namen verflucht, sich göttliche Stellung und Würde anmaßt." O. HOFIUS, "βλασφημία", EWNT, I, 530. Blasphemy is punishable by death (see Lev 24:10–16:23). The Mishnah later narrows the definition of blasphemy punishable by death to the blasphemer who has fully pronounced the divine name. See m. Sanh. 7:5.

[30] ROWE, Early Narrative Christology, 99 points to 4 Kgdms 19:15; Ps 85:10 [86:10 MT]; Isa 37:16; 2 Macc 7:37; Philo Conf. 93; Somn. 2.193–194; Josephus Ant. 8.335; Let. Aris.132 and demonstrates that μόνος ὁ θεός is a fundamental Jewish affirmation about the God of Israel's uniqueness. This leads him to state that "it is thus rather doubtful that the christology that underlines the portrayal of this first face-off with the scribes and Pharisees is an agent christology – Jesus is God's agent in the same way as, for example, the prophet Nathan in 2 Sam 12 and in this capacity can forgive sins. [...] Luke is making a much stronger claim – if indirectly – about the person of Jesus, one capable both of eliciting and answering the charge levied against him. [...] The person of Jesus embodies in his action the Lord of Israel: by the power of the Lord are the paralytic's sins forgiven – δύναμις κυρίου is the theological response to τίς δύναται" (ibid. 103–104).

[31] C. F. EVANS, Saint Luke, 301, thinks the criticism of Jesus is less radical. According to him, "the issue here would seem to be, 'Who has the right to declare authoritatively and

this hypercritical interpretation will be proven correct. As religious leaders feel obliged to defend the uniqueness of Israel's God, Jesus obliges them to recognize the uniqueness of his relationship with Israel's God. The unexpected declaration of forgiveness becomes now a cause of controversy, with the identity of Jesus, and the identity of God, at its center.

The scribes and the Pharisees do not question Jesus directly. Nevertheless, his immediate response to them in 5:22 – "Why do you raise such questions in your hearts?" – confirms that he knows what transpires in the hearts of his critics.[32] Jesus' next question – "Which is easier, to say, 'Your sins are for-

---

with privy knowledge that God has forgiven?'" Since, as Evans argues, the priests exercised such a right within the sacrificial ritual, Jesus' offence consists in declaring the forgiveness authoritatively "outside the prescribed ritual" (*ibid.* 301). This interpretation is problematic at least on two grounds. First of all, it downplays the fact that the scribes and the Pharisees ask 'who can forgive' and not 'who can declare forgiveness.' Secondly, the declaration of forgiveness was not necessarily limited to the setting of the sacrificial ritual. Other than 2 Sam 12, see the discussion of the prophetic mediation of forgiveness in intertestamental Judaism in HÄGERLAND, *Jesus and the Forgiveness of Sins*, 142–166, particularly Hägerland's analysis of Josephus, *Ant.* 6.91–93, and of the *Prayer of Nabonidus* (4Q242).

[32] Jesus' prophetic clairvoyance is attested throughout the narrative of Luke. Jesus possesses foreknowledge of his audience's reactions (4:23), knowledge of his opponents' intentions (6:8), awareness of his host's thoughts (7:40), and of his disciples' doubts (24:38), not to mention his predictions regarding his own passion, the fate of the temple, the denial of Peter, and his own future coming. Are we to explain Jesus' reaction in 5:22 as a similar manifestation of his prophetic powers? Is this a case of Jesus' prophetic knowledge of things secret? A negative answer seems to be suggested by the fact that Luke's account in 5:21 gives the impression of an open, audible objection on the part of the Pharisees and the scribes. Unlike the reactions described in 1:21, where the people wondered (ἐθαύμαζον) about Zechariah's delay, or in 1:66, where they pondered things in their hearts (ἔθεντο... ἐν τῇ καρδίᾳ αὐτῶν), or in 3:15, where they were questioning in their hearts concerning John (καὶ διαλογιζομένων πάντων ἐν ταῖς καρδίαις αὐτῶν), Luke does not indicate that the questioning that arose among the scribes and the Pharisees (καὶ ἤρξαντο διαλογίζεσθαι) was strictly internal. That said, Luke makes clear that their questioning is not addressed to Jesus; they refer to him in the third person – "Who is this one, who...?" (τίς ἐστιν οὗτος ὃς...) – not in the second: "Who are you?" Even though it is not directed to Jesus, he comes to know it (ἐπιγνούς) and, in responding, qualifies it as something that transpires in their hearts (ἐν ταῖς καρδίαις ὑμῶν), that is, as something internal to their group. His knowledge of their opinions appears then to be prophetic. The reader will encounter a similar presentation of Jesus' prophetic powers in Lk 9:46–47. The information about the argument (διαλογισμός) among the disciples, presumably an open and audible exchange of views, is followed by the reference to Jesus' awareness of their inner thoughts (εἰδὼς τὸν διαλογισμὸν τῆς καρδίας αὐτῶν), that is, to his prophetic coming to know about their quarrel. Speaking of the prophetic competence of Jesus, GREEN, *The Gospel of Luke*, 242, points to its connection with Lk 2:35 and 4:23. WOLTER, *Das Lukasevangelium*, 223 notes how the cognizance of hidden thoughts characterizes the divine mode of knowing in 1 Sam 16:7; 1 Kgs 8:39; Ps 94:11; 19:2. See similar observa-

given you,' or to say, 'Stand up and walk'?" – refers to the doubt expressed
by the scribes and the Pharisees. For them, only God can forgive sins, and so
the declaration of forgiveness pronounced by Jesus is just an empty talk, or
words without effects. Following their logic, the words of healing would be
equally empty, their emptiness being seen in the lack of healing. If anything
could be easier to say, it would be the words of forgiveness since their effects, unlike the effects of healing, would not be directly verifiable.[33] In 5:23
then, Jesus lays the ground for the authenticating function of the healing miracle he is about to perform. In 5:24, he makes that function explicit: the healing takes place so that the scribes and the Pharisees may know[34] "that the Son
of Man has authority on earth to forgive sins."

For the first time in the Gospel, Jesus refers to himself as the Son of Man
(ὁ υἱὸς τοῦ ἀνθρώπου). Although echoes of the use of that title in the book
of Daniel can be detected here, particularly the connection between the Son
of Man and the notion of authority (ἐξουσία) in Dan 7:13–14,[35] not much

---

tions in RADL, Lukas, I, 319; P. ROLLAND, "Jésus connaissait leurs pensées", EThL 62
(1986) 121, SCHÜRMANN, Das Lukasevangelium, I, 283.

[33] See FITZMYER, Luke, I, 584.

[34] Some commentators, among others FITZMYER, Luke, I, 579, NOLLAND, Luke, I, 237;
and SCHÜRMANN, Das Lukasevangelium, I, 283, propose to read the first part of the verse
as an editorial comment to the reader: "But so that you (the readers) may know that the
Son of Man has authority on earth to forgive sins, he said to the one who was paralyzed: 'I
say to you…'" Their proposal attempts to solve the problem of the anacoluthic ending of
the final clause, which creates a shift of addressees from the second person plural (you, the
scribes and the Pharisees) to the second person singular (you, the paralyzed man): "But so
that you may know that the Son of Man has authority on earth to forgive sins – he said to
the one who was paralyzed – I say to you…" WOLTER, Das Lukasevangelium, 224, however, provides examples from Greek literature where the final clause is followed not by the
main clause but by the change of addressee. (Demosthenes, Orationes 45,19; 46,10; Aeschines, Ctes. 93). There is no need then to postulate an editorial comment to the reader.
Besides, as BOVON, Luke 1, 184, rightly observes, "a sudden switch here would be just as
clumsy as the anacolouthon." Finally, an editorial comment to the reader would create an
otherwise unwarranted impression that the readers need to be persuaded of Jesus' authority
as much as the hypercritical scribes and Pharisees do.

[35] Connection between Jesus and the Danielic son of man is explored by A. FEUILLET,
"L'Exousia du fils de l'homme (d'après Mc. II, 10–28 et parr.)", RSR 42 (1954) 161–192.
Regarding the scene of the Healing of the Paralytic, Feuillet admits that Jesus' reference to
the Danielic vision remains extremely discreet. See ibid. 171. HÄGERLAND, Jesus and the
Forgiveness of Sins, 171, thinks the Danielic influence is much stronger and points in addition to the resemblances between the Greek versions of Dan 4:14 and the Synoptic form of
Jesus' saying. There is a correspondence between the syntactical structure of the final
clause "but so that you may know that" (ἵνα δὲ εἰδῆτε ὅτι; Mark 2:10; Lk 5:24) and The-
odotion's "so that those who live may know that" (ἵνα γνῶσιν οἱ ζῶντες ὅτι; 4:17 The-
od), as well as between the LXX wording (ἐξουσίαν ἔχειν … τῶν ἐπὶ τῆς γῆς; 4:17
LXX) and the Gospel's phrases "has authority" (ἐξουσίαν ἔχει) and "on earth" (ἐπὶ τῆς
γῆς).

more beyond the general designation of God's representative endowed with authority can be discerned in the Lukan context. It is rather the present context that gives contours to the title of the Son of Man. The Son of Man is endowed with authority to forgive sins. In the mind of the scribes and the Pharisees this authority belongs exclusively to God, that is, to the realm of heaven, but in Jesus' understanding it is exercised now on earth by the Son of Man. The Son of Man then does what God alone can do. In other words, the Son of Man appears as a self-designation chosen by Jesus to capture his identity as revealed in his authority to forgive sins. It is "distinguishing Jesus in his singularity."[36]

That the authority of the Son of Man regards the forgiveness of sins is not to be overlooked. The controversy at the heart of the story serves to highlight this aspect of Jesus' characterization that is crucial. Here it is clearly Jesus' share in God's prerogative to forgive sins. It is equally a controversy about God: God's decision to forgive is not something postponed until the fruits of repentance and the rituals of repentance are accomplished, as suggested by the preaching of John the Baptist. God grants forgiveness in response to faith in Jesus.

## 5.4. Reactions to the Miracle (5:25–26)

It is only now that the healing takes place. The effectiveness of Jesus' words of healing is rendered visible by the exact parallel between Jesus' command in 5:24 and its realization in 5:25. To the three elements of Jesus' command – stand up (ἔγειρε), take your bed (ἄρας τὸ κλινίδιόν σου), and go to your home (πορεύου εἰς τὸν οἶκόν σου) – correspond the three distinct actions of the healed man: he stood up (ἀναστάς), took what he had been lying on (ἄρας ἐφ᾽ ὃ κατέκειτο), and went to his home (ἀπῆλθεν εἰς τὸν οἶκον αὐτοῦ). Finally, the healed man and then all[37] those present glorify God. The theocentric perspective established in 5:17 with the reference to the power of the Lord is reaffirmed with the double reference to the glorification of God (5:25,26). Thus the transition from the presence of God's power to heal to the glorification of God passes through Jesus' ministry of forgiveness and healing. The theocentric framing of Jesus' ministry is reaffirmed at the point at

---

[36] GREEN, *The Gospel of Luke*, 242.

[37] With no indication to the contrary, the Pharisees and the scribes are to be included among all those seized by amazement who give glory to God (5:26). "Pharisees appear to have capitulated, joining the chorus in God's praise." CARROLL, "Luke's Portrayal of the Pharisees", 608. Similarly, LEVINE, "Luke's Pharisees", 116; ECKEY, *Das Lukasevangelium*, I, 257; C. F. EVANS, *Saint Luke*, 297. For a contrary opinion, see MEYNET, *L'Évangile de Luc*, 257.

which the objections of the religious leaders attempt to drive a wedge between Israel's God and Jesus. The glorification of God vindicates both God, who acts through Jesus, and Jesus, who acts in God's place.[38]

## 5.5. The Theme of Sinfulness and the Likely Effects of Lk 5:17–26

The scene is populated with many characters. Their functions allow us to group them into four categories: 1) Jesus (and God), 2) the paralytic (and his friends), 3) the scribes and the Pharisees, 4) and the crowd. The healing story, in which the paralytic (group 2) wants to obtain a favor from Jesus (group 1) by overcoming the obstacle of the crowd (group 4), is intercepted by the controversy, in which the challenge of the scribes and the Pharisees (group 3) is overcome by Jesus (group 1) to the applause of the crowd (group 4). Both dramatic developments, the controversy and the quest for healing, are so arranged that their final explanation and resolution – their dramatic denouement – is performed by Jesus. Jesus is the ultimate hero. As in the story of the Calling of Peter, the multiplicity of the characters does not detract from but rather points to Jesus. Let us recapture this dynamic orientation by which various personages in the story point to the mystery of Jesus.

The crowd as a category includes all those initially present, that is, among others the scribes and the Pharisees. The disciples, although not mentioned, should be assumed to form part of the crowd gathered around Jesus. Other than forming an obstacle to the paralytic's access to Jesus, the members of the crowd are to be included among all (ἅπας) seized with amazement at the miracle. The crowd's function is limited to these two elements. The first of them helps display the value of faith in Jesus. The second serves as a demonstration of Jesus' success.

The paralyzed man, around whose need for healing the resolution plot is structured, functions as a recipient of divine favor. His helpers have no independent existence in the story. Their function consists in demonstrating an attitude of faith in overcoming obstacles that separate their friend from reaching the presence of Jesus. A far as the trait of faith is concerned, they and the paralytic act as one group character. The sick man remains passive. He does not participate in the dispute between Jesus and the religious leaders. Like the

---

[38] What I. MAISCH, *Die Heilung des Gelähmten.* Eine exegetisch-traditionsgeschichtliche Untersuchung zu Mk 2,1–12 (SBS 52; Stuttgart 1971) 128, states about the Markan version of the story is applicable here as well. The pericope shows "*was* Jesus kann, *wie* er ist und *wer* er ist: Er tut, was Gott tut; er handelt, wie Gott handelt; er ist wie Gott – er ist der gottgleiche Herr." Or as ROSSÉ, *Luca,* 180, n. 50, puts it: "Gesù offre in nome proprio il perdono di Dio".

leper in the previous scene, he illustrates the benefits of faith in Jesus: his faith brings him healing. Like Peter, he receives divine forgiveness because of his faith.

Related to and integrated with the characterizations of Peter and the leper, the presentation of the paralytic draws attention to the function of space in the narrative. Space as a modality of the narrated world becomes an eloquent means of expressing the workings of forgiveness. Peter's awareness of sin was expressed as a need for distance from Jesus ("go away from me, Lord," 5:8), while forgiveness was enacted as inclusion in the company of Jesus ("they followed him," 5:11). For the leper, the purification from leprosy happened through the complete elimination of the required distance (Jesus "touched him," 5:13). The paralytic and his friends persevere now in reducing the space that separates them from Jesus. Being placed in the presence of Jesus occasions the gift of forgiveness of sins.[39] Finally, although the man's paralysis is not presented as resulting from sin[40] – if it were, the forgiveness itself would have brought about the healing – the condition plays into the symbolic function of alienation that is proper to the one who sins.[41]

The scribes and the Pharisees are bound together in everything they do in the story. Their basic function is to be a foil against which the identity of Jesus as a bearer of divine authority to forgive sins is sharpened and enhanced. The objection of the scribes and the Pharisees serves only to enhance our understanding of Jesus' participation in what "God alone" can do. Their overall characterization, however, remains somewhat ambiguous. There is no lack of irony in how their role in the story is presented. They are clearly attracted to Jesus in the first place. But it is not clear whether they come to be taught by Jesus or to investigate his teaching. Their radical criticism of Jesus' declaration of forgiveness suggests the latter. But when they are filled with amazement over the strange (παράδοξα)[42] things they had seen, they appear to be won over by Jesus' arguments. In praising God, they indirectly acclaim Jesus as teacher. Secondly, and even more ironically, if Jesus brings everyone to glorify God, and if blasphemy means anything that denies God's glory,

---

[39] That in the end the healed man goes home and thereby distances himself from Jesus is mitigated by the fact that, as he goes, he glorifies God, presumably for what God has done for him through Jesus. In this sense, the man's relationship with Jesus is not ruptured.

[40] Paralysis is a punishment for sin in 1 Macc 9:55; 2 Macc 3:22–28; 3 Macc 2:22. Cf. C. F. EVANS, *Saint Luke*, 301.

[41] According to Lev 21:18–24; 1QM 7,4–6; 1QSa 2:5–7 the lame were banned from priesthood in Israel and excluded from full participation in the Qumran community. Cf. GREEN, *The Gospel of Luke*, 239.

[42] According to BUSSE, *Die Wunder*, 124, παράδοξα is used in the plural to refer to both healing and forgiveness of sins.

then the real blasphemy is found in those who oppose Jesus' service to the paralyzed man.[43]

Jesus is clearly the protagonist. He acts as the representative of God and, in a certain sense, alongside God. He appears in easily identifiable roles. He acts as a teacher, prophet, healer, and finally as the Son of Man, endowed with divine authority to forgive sins. His characterization comes from the narratorial description of his external action (Jesus "was teaching" in 5:17), his God-granted capacity ("the power of the Lord was with him to heal" in 5:17) and his interior perceptions (Jesus "saw their faith" in 5:20; he "perceived their questioning" in 5:22). At crucial junctures the narrator leaves it to Jesus to characterize himself by words that first manifest his power to forgive sins ("your sins are forgiven you" in 5:20), and then confirm the radical character of this power ("the Son of Man has authority" in 5:24). Along the same line, it is left to Jesus to characterize the attitude of the paralytic and his companions as an attitude of faith, to characterize the paralytic as a sinner, and to characterize himself as the Son of Man authorized to forgive sins. Jesus clearly holds the key to how others and himself are to be understood.

The reader of the preliminary narrative of Luke 1–4 can be expected to undergo a dynamic process of moving from (1) perceiving the sinfulness as a condition to be addressed by God's eschatological intervention, to (2) realizing that the sinfulness can be properly perceived only from the perspective of God's eschatological agent. Lk 5:17–26 enhances this dynamic effect. Sinfulness as a literary characteristic is inserted into the fabric of the narrated world at a very well-staged moment: through the surprising declaration of forgiveness Luke lets Jesus redirect the plot of the story subordinating the quest for healing to the controversy about power to forgive sins. Jesus, the authoritative interpreter of himself and therefore of God's redemptive intervention, decides to make explicit that which until now has been only indirectly expressed, namely, his power to forgive sins.[44] Sinfulness then appears as the object of Jesus' attention: he indirectly declares someone to be sinful, and he frees the individual from the condition of sin. In this way the characteristic of sinfulness emerges in the consciousness of the reader as mediated by the authoritative perception of Jesus. Secondly, the trait of sinfulness is used as an ideological label, which the scribes and the Pharisees try to impose on Jesus. In their minds, Jesus blasphemes by claiming for himself a divine prerogative.[45] To the scribes and the Pharisees he is a sinner. The fact that sin-

---

[43] See R. A., CULPEPPER, *The Gospel of Luke*. Introduction, Commentary, and Reflections (The New Interpreter's Bible Volume IX; Nashville, TN 1995) 126.

[44] According to C. F. EVANS, *Saint Luke*, 296, the deliverance from paralysis and from sin supplies the most direct fulfillment of Lk 4:18.

[45] Jesus then, by forgiving sins, risks being viewed as a sinner. This is somewhat similar to the situation where by touching the leper Jesus accepts the risk of contagion without becoming a leper himself.

fulness as a characteristic is predicated of Jesus is not just ironic. It makes of sinfulness an issue upon which Jesus' identity hinges. For, the question of whether he can forgive sins or not gives way to a more dramatic predicament about Jesus: either he can forgive sins or he is himself a sinner. Ultimately, Jesus' authoritative view is miraculously confirmed, silencing his opponents, at least for now. It becomes clear that *their* view of sin and sinners is inadequate.

In the Calling of Peter, Jesus triggered both the realization and confession of Peter's sinfulness, and also corrected Peter's understanding of what his own sinfulness entailed. Here Jesus prophetically reveals and divinely remits the sins of the paralytic. He also challenges the mistaken notion that the scribes and the Pharisees have about his allegedly sinful conduct. Jesus remains the one who chooses to trigger the revelation, or simply chooses to reveal sin. At the same time, he corrects the mistaken understanding of sin's consequences, or of its attribution. The operations seen in 5:1–11 are repeated with an added emphasis on Christological explicitness, in particular on Jesus' power to forgive sins. The contextual frame in which the characteristic of sinfulness operates is largely replicated: the connection that faith in Jesus has with the revelation of one's sinfulness and its subsequent remittal is reaffirmed for the reader. A new emphasis is placed on sin's connection with sickness. Jesus, who has forgiven the sins of Simon and healed the illness of the leper, now ministers to someone who is both sick and sinful. Thus, on the one hand, Jesus' ministry of release from sins remains embedded in his larger program of procuring liberation from various alienating and oppressive forces. On the other hand, the physical paralysis, as a concrete representation of the debilitating character of those forces, comes to illustrate the "sickness-like" nature of sin.[46]

The mimetic content of the characteristic of sinfulness remains unspecified and thus potentially within the range of the reader's pre-existing beliefs. Finally, the reader becomes alert to the fact that, broadly, Jesus' handling of sin and sinners causes controversies, a theme that will receive much attention in the subsequent scenes.

---

[46] Soon, in 5:31, Jesus will explore the power of this metaphor.

Chapter 6

# The Call of Levi (5:27–39)

Lk 5:27–39 is the first episode in the Galilean ministry of Jesus where the theme of sinfulness runs through every dramatic segment of the account. From Jesus' look at the potentially sinful tax collector, through the table fellowship with tax collectors and sinners, to Jesus' double address to the implicitly sinful Pharisees, sinfulness as a characteristic becomes declared, debated, and even denied. For the most part, Luke the narrator withdraws, allowing Jesus and his interlocutors to speak directly. But even then there is much indirectness in what they say about sinners and sin.

Lk 5:27–39 consists of two scenes, the scene of the call in 5:27–28 and the scene of the banquet in 5:29–39. Within the episodic plot of the Galilean ministry of Jesus, the call of Levi (5:27–28) and the meal scene[1] that follows (5:29–39) stand out as causally connected: the call occasions the meal, which in turn creates a setting for the table conversation that follows. The interaction between Jesus and Levi, initiated in 5:27–28, continues in 5:29;[2] in fact it now expands to include a crowd of Levi's fellow tax collectors and others gathered together in a meal scene setting. The reaction of the Pharisees and their scribes directed toward Jesus' disciples in 5:30 receives a response from Jesus in 5:31–32. A new question from the Pharisees[3] in 5:33 receives anoth-

---

[1] Although "Greco-Roman and Jewish meals owe much of their structure to the classical form of the symposium" [J. H. NEYREY, "Ceremonies in Luke-Acts: The Case of Meals and Table Fellowship", *The Social World of Luke-Acts*. Models for Interpretation (ed. J. H. NEYREY) (Peabody, MA 1991) 364], Lk 5:29–39 should not be pressed to fit the narrow frame of the symposium genre only. After all, in the context of the meal in question, Jesus will refer to the image of the wedding (5:34) and not that of a symposium. It is better, then, to speak of a table fellowship theme in which use is made of meal symbolism. On the table fellowship theme in Luke, and particularly on various elements of meal symbolism present in Luke's Gospel, see D. E. SMITH, "Table Fellowship as a Literary Motif in the Gospel of Luke", *JBL* 106 (1987) 613–638.

[2] "Luke creates one story by making Levi a point of continuity." JOHNSON, *The Gospel of Luke*, 97.

[3] It is not immediately clear who poses the question in 5:33. Many commentators are hesitant to perceive the Pharisees as the subject of οἱ δὲ εἶπαν because of the awkwardness of the self-referential phrase contained in their question: "and the disciples of the Pharisees" as opposed to a more natural "our disciples." See, for example, BOCK, *Luke*, I, 515, for whom the remark in 5:33 is coming from the crowd. This awkwardness, however, is lessened when we notice that the same asking subject in 5:30 and 5:33 are not just the

er response from Jesus in 5:34–35, followed by a parable involving three different images in 5:36–39. The literary unity of the episode is additionally manifested by references to eating and drinking in 5:30 and 5:33, and again to drinking in 5:39.[4] After the narratorial *telling* in 5:27–29 about Levi's encounter with Jesus and its consequences, the narrator resorts to *showing* by having Jesus and the Pharisees present themselves through direct speech in 5:30–39. Thus the plot moves from attention to actions performed by Jesus and Levi in 5:27–29 to attention to information revealed through the characters' words in 5:30–39. A plot of revelation comes to govern the unfolding of the story. Our analysis will be conducted in three steps. We will start with the scene of the call in 5:27–28. Our examination of the banquet scene will be divided into 5:29–32 and 5:33–39, that is, according to the challenge-response format discernible in the interaction between Jesus and the Pharisees.

## 6.1. Call and Response (5:27–28)

This time the scene does not begin with the καὶ ἐγένετο formula nor with space or time indications: "in one of the cities" (5:12); "on one of those days" (5:17). There is no indication that much of Jesus' activity has gone unreported. Instead, a new episode is announced by chronological and topographical indications: "and after this he went out and saw" (καὶ μετὰ ταῦτα ἐξῆλθεν καὶ ἐθεάσατο). This creates an impression of consecutive events. As readers we are encouraged to view the call of the tax collector as the very first thing Jesus does after having had his power to release from sin disputed. In this sense, Jesus does not walk out of the disputed issue. He reenters it.

Indeed, unlike in previous episodes, the topic of sinfulness enters the scene right away. Even before Levi's name is mentioned, the reader finds out through the authoritative perception of Jesus (ἐθεάσατο, 5:27) that he is a tax collector. Is this enough to consider him sinful? John the Baptist's instruction given to the tax collectors in 3:13 – "collect no more than the amount prescribed for you" – points to extortion as the typical sin of tax collectors. But the same instruction also indicates that the profession of the tax collector is not necessarily sinful: they are not told to abandon their profession. Nevertheless, the fact that the tax collectors receive the baptism of re-

---

Pharisees but the Pharisees and their scribes. The self-referential phrase ("and the disciples of the Pharisees") might serve to clarify that the scribes *as such* are not compared with the disciples of Jesus. For BOVON, *Luke 1*, 187, since the reference to the disciples of the Pharisees is placed at the end of the sentence, Luke no longer needs to put it in direct speech ("our disciples"). On οἱ δέ, as a mark of continuation of a narrative, see BDF, §251.

[4] Cf. J. DUPONT, "Vin vieux, vin nouveau", *CBQ* 25 (1963), 300.

pentance for the forgiveness of sins (3:3) means that they are actually sinful, which, given the likelihood of them committing a sin of extortion, is not surprising. The reader then is warranted in seeing the indication of sinfulness in the characterization of Levi as a tax collector. When Jesus later speaks of having come to call sinners to repentance (5:32), it is logical to include Levi in this category.

Unlike in previous scenes, Jesus does not trigger the recognition of sinfulness nor declare the sinful state of the person he interacts with. Nevertheless, he is still the one who perceives it (ἐθεάσατο τελώνην), and it is through his authoritative perception that the reader is presented with the characteristic of sinfulness. Inasmuch as Levi's profession is associated with sinfulness, Jesus' call to discipleship must signify an offer of forgiveness. It is the link between the acceptance of the call to discipleship and the status of being reconciled with God, first forged in the scene of the Calling of Simon Peter, that now invites such a conclusion. Other lexical parallels point in the same direction. Like the forgiven paralytic (5:25), Levi stands up; like Peter and his companions earlier (5:11), he leaves everything behind and follows Jesus. The following disposition of the text highlights the lexical and semantic links between the reactions of Levi (5:28), the paralytic (5:25), and Peter and his companions (5:11).

*Table 4:* Lexical and semantic links between Lk 5:28, 5:25, and 5:11.

| Lk 5:28: | Lk 5:25: | Lk 5:11: |
|---|---|---|
| | | καὶ καταγαγόντες τὰ πλοῖα |
| καὶ | | ἐπὶ τὴν γῆν |
| καταλιπὼν πάντα | καὶ παραχρῆμα | ἀφέντες πάντα |
| ἀναστὰς | ἀναστὰς | |
| ἠκολούθει αὐτῷ | ἐνώπιον αὐτῶν, ἄρας | ἠκολούθησαν αὐτῷ |
| | ἐφ' ὃ κατέκειτο, ἀπῆλθεν | |
| | εἰς τὸν οἶκον αὐτοῦ | |
| | δοξάζων τὸν θεόν | |

Levi's new identity is formed and revealed through his actions. These actions, in turn, bespeak his faith understood here as trustful obedience to the command of the one who calls him.[5] In this short scene (5:27–28) the charac-

---

[5] We have characterized Simon Peter's trustful obedience to Jesus' command (5:5) as an act of faith by virtue of its affinity with the similar attitude of Mary, whom Elizabeth characterized as believer (1:45). The faith of the paralytic and his companions, identified as such by Jesus (5:20), did not imply obedience to a command. It rather referred to their attitude of unrelenting trust in the healing powers of Jesus. Levi's submission to Jesus' call follows the type of faith exemplified by Simon Peter. Both types of faith, the one represented by Mary and Simon Peter and the one exemplified by the paralytic and his companions, have in common an element of decision by which the characters act upon their recognition of God's/Jesus' authority/truthfulness/power: Mary's decision to collaborate with

teristic of sinfulness functions in a familiar contextual frame: the theme is repeated in connection with the same theme of faith as before. Jesus performs a familiar operation: he notices Levi's sin and then offers a release from sin in virtue of his own association with Levi. Levi's sin, specified through the likelihood of sinfulness inherent in his profession, conforms to the reader's preexisting beliefs. What is missing now is Jesus' action of challenging the received understanding of what sinfulness entails. In the case of Peter, Jesus challenged his view that a distance was to be kept between a sinner and Jesus. In the case of the Pharisees who accused him of blaspheming, Jesus challenged their view that the sin of the paralytic could not be removed by Jesus' word. An occasion for a similar challenge regarding an opinion about what Jesus should and should not do vis-à-vis sinners is created right away by the Pharisees' objection voiced in 5:30.

## 6.2. Meal – First Objection – Response (5:29–32)

In 5:29 the narrator simply informs us that "Levi gave a great banquet for him in his house; and there was a large crowd of tax collectors and others sitting at the table with them." The Pharisees' complaint betrays a different perception of what is happening. They ask: "Why do you eat and drink with tax collectors and sinners?" (5:30). Where the narrator speaks of "tax collectors and others," the Pharisees see "tax collectors and sinners."[6] Neale discusses four

---

God's plan, Peter's decision to lower the nets for a catch, the paralytic and his friends' decision to move toward Jesus, and Levi's decision to follow Jesus.

[6] NOLLAND, *Luke*, I, 245, argues that the disciples of Jesus are to be included among the narratorial "others" in 5:29 for they will not be separately introduced by Luke. ROSSÉ, *Luca*, 187, sees the disciples among "others" on different grounds. The "others" are called "others" and not "sinners" to signify that, like the disciples whom they include, they had already been converted. We shall challenge Rossé's assertion as we analyze Jesus' response in 5:31–32. Let us, for now, state our reasons for opposing Nolland's view. First of all, when both the Pharisees with their scribes and the disciples are mentioned in verse 30, it must be assumed that, since the Pharisaic party objects to the table fellowship taking place at Levi's house, they are not to be included among "others" reclining at Levi's table. Since the Pharisees and their scribes are not separately introduced and since they are not among the "others," we must assume that they are introduced by virtue of posing the question to the disciples in 5:30. This way of introducing the Pharisees suggests that their interlocutors in 5:30 are similarly introduced at the same point. Secondly, the narratorial "tax collectors and others" modifies "a large crowd," that is, "others" refers to others *in the crowd* and not necessarily to all non-tax collectors reclining at table. It seems then more natural to assume that Luke introduces the crowd (of tax collectors and others) in 5:29 and then moves to introduce the Pharisees (with their scribes) and the disciples in 5:30 apart from the crowd. That the crowd of "tax collectors and others" stands apart from the rest of the characters populating the scene is additionally suggested by the Lukan use of ἄλλος

different reasons that have been proposed as the historical grounds for the objection against eating and drinking with tax collectors and sinners: political issues, legal issues, moral issues, religious symbolism. He concludes that at the level of history the nature of the offense remains unresolved.[7] In the narrative world, however, the cause of the offense is made clear when we notice the grouping together of tax collectors and sinners. The offense, in other words, appears to have moral grounds, just as the sinfulness of tax collectors has moral underpinnings in Luke's narrative (3:13). The Pharisees' understanding of sinfulness seems to conform to the reader's pre-existing belief about what made one sinful and about the danger of consorting with sinners.[8] Nevertheless, the difference between the narrator's and the Pharisees' points of view needs to be resolved. As can be expected, the reader will find the solution in Jesus' normative view of the issue.

Jesus' response in 5:31–32 accomplishes two things at the same time: on the one hand it answers the Pharisees' objection, and on the other it attempts to win them over. How is Jesus trying to win them over? He acknowledges their perception, at least partially: the narratorial "others" become "sinners" in Jesus' mouth.[9] Secondly, he speaks about bringing sinners to conversion, a value no one would object to. But as he partially aligns himself with the Pharisees' view, the sinners and the conversion he speaks of are not what the Pharisees understand them to be. For Jesus, the conversion is not a condition placed on the sick before they can meet their physician. Rather, it becomes a description of an encounter between the sick and their physician. And thus sinners are no longer sinful; their sin is already forgiven.[10] They are the sick

---

instead of ἕτερος to refer to "others." As V. R. SANDIYAGU, "Ἕτερος and Ἄλλος in Luke", *NT* 48 (2006) 129, demonstrates, "when Luke uses ἕτερος it means 'another of a different kind' having also connotation of 'another in enumeration', and when he uses ἄλλος it means 'another of the same kind.'" Accordingly, in 5:29 Luke describes the crowd of "tax collectors and others" *of the same kind* sitting at the table "with them" (μετ' αὐτῶν), that is, with Levi and Jesus, and, as we learn in 5:30, with Jesus' disciples as well. Finally, the parallelism between two expressions, the narratorial "tax collectors and others" and the pharisaic "the tax collectors and sinners," invites considering "sinners" as the Pharisees' word for the narratorial "others" and discourages considering the καί in "the tax collectors and sinners" as epexegetic: "the sinful tax collectors;" against RADL, *Lukas*, I, 329. For the Pharisees, the disciples and the sinners are two separate groups. They speak to the former about the latter.

[7] See NEALE, *None but the Sinners*, 118–129.

[8] See §1.4 above, where the violation of the rules of human relationships (e.g. Lev 19) and the need for keeping at a distance from those publicly acknowledged as sinners (e.g. Ps 1) are listed among the basic components of the discourse on sinfulness.

[9] This does not show that the narrator is not reliable but simply that he leaves to Jesus the ultimate evaluative conclusion.

[10] "By celebrating with these people, Jesus indicated that they had received God's forgiveness and would share in the reign of God." TANNEHILL, *Luke*, 109.

meeting their physician. In their table fellowship with Jesus their repentance is accomplished.[11] We note how again the correction of the Pharisees' view of sinfulness is combined with the amplification of Christological claims. In correcting the Pharisees' perception of how sinfulness is to be treated, Jesus presents himself as the criterion of conversion: conversion, in Jesus' understanding, is not a condition for community with him, but rather a turn toward him as the one authentically representing God.

But it is not just conversion that is Christologically redefined. Sinfulness itself, which until now has received a Christological framing – that which Jesus reveals and remits – begins to receive a new Christological content. The refusal to believe in Jesus is now indirectly characterized as something sinful. In other words, it is not just *how* sin is to be remitted but also *what* is to count as sin that is now Christologically determined. Let us spell out this development in more detail.

With the correction of the Pharisees' perception of others, Jesus combines a correction of the Pharisees' perception of themselves. First of all – and the reader should see it sooner than the Pharisees – by repeatedly directing himself to the Pharisees and by identifying himself as one sent to call sinners to repentance, Jesus treats the Pharisees as the sick in need of a physician. The reader is led to see them as, in some way, marked by sinfulness, since it is to the sinners that Jesus directs his attention.[12] But their implied sinfulness is compounded by their refusal to accept Jesus' ministry to them (and to other sinners). The reader can see again how, by ironically employing the Pharisees' self-perception as those who are well and in no need of a physician, Jesus subtly accuses them of alienating themselves from the one who can heal them.[13]

---

[11] See MÉNDEZ-MORATALLA, *The Paradigm*, 98, who accurately observes that "the offense for the religious groups representing largely accepted views within Judaism is that Jesus by-passes traditionally accepted demands concerning repentance and becomes himself the criterion for inclusion into the kingdom he claims to herald." The same line of interpretation is found in WOLTER, *Das Lukasevangelium*, 230; and BUSSE, *Die Wunder*, 128–129. Against ERNST, *Das Evangelium nach Lukas*, 199 who claims that "Die Busse ist die Voraussetzung für die Zulassung zur Mahlgemeinschaft." And similarly, against SCHÜRMANN, *Das Lukasevangelium*, I, 291; ROSSÉ, *Luca*, 187; and SELLNER, *Das Heil Gottes*, 135, for whom this meal is not yet salvation, but rather a reason to feel called to conversion.

[12] POWELL, "The Religious Leaders in Luke: A Literary-Critical Study", 104, taking into account the entire Lukan narrative, observes that "by eating with the religious leaders and by continuing to challenge them, Jesus shows that he regards them, like the tax collectors with whom he also eats (5:29; 15:1; 19:7), as lost persons and as sinners who need to repent."

[13] Many commentators postulate an irony here. See, for instance, BOCK, *Luke*, I, 498. See also J. L. RAY, *Narrative Irony in Luke-Acts*. The Paradoxical Interaction of Prophetic Fulfillment and Jewish Rejection (Mellen Biblical Press Series 28; Lewiston, NY 1996)

## 6.3. The Second Objection and the Response Followed by a Parable (5:33–39)

Jesus' dialogue with the Pharisees continues in 5:33–39. The question about fasting is a continuation of the first question about eating with sinners. It is Jesus' same attitude of not distancing himself from the sinners that continues to be questioned.[14] When a penitential connotation[15] of fasting is recalled, then it becomes clear that Jesus opposes the necessity of fasting because in his presence forgiveness has already taken place: either by table fellowship with him or by following him as a disciple as in the case of Peter and Levi. But here something more than just table fellowship is at stake. Jesus describes this table fellowship as the bridegroom's wedding feast. To the degree to which the image of the bridegroom and the wedding banquet is to be understood as the image of the Messiah and the arrival of messianic times,[16] the drama of the Pharisees' refusal of Jesus is heightened. The sickness of the Pharisees appears all the more serious since it places them outside the celebration of the messianic banquet. At the same time, Jesus' attempt to win the Pharisees over, to heal their sickness, also intensifies. The parable to which Jesus resorts in the final part of his speech constitutes such an attempt. This

---

55. For the discussion of other examples of verbal, dramatic, and situational irony in Luke-Acts see *ibid.* 53–66.

[14] Against LEVINE, "Luke's Pharisees", 117, for whom the Pharisees shift the question from table fellowship to fasting because they seem to be satisfied with the first answer, and with NAVE, *Repentance in Luke-Acts*, 171, who states that "the controversy is not about a different perspective on fasting but rather a different perspective on repentance."

[15] Lev 16:29,31; 1 Kgs 21:27; Isa 58:3–5; Sir 34:26. See other references in WOLTER, *Das Lukasevangelium*, 230.

[16] Jeremias' categorical rejection of the Messiah-Bridegroom association – according to him, "the allegorical representation of the Messiah as a bridegroom is completely foreign to the whole of the Old Testament and to the literature of late Judaism" [J. JEREMIAS, *The Parables of Jesus* (London ³1972) 52] – has been questioned. See R., ZIMMERMANN, *Geschlechtermetaphorik und Gottesverhältnis*. Traditionsgeschichte und Theologie eines Bildfelds in Urchristentum und antiker Umwelt (WUNT 2.R 122; Tübingen 2001) 227–276, where he discusses the use of the bridegroom-metaphor within the frame of Jewish messianic expectations, in particular the image of the wedding of the Royal Anointed One in Ps 45 (LXX 44), the messianic (High) Priest as bridegroom according to 1QIs^a 61:10 and Targum Zechariah 3:1–10. Zimmermann concludes that even though our knowledge remains fragmentary, the likelihood that Jesus, and in particular the NT authors, used the bridegroom metaphor in relation to the background of the early Jewish image is not small (*ibid.* 276). With K. R. SNODGRASS, *Stories with Intent*. A Comprehensive Guide to the Parables of Jesus (Grand Rapids, MI 2008) 514, we can add that, if properly restored, 4Q434^a fragments 1–2, lines 6–7 compel us even more to conclude that the association of a bridegroom with the messianic idea is not as late as is usually suggested.

claim, however, must be both elaborated and justified in light of various proposals regarding the interpretation of 5:36–39.

Three main lines of interpretation can be discerned in the study of this passage. The first line of interpretation sees a superior novelty in the teaching of Jesus and treats 5:39 as an observation about some peoples' unfortunate attachment to the old pharisaic ways,[17] an observation additionally interpreted by some to be nostalgic,[18] humorous[19] or ironic.[20] The second line of interpretation reverses the valuation of old and new in light of 5:39 and sees the teaching of Jesus as the true old.[21] The third line of interpretation claims that verse 5:39 is neither about an attachment to the old nor about Jesus' way being genuinely ancient, but simply about the fact that the old and the new cannot be mixed.[22] Finally, there are individual views that escape this tripartite classification.[23] All of these interpretations, however, rest on the same pre-

---

[17] See F. HAHN, "Die Bildworte vom neuen Flicken und vom jungen Wein (Mk. 2,21f parr)", *EvTh* 31 (1971) 374; M. G. STEINHAUSER, *Doppelbildworte in den synoptischen Evangelien. Eine form- und traditionskritische Studie* (FzB 44; Würzburg 1981) 50–51; BOCK, *Luke*, I, 519; F. B. CRADDOCK, *Luke* (Interpretation, a Bible Commentary for Teaching and Preaching; Louisville, KY 1990) 80; NOLLAND, *Luke*, I, 250; ERNST, *Das Evangelium nach Lukas*, 201; GRASSO, *Luca*, 176–177; JOHNSON, *The Gospel of Luke*, 99–100; RADL, *Lukas*, I, 334; ROSSÉ, *Luca*, 194; SCHNEIDER, *Lukas*, I, 140–141; SCHÜRMANN, *Das Lukasevangelium*, I, 299–300; TANNEHILL, *Luke*, 109.

[18] According to P. ROLLAND, "Les prédécesseurs de Marc: Les sources présynoptiques de Marc II,18–22 et parallèles", *RB* 89 (1982) 370–405, Luke, an old missionary, knows firsthand how difficult it has been for the Jews to accept the Gospel. Thus his nostalgic remark.

[19] CULPEPPER, *The Gospel of Luke*, 131.

[20] FITZMYER, *Luke*, I, 602; MARSHALL, *The Gospel of Luke*, 228.

[21] S. R. GOOD, "Jesus, Protagonist of the Old, in Lk 5:33–39", *NT* 25 (1983) 32f; D. FLUSSER, "Do You Prefer New Wine?", *Imm* 9 (1979) 26–31; GREEN, *The Gospel of Luke*, 249–250; ECKEY, *Das Lukasevangelium*, I, 264–5; KLEIN, *Das Lukasevangelium*, 227–228. Finally, BOVON, *Luke 1*, 194, seems to lean this way, too.

[22] See A. JÜLICHER, *Die Gleichnisreden Jesu. Zweiter Teil. Auslegung der Gleichnisreden der drei ersten Evangelien* (Tübingen ²1910) 201; J. DUPONT, "Vin vieux, vin nouveau", *CBQ* 25 (1963) 303; J. FLEBBE, "Alter und neuer Wein bei Lukas: zum Verständnis der sogenannten 'Weinregel' Lk 5,39", *ZNW* 96 (2005) 187. For L. P. TRUDINGER, "Un cas d'incompabilité: Marc 2:21–22: Luc 5:39", *FV* 72/5–6 (1973) 7, incompatibility is expressed in 5:39; the view expressed in the preceding verses is that the old is adaptable to the new but after some preparation.

[23] For a claim that the parable is not about old versus new but about the danger of loss through inappropriate action, and thus functions as a wake-up call directed toward repentance, see A. KEE, "The Old Coat and the New Wine: A Parable of Repentance", *NT* 12 (1970) 13–21. For a suggestion that some sayings of Jesus are inconsistent and in 5:39 Jesus could be endorsing a common view that the old is better, despite what he said in a previous saying, see A. H. MEAD, "Old and New Wine: St Luke 5:39", *ET* 99 (1988) 234–235. Similarly, for a view that the new in 5:36–38 refers to the teachings of Jesus, while in 5:39, under the meaning of "inferior," it points to Pharisaic practices, see C. H. TALBERT,

supposition: the main issue is the opposition between the way of Jesus (or more generally, the Christian movement) and the pharisaic way (or more generally, the Jewish traditions). In other words, Jesus, who in 5:31–32 shared the Pharisees' perception by using their term "sinners" and by speaking of the sinners' conversion, a value no one would object to, is now allegedly distancing himself from the Pharisees, their practices, and their religious concerns by stating a radical, old versus new, opposition between himself and them. Naturally, even while highlighting the difference, he continues to address them and thus call them to embrace his perspective.

While such a view is not unreasonable, it seems that a better explanation of the meaning of 5:33–39 could be offered, one that harmonizes more with the dynamic we discovered in 5:31–32. We can see the referents of new and old not in the teachings of the Pharisees and of Jesus but in the two situations described in 5:34–35, the fasting and non-fasting of Jesus' disciples.[24] Jesus acknowledges the Pharisees' concern with the religious practice of fasting. Like before, he shares, at least partially, their perspective. He states that his disciples will indeed fast. But, again like before, he makes himself the criterion of a religious practice, this time of fasting and abstaining from fast. Jesus' absence calls for fast, Jesus' presence calls for celebration. To apply practices marking Jesus' absence to the time of Jesus' presence is not to be done, just like a patch from a new coat is not to be put on an old one, or new wine is not to be poured into old wineskins. New wine is poured into new wineskins, that is, fasting will be appropriate at the time of Jesus' absence. Finally, the statement that no one who has just drunk the old wine will be

---

*Reading Luke*. A Literary and Theological Commentary on the Third Gospel (New York 1986) 67. GRUNDMANN, *Das Evangelium nach Lukas*, 133–134, states that Luke wants to assert the greatness of two separate traditions, Christian and Jewish. Then there are those who like J. M. CREED, *The Gospel According to St. Luke* (London 1930) 83, bracket 5:39, on the basis of this verse being omitted in D.

[24] This very original interpretation has been proposed by A. ERIKSSON, "The Old is Good: Parables of Patched Garment and Wineskins as Elaboration of a Chreia in Luke 5:33–39 about Feasting with Jesus", *Rhetoric, Ethic, and Moral Persuasion in Biblical Discourse* (ed. T. H. OLBRICHT – A. ERIKSSON) (Emory Studies in Early Christianity; London 2005) 52–72. Eriksson does not develop the type of narrative connection between 5:31–32 and 5:33–39 we have observed on the basis of parallel tactics of Jesus vis-à-vis two challenges coming from the Pharisees. Eriksson's proposal, instead, is based on the observation that in 5:36; 6:39; 12:16; 13:6; 14:7; and 18:9 the formula εἶπεν/ἔλεγεν παραβολὴν functions to introduce analogies to a point already made in the text (*ibid.* 55). So in 5:39 it refers to what Jesus said in 5:34–35. See also ZIMMERMANN, *Geschlechter-metaphorik*, 293, whose observation regarding Mark – "Es geht dabei nicht um die Frage, wer Subjekt des Fastens oder Nichfastens ist, sondern worin der Grund des Fastens liegt" – could have been easily used by Eriksson were it not for the fact that Zimmermann refers it in the first place to the difference between the disciples of Jesus and the disciples of other Jewish groups.

willing to taste the new one speaks to the incompatibility of the two tastes
– taste-wise they do not go together.[25] But it also[26] affirms the natural prefer-
ence for the old,[27] for the time of feasting in Jesus' presence, the time of
wedding guests sharing the company of the bridegroom, the time of the sick
with their physician. Directed to the Pharisees, the concluding image of verse
39 comes across as an invitation to join in tasting the good old wine.[28]

Sinfulness as a characteristic is at the center of narrative attention in 5:27–
32: the call of a tax collector, someone always suspected of sin, and the controversy about eating and drinking with sinners. What is discussed in 5:33–
39, in contrast, is an element of Jewish piety. Still the way the discussion is
conducted in 5:33–39 puts the question of the sinfulness back in the center:
the reader can see in this discussion the physician's attempt to reach out to
those who are sick. The discussion of Jewish piety is conducted by Jesus as
an act of persuasion directed toward the Pharisees who resist entrance into
the messianic banquet.[29] Jesus again acknowledges their concern, shares their
perspective, answers their objection, and tries to win them over. While their
resistance is thus indirectly described as sinful, their sinfulness continues to
be addressed by Jesus' call to (redefined) repentance. There is a growing intensity with which Jesus' self-revealing statement ("I have come...," 5:31–
32) is acted out just as it is uttered.

## 6.4. The Theme of Sinfulness and the Likely Effects of Lk 5:27–39

Like in the previous scenes, the multiplicity of the personages does not detract from but rather points to Jesus. Thanks to Levi, Jesus is again presented
as a charismatic leader choosing his own followers. Thanks to the opposition

---

[25] FLEBBE, "Alter und neuer Wein bei Lukas", 185.

[26] J. W. SIDER, "Proportional Analogy in the Gospel Parables", *NTS* 31 (1985) 1–23,
rightly argues that Jülicher's theory that a parable has only one point and an allegory many
must be rejected. "We can maintain the one-point theory only by confusing unity of effect
with simplicity of meaning, or by concentrating attention on one unit of meaning and ig-
noring the rest" (*ibid.* 19).

[27] On the ancients' appreciation of that which was old rather than new see an excursus
by ECKEY, *Das Lukasevangelium*, I, 266.

[28] ERIKSSON, "The Old is Good", 69–70, sees in 5:39 either a rebuke of the Pharisees
(they should know better than to call for fasting during a wedding) or an invitation to taste
old wine, that is, to join with Levi, the disciples and the sinners, and to see that it is good.

[29] Even in his attempts to persuade, Jesus continues to favor indirectness in pointing out
his own identity; see ALETTI, *L'art*, 96: "Si Jésus ne dit jamais explicitement qu'il est
prophète ou messie, c'est parce qu'il laisse à ses auditeurs l'entière liberté d'accepter ou
non les signes. La reconnaissance est donc sollicitée."

of the Pharisees and their scribes, triggered by Jesus' association with tax collectors and sinners, Jesus articulates his authoritative understanding of his person and his mission (the physician healing the sickness of sin, the bridegroom celebrating his wedding feast). In all that, Jesus as a character remains static. He does not change or evolve. But, as has been seen before, his characterization does. The reader's acquaintance with him constantly grows. In the growth of the reader's knowledge of Jesus, new elements are integrated with what has already been established as his traits. Thus, when Jesus is portrayed as the leader of a group of disciples calling an individual to follow him, or as a teacher engaged in disputes with the religious authorities, he assumes roles familiar to the reader. What is new is Jesus' self-referential use of metaphors such as physician or bridegroom to describe his table fellowship with guests at Levi's house.

A similar effect of consolidating and refining through repetition pertains to Jesus' relationship with sinners. One can discern a certain repetitiveness of operations through which the narrative organizes and expresses Jesus' perception of sinfulness. The following schematization illustrates this:

*Table 5:* Jesus' relationship with sinners in Lk 5:1–39

| Scene:<br><br>Jesus: | Calling of Peter 5:1–11 | Healing of the Paralytic 5:17–26 | Calling of Levi 5:27–39 |
|---|---|---|---|
| Prompts recognition of sinfulness or declares sinfulness | of Peter | of the Paralytic | of the tax collectors and sinners |
| Remits sin | by call to discipleship | by announcement of forgiveness | by call to discipleship; by table fellowship |
| Challenges and corrects the views regarding the proper treatment of sinfulness | Peter's view of the need for a distance from Jesus | Pharisees' view of Jesus' inability to forgive sins | Pharisees' view of the need for a distance from tax collectors' and others' sinfulness |
| Attempts to elicit recognition of one's own sinfulness | | | Pharisees |

This repetition produces rhetorical effects. It reinforces the characterization of Jesus as someone who reveals, correctly interprets, and frees from sin. As the narrative presents and consolidates the main elements of Jesus' treatment of sinners, it becomes clear that his ministry departs from the pattern established by John the Baptist. Forgiveness of sins is no longer anticipated but rather enacted. The call for ethical conduct, understood as a condition of forgiveness, gives way to the turning in faith toward Jesus. In addition, the contextual connection between faith in Jesus and the revelation and remission of sin – repeated in the Calling of Peter, the Healing of the Paralytic, and the Calling of Levi – reinforces the theological claim about faith in Jesus as a prerequisite for release from sin. Conversely, it points to the lack of faith in Jesus as the main characteristic of those who are otherwise self-righteous and judgmental.[30]

The repetition of known elements is combined with the introduction of new ones. There is a new referential content of what is implied by sinfulness. Until now very little has been said about what concrete sin Peter, the paralytic, or even the tax collectors and sinners had fallen into. The only specific content of sinfulness is that attributed to the Pharisees: they are sinful because they fall into the rejection of Jesus. Such a Christological expansion of the content of sinfulness makes faith in Jesus an act of the highest religious import, since refusal of that faith amounts to sin.

This presentation of new and old traits in Jesus does not exhaust the effects Lk 5:27–39 is likely to have on the reader. The consolidation and expansion of the reader's knowledge about Jesus is coupled with the formation of an attitude best described as an attitude of searching. The reader is invited to search for the normative view of Jesus. Let us retrace the strategy by which Luke's text tends to produce this effect.

Although Luke populates the scene with numerous personages endowed with various traits and functions, these can be grouped and analyzed in terms of two basic configurations: the personages are either with Jesus or against him. As noted, the miniature scene of the Call of Levi (5:27–28) functions as a set up for the banquet scene that follows. Levi's brief presentation recalls the story of Peter and his companions who also left everything behind and followed Jesus. In the later part of the story, 5:29–39, Levi, the tax collector turned disciple, acts as a host. In this way, the two elements of his characterization, his having been a sinful tax collector and his being a disciple, justify the grouping together of the disciples, tax collectors and sinners at Levi's table. The Pharisees and their scribes' complaint in 5:30 highlights the functional unity of all those gathered at the table: "Why do you [the disciples] eat and drink with tax collectors and sinners?" In the mind of the Pharisees, the table fellowship unites the disciples with the tax collectors and sinners. Jesus' answer in 5:31 tacitly confirms the common categorization of all those gathered at Levi's table. In Jesus' view, all of them form one category: they are the sick attended by their physician. The Pharisees and the scribes form the

---

[30] For POWELL, "Religious Leaders in Luke: A Literary-Critical Study", 95, their main trait is self-righteousness. For DARR, *On Character Building*, 86, they are "a paradigm of imperceptiveness." Inasmuch as lack of faith equals inability to see who Jesus truly is, our claim that the lack of faith is their main trait agrees with Darr's description of the Pharisees as imperceptive.

opposite group. They protest against the practice of Jesus and his disciples. As a group character, they are set in contrast with the rest of those gathered at Levi's table. In Luke's presentation of the personages, the reader discerns an ordering. The characters form three groups: (1) Jesus, (2) the Pharisees and their scribes, (3) the disciples, tax collectors and sinners gathered at Levi's table.

As this order is being created, it is also constantly being subverted. There are instances of an overlap – presumed or intended – between the three groups. Jesus positions himself as distinct from his disciples when he speaks of their practices of feasting or fasting on account of his presence or absence. But he aligns himself with his disciples when he steps in to answer the words of critique directed against them – "Why do you eat and drink with tax collectors and sinners?" (5:30). Similarly, being opposed by the Pharisees and their scribes, Jesus does not negate their opinions and practices. He acknowledges their concerns and their perceptions, while constantly inviting them to cross over to the community of those who share table fellowship with him. He wants them to understand that they have a right to belong to the category of tax collectors and sinners. Naturally, these overlaps between the three basic groups do not negate the underlying differences; they rather assume them.[31] Still, they work together to create an interplay of similarity and difference that asks to be unraveled. This is the engine that powers the rhetorical effectiveness of the scene. The reader is invited to untangle crisscrossing viewpoints, follow implicit references, and thus engage in the task of discovering the normative view of Jesus. The reader is forced to search.

The gap between Jesus' normative view and the human ability to grasp it never disappears. It is now sustained and exploited by the text's tactic of maneuvering the reader into an activity of searching. Recognition of and submission to Jesus' authority are not passive; they have their active component: the search. Jesus' identity is seen as reflected and refracted by the relations he forges with characters known as sinners, as forgiven sinners, as sinners who refuse to recognize their sinfulness. Conversely, insinuations, denials, partial confirmations are among the numerous operations by which sinfulness enters the narrative world and, within it, the world of Jesus' relationships. To know Jesus' view of sin and sinners, the reader must disentangle it from the web of conflicting, overlapping, or ambiguous perceptions exhibited by the narrator

---

[31] At the structural level, the three basic categories of the characters – (1) Jesus, (2) the Pharisees and their scribes, (3) the disciples, tax collectors and sinners gathered at Levi's table – function as a so-called dramatic triangle. The rhetorical effect of the use of the dramatic triangle in Luke is well captured by M. CRIMELLA, *Marta, Marta!* Quattro esempi di 'triangolo drammatico' nel 'grande viaggio di Luca' (Assisi 2009) 57: "Attraverso il triangolo drammatico, [Luca] obbliga il suo lettore a paragonare il proprio punto di vista coi differenti punti di vista dei personaggi di parabole e racconti e dunque a distinguere, a discernere, a diventare un interprete, un ermeneuta di quelle medesime narrazioni."

and other characters. Thus it is not just knowing who Jesus is, but it is the *coming* to know that is dramatically reenacted for the reader. In other words, to know Jesus the reader must *search for* Jesus and concomitantly replicate in his or her own reading the same attitude that many of the Gospel characters so vividly represent.[32] Luke's sophisticated use of the characteristic of sinfulness both creates and facilitates such a search.

The preliminary narrative of Luke 1–4 has prompted in the reader the dynamic effect of moving from perception of sinfulness as a condition to be addressed by God's redemptive intervention to realization that sinfulness can be properly perceived only from the perspective of God's agent. Peter's submission to Jesus' implicit offer of forgiveness meant his capitulation to Jesus' view of how sin is to be forgiven. The opposition Jesus faced in the Healing of the Paralytic scene served to clarify and confirm that Jesus' view, not that of the Pharisees and scribes, represents God's perception. In the present scene, the reader is unable to simply assimilate Jesus' divine perspective. He or she must first discover it. The multiplicity of overlapping and conflicting views combined with the indirectness with which Jesus engages the issue of sin in his dialogue with the Pharisees, leaves the reader no choice but to search for Jesus' view of sin. That the Pharisees function as open-ended constructs – no reaction of them to the words of Jesus in 5:34–39 is reported[33] – creates a dramatic suspense as to their future interactions with Jesus. It also leaves the reader wondering whether they have truly grasped the indirect message Jesus has delivered to them. The need to struggle with Jesus' indirectness is subtly reaffirmed.

---

[32] That the search for Jesus (ζητεῖν Ἰησοῦν) constitutes a theme and a compositional pattern by which the Gospel, as a Christological memory, is governed, has been argued by R. VIGNOLO "Una configurazione da non perdere. Il Vangelo come racconto di ricerca cristologica", *Non mi vergogno del Vangelo, potenza di Dio. Studi in onore di Jean-Noël Aletti SJ, nel suo 70° compleanno* (ed. F. BIANCHINI – S. ROMANELLO) (AnBib 200; Roma 2012) 371–389. According to Vignolo, "per i contemporanei di Gesù raffigurati nei personaggi del racconto evangelico, la posta in gioco infatti no fu mai riducibile solo alla questione di sapere chi effettivamente sia mai Gesù, ma piuttosto al tentativo di *cercare Gesù per averlo*" (*ibid.* 375).

[33] For examples of how the ancient rhetoricians, historians, biographers, and novelists used such audience engaging literary techniques as omission, open-ended comparisons, privileged access to information, hidden meaning, allusion see K. R. MAXWELL, *Hearing Between the Lines. The Audience as Fellow-Worker in Luke-Acts and its Literary Milieu* (LNTS 425; London 2010) 80–117.

Chapter 7

# The Sabbath Disputes (6:1–11)

The first cycle of episodes within the narrative proper of Luke concludes with two Sabbath scenes: 6:1–5 and 6:6–11. Just as the preliminary narrative of Luke 1–4 culminated in the Nazareth-Capernaum prelude to Jesus' ministry, enacted in the time-frame of two Sabbath days (4:16–30 and 4:31–41), two Sabbath days bring the initial stage of Jesus' ministry to a close.[1] In our effort to disclose the strategies by which Luke evokes for the reader the characteristic of sinfulness, we have noted how in the Nazareth-Capernaum scenes the references to sin or sinners were present but only implicitly. They were imbedded in Jesus' general program of release. Similarly, in the two Sabbath episodes we are about to analyze, the explicit references to sin or sinners are lacking. Nevertheless, the fact that by now the reader has learned to infer that the scribes and the Pharisees who oppose Jesus are to be seen as sinners – Jesus' treatment of them implies that they are the sick in need of the physician – means that the theme of sinfulness will continue to be present. How exactly Luke makes it present and in connection with what theological concerns will now need to be examined.

The two Sabbath scenes, 6:1–5 and 6:6–11, are closely related. In each scene the word Sabbath is mentioned three times: 6:1,2,5 and 6:6,7,9. In both scenes – in 6:2,4,9 – there is talk about what is lawful (ἔξεστιν). Finally, the lack of denouement in the first scene – no final reaction of the Pharisees is reported – makes of 6:6–11 a continuation of the same dispute.[2] To account accurately for this continuity, we propose to treat the two scenes together while respecting the structural elements peculiar to each of them.

The compositional arrangement of Lk 6:1–5 is rather straightforward. The scene opens with the initial situation (6:1) to which the Pharisees react with a critical question (6:2). Jesus' response, which takes up the rest of the perico-

---

[1] The connection with the Nazareth-Capernaum Sabbath episodes is additionally strengthened by the fact that Jesus again enters a synagogue (6:6; 4:16,33) to teach (6:6; 4:31). His activity of healing on a Sabbath day evokes his prior Sabbath healings in Capernaum (6:10; 4:33–37,38–39,40–41).

[2] Cf. GREEN, *The Gospel of Luke*, 251, 254. The thematic combination of a healing miracle with a dispute sets 6:6–11 in parallel to the scene of the Healing of the Paralytic in 5:17–26 where the very first dispute with the Pharisees and the scribes was resolved through a miraculous healing.

pe, draws on a scriptural precedent (6:3–4) and seals the argument with a self-referential claim to authority (6:5). Our analysis of this scene will advance in three steps corresponding to its situation-critique-response structure.

In 6:6–11, Luke dedicates two verses, 6 and 7, to describing the setting of the scene. This description is ripe with narrative expectations. The presence of the sick man, mentioned in 6:6b, sets up the expectation of healing. The presence of the scribes and the Pharisees, and in particular their desire to find a charge against Jesus, sets up the expectation of a clash between Jesus and his opponents. In verses 8–10 the initiative belongs to Jesus. He is the only one speaking. In what he says and does, he responds to both expectations created in the setup of the story. In speaking to the sick man in 6:8, he responds to the scribes and the Pharisees. In speaking to the scribes and the Pharisees in 6:9, he describes his ministry to the sick man. In addressing the sick man again in 6:10, he first fixes his gaze upon all those present, that is, in addressing the sick man he again responds to all. The final reaction of the Pharisees and the scribes is reported in 6:11. As we analyze the second Sabbath scene, we will divide it into the three segments corresponding to the three narrative interests just expounded: how the expectations are created (6:6–7), how they are met by Jesus (6:8–10), and how the Pharisees and the scribes react to it (6:11).

## 7.1. The Initial Situation (6:1)

The new episode is announced by the ἐγένετο δέ formula followed by the chronological marker. Before any of the characters are presented, the reader is informed that the new episode takes place on a Sabbath (ἐν σαββάτῳ). Naturally, the new episode is an episode in the life of Jesus and so the use of the personal pronoun – "*he* was going through the grainfields" – is enough for the reader to conclude that it is Jesus who is now walking through the fields. The fact that the disciples are introduced afterwards – they are plucking[3] the heads of grain, rubbing them in their hands and eating – suggests an image of them walking behind Jesus in the same grainfield.[4] If correct, this

---

[3] Plucking the grain (ἔτιλλον ... τοὺς στάχυας) could mean removing the whole stalks of grain or, as É. DELEBECQUE, "Les moissonneurs du Sabbat (6,1)", *Études grecques sur l'Évangile de Luc* (Paris 1976) 76–83, demonstrates, it could refer to simply shelling the grain out of the heads of grain. Cf. C. SPICQ, "τίλλω", *Theological Lexicon of the New Testament* (tr. and ed. D. ERNEST) (Peabody, MA 1994) III, 379–380. In the latter case, the action of rubbing would then just separate the grain from the husks. RADL, *Lukas*, I, 340, posits a third possibility: breaking off the heads of grain without pulling out the stems.

[4] See a similar observation by KLEIN, *Das Lukasevangelium*, 230: "Die umständliche Formulierung [...] zeichnet Jesus als voranschreitend und die Jünger als ihm nachfolgend."

image presents the disciples in their primary role. Like in 5:11 and 5:27, they act as followers of Jesus. The prior narrative gives no grounds for seeing the disciples as ignorant or disobedient. It is then only natural to assume that their current actions are congruent with the will of their master.[5] Though, significantly, within the bond that unites them with their teacher, there is also the distinction that separates them from him. As we have seen, Jesus is introduced before them and he does not share in their activities of plucking and eating. A "distinction-yet-connection"[6] pattern underlies the leader's relation to his followers. A similar pattern will emerge soon in the reference to David's relation to his followers.


## 7.2. The Critique of the Pharisees (6:2)

The sudden appearance of the Pharisees is not as artificial as some assume.[7] As far as we know, it was not forbidden for the Pharisees to enter the fields on the Sabbath.[8] What is more, Luke speaks of "some of the Pharisees," a realistic detail indicating that some Pharisees simply happened to witness the transgression.[9] Naturally, the fact that they do react to it harmonizes well

---

[5] BOVON, *Luke* 1, 198–199.

[6] I take this felicitous phrase from J. P. MEIER, *A Marginal Jew. Rethinking the Historical Jesus.* Volume IV Law and Love (AncBRL; New Haven, CT – London 2009) 271, who uses it in his discussion of the Markan version of the same scene.

[7] What H. WEISS, "The Sabbath in the Synoptic Gospels", *JSNT* 38 (1990) 21, says of the Markan version of the story could, in principle, be said of Luke's account: "The story of the disciples plucking grain on the Sabbath [...] is notorious for its artificiality. It is not easy to imagine the Pharisees trailing Jesus and his disciples on the open fields on a Sabbath day."

[8] Even the restrictive Sabbath laws of the Damascus Document stipulate that one is forbidden to walk in the field (שדה) *to do the work* that he desires (CD X, 20). It follows that walking in the field, as such, is not prohibited, of course assuming that one does not travel beyond the designated limit of one thousand cubits (CD X, 21). This conclusion remains valid even if we agree with the suggestion of L. DOERING, *Schabbat. Sabbathalacha und -praxis im antiken Judentum und Urchristentum* (TSAJ 78; Tübingen 1999) 144, that the prohibition must refer to the work that would begin after the Sabbath. Interestingly, one could on the Sabbath, according to CD X, 22b–23a, eat what has fallen to the ground and started to decay (אבד). This stipulation implies someone's presence in the fields. Cf. S.-O. BACK, "Jesus and the Sabbath", *Handbook for the Study of the Historical Jesus.* Volume 3. The Historical Jesus (ed. T. HOLMÉN – S. E. PORTER) (Leiden – Boston 2011) 2607; DOERING, *Schabbat,* 155–156.

[9] While interpreting Luke's reference to "some of the Pharisees" as opposed to "the Pharisees," commentators often speak of Luke's desire to differentiate between the members of that group. See WOLTER, *Das Lukasevangelium,* 234; GREEN, *The Gospel of Luke,* 253. A. J. MAYER-HAAS, *„Geschenk aus Gottes Schatzkammer" (bSchab 10b). Jesus und der Sabbat im Spiegel der neutestamentlichen Schriften* (NTA.NF 43; Münster 2003) 304,

with their consistent trait as a group character[10]: they are guardians of the legal tradition. They cannot remain indifferent to the breach of the Sabbath law.[11]

Obligation to desist from any kind of labor on the Sabbath day,[12] which the later rabbinic tradition spells out as, among others, an explicit prohibition of reaping, threshing and winnowing,[13] appears to be at stake here.[14] In the Pharisees' eyes, the disciples work by plucking grain. There is no doubt in the Pharisees' mind that the law is violated.[15] Interestingly, Jesus' response will affirm that the violation has indeed taken place.

As the Pharisees assume their typical role as Jesus' opponents, the question of their final stance toward Jesus remains open. They had earlier joined

---

perceives here Luke's intent to create in the end an ambivalent image of the Pharisees with the negative and positive traits mixed together. While the use of the indefinite pronoun with partitive genitive (τινὲς δὲ τῶν Φαρισαίων) could signify an attempt to differentiate between the members of the Pharisaic party, it seems that a more natural explanation in the case of Lk 6:2 is simply to see it as a realistic touch: only some of the Pharisees happened to see and react to the incident. One could recall a similar instance in Acts 17:18 where "some Epicurean and Stoic philosophers" (τινὲς δὲ καὶ τῶν Ἐπικουρείων καὶ Στοϊκῶν φιλοσόφων) debated with Paul. The fact that only some of them engaged in the debate does not necessarily mean that other Epicurean and Stoic philosophers had nothing to debate about with Paul, or that they found themselves convinced by his claims. It, again, can be seen as a realistic detail in the sense that only some of them *happened* to debate with Paul. All this makes superfluous an interpretation proposed by MARSHALL, *The Gospel of Luke*, 231: "We are not told at what point the Pharisees commented on the action, and it is nonsensical to find in this a historical difficulty, since the details of the story have been pared away, and one can easily visualise gossip about the behaviour of the disciples reaching their ears (cf. 5:30)."

[10] On the dynamics of consistency building in characterization by which a single figure or a limited number of figures can represent an entire group, see DARR, *On Character Building*, 94.

[11] E. LOHSE, "σάββατον", *TDNT* VII, 5 states: "In the post-exilic community the Sabbath commandment is indeed the most important part of the divine Law."

[12] See Exod 20:8–11. See also Exod 16:22–26; *Jub.* 2.19 and *Jub.* 50.9 on the obligation to prepare Sabbath meals the day before.

[13] *m. Šabb.* 7:2 list activities prohibited on the Sabbath, among them reaping, threshing, and winnowing.

[14] Plucking someone else's grain was not a problem. See Deut 23:26 MT: "If you go into your neighbor's standing grain, you may pluck the ears with your hand, but you shall not put a sickle to your neighbor's standing grain" (NRSV). Nor is there a suggestion in the text that the disciples were violating the limits of the distance one was permitted to walk on the Sabbath.

[15] DOERING, *Schabbat*, 428–429, draws on CD X, 22–23; Philo, *Mos.* 2.22 and *t. Šabb.* 9:17 to argue that, historically, various Jewish groups would find plucking of the grain objectionable. Commenting on Philo, *Mos.* 2.21–22, MEIER, *A Marginal Jew*, IV, 247, says: "This text supplies the closest pre-70 parallel to the dispute about plucking grain in Mark 2:23–28."

the choir of praise at the end of the first confrontation with Jesus (5:26). No reaction of theirs was reported at the end of the second confrontation over eating with sinners and not fasting. Now they voice criticism, but without hostility. Their dialogue with Jesus continues.

## 7.3. Jesus' Response (6:3–5)

The refutation of the Pharisees' critique comes from Jesus. Like in 5:31, the teacher answers the question directed to his disciples, freely intervening on their behalf.[16] The question – "Have you not even[17] read what David did? – is ironic[18] in that it imputes the ignorance of the Scriptures to those allegedly versed in scriptural traditions. But behind the irony one can detect a tone of rebuke.[19] Despite prior disputes with Jesus, they continue to be blind to his true identity. Jesus' willingness to treat "the sick" (οἱ κακῶς ἔχοντες; 5:31) is, nevertheless, evident. One more time he explains to them the mystery of his person. This time, Jesus' explanation involves his peculiar retelling of an OT story.

As it stands in 1 Sam 21:2–7 the story recounts an incident in the life of David, when, fleeing from Saul, he entered the sanctuary of Nob. There the priest gave the "holy bread" for him and his companions to eat. In accordance with Lev 24:5–9, every Sabbath twelve freshly baked loaves were to be placed on the table before the Holy of Holies and then consumed by "Aaron and his decedents." David then ate what he was not allowed to eat. As Jesus recounts this story he makes sure to stress the unlawfulness of the act. David, Jesus says, ate the bread "which it is unlawful (οὓς οὐκ ἔξεστιν) to eat" (6:4). This way the story of David echoes the Pharisees' charge of doing what is unlawful (ὃ οὐκ ἔξεστιν) on the Sabbath (6:2). The main connection, however, between the situation the Pharisees criticize and the situation Jesus describes lies somewhere else. It is to be found in the "distinction-yet-

---

[16] On teachers being held answerable for his disciples' actions, see Josephus, *J.W.* 1.648–655; Plato, *Apol.* 24b; Xenophon, *Mem.* 1.1.1. Cf. D. DAUBE, "Responsibilities of Master and Disciples in the Gospels", *NTS* 19 (1972–73) 1–15.

[17] On "not even" as the English rendering of οὐδέ, see BDAG, 734. NOLLAND, *Luke*, I, 256 notes that the combination of the negative particle and the demonstrative pronoun (οὐδὲ τοῦτο) sharpens the suggestion of ignorance found in Mark's "never" (οὐδέποτε; 2:25). Cf. M. M. CULY – M. C. PARSONS – J. J. STIGALL, *Luke. A Handbook on the Greek Text* (BHGNT; Waco, TX 2010), 183.

[18] BOVON, *Luke 1*, 199, n. 24.

[19] This tone has been noted by the commentators. JOHNSON, *The Gospel of Luke*, 101, states: "Luke sharpens the implied rebuke by his use of *oude.*" BOCK, *Luke*, I, 524, notes: "He words the question in a way to suggest rebuke."

connection"[20] pattern underlying the relationship between the leader and his followers. We saw this pattern emerge in the set-up of the dispute in 6:1.

In Jesus' retelling of the story of 1 Samuel 21, both David and his companions receive much more emphasis than in the original account. David enters the House of God and taking the bread eats it and gives it to his companions. As the priest is no longer mentioned as an agent,[21] the participle and the three finite verb forms in 6:4 have David as their subject.[22] David's companions, who in the original story are not present but only mentioned – and most likely only as an element of deception aimed at securing more food – become now explicit sharers of his predicament. David is hungry, and so are "those with him" (οἱ μετ' αὐτοῦ). David takes the holy bread, and gives it to "those with him" (τοῖς μετ' αὐτοῦ). The repetition of μετ' αὐτοῦ in 6:3 and 6:4 binds David and his companions in the same pattern of "distinction-yet-connection" seen in Jesus' stance toward his followers. The main line of Jesus' defense, then, is not halakhic. He is not quoting any actual precept of the law.[23] He steers the argument in a different direction.[24] Just as the followers of David (οἱ μετ' αὐτοῦ) were justified in breaking the law by their participation in the authority of David, their leader, so the disciples of Jesus (οἱ μαθηταὶ αὐτοῦ) are justified in their actions in view of their participation in the authority of Jesus. The implicit link in this type of argumentation is the claim that Jesus actually possesses an authority comparable to the one possessed by David, "the anointed but as yet unrecognized king of Israel."[25] Jesus supplies this link in 6:5.

---

[20] See MEIER, *A Marginal Jew*, IV, 271, for discussion of the role of this pattern in Mark 2:23–28.

[21] Cf. 1 Sam 21:7 LXX καὶ ἔδωκεν αὐτῷ Αβιμελεχ ὁ ἱερεὺς τοὺς ἄρτους τῆς προθέσεως.

[22] It is David who entered (εἰσῆλθεν) the house of God, and having taken (λαβὼν) the bread of the Presence, ate it (ἔφαγεν) and gave some (ἔδωκεν) to his companions.

[23] According to D. M. COHN-SHERBOK, "An Analysis of Jesus' Arguments Concerning the Plucking of Grain on the Sabbath", *JSNT* 2 (1979) 34–36, Jesus' argument is not valid from the halakhic point of view because there is no real analogy between the situation of David and that of Jesus' disciples (the disciples' breach of law takes place on the Sabbath, while David's violation of law does not; secondly, David's life is in danger, while the disciples' lives are not), and because Jesus' argument against Sabbath observance is not based on any actual precept promulgated in Scripture (Jesus makes reference to a historical narrative, not to a legal text). Similarly DOERING, *Schabbat*, 432: "Trotz seines jüdischen Hintergrunds kann das Argument aufgrund seiner nicht auf Lebensgefahr weisenden Beanspruchung der Stichworte 'Not' und 'Hunger' nicht in einer im 1.Jh. n.Chr. geltenden jüdischen Sabbathalacha verortet werden."

[24] M. TAIT, *Jesus, The Divine Bridegroom, in Mark 2:18–22*. Mark's Christology Upgraded (AnBib 185; Rome 2010) 107, speaks of Jesus' "deliberate attempt to steer the controversy in a different direction since *haggadah* can only illuminate but not establish *halakhah*."

[25] C. F. EVANS, *Saint Luke*, 315.

In the crowning statement of the argument, Jesus the Son of Man proclaims himself to be the Lord of the Sabbath. Luke the narrator makes the statement stand out. By briefly interrupting the flow of direct speech with a redundant "and he said to them," he creates a delay that draws the reader's attention to what follows.[26] Jesus is no less rhetorically effective in how he delivers the final point of his argument. He begins his statement with the emphatic "the Lord of the Sabbath is..." To those versed in Jewish scriptures there is only one Lord of the Sabbath, the one who gave it to Israel in the first place, the God of Israel.[27] When Jesus finishes the sentence by pointing to himself as the *kyrios* of the Sabbath he effectively establishes the God of Israel as the source of his own power over the holy day of rest. Like in 5:17–26, here again Jesus claims to participate in the authority that belongs to God alone.

Jesus' statement resounds as the final word of the pericope. The reactions of the Pharisees are not reported. Nothing is said about the disciples whose behavior triggered the controversy in the first place. Jesus' use of the self-referential title, the Son of Man, harkens back to his claim to have the authority to forgive sins, and thus to the issue that initiated Jesus' dispute with the Pharisees. As we have seen, both kinds of authority, to forgive sins and to regulate the Sabbath, have the God of Israel as their source. For the reader it is clear that whatever response the Pharisees will give to Jesus, they will give it also to the God of Israel in whose authority Jesus acts.

## 7.4. The Theme of Sinfulness and the Likely Effects of Lk 6:1–5

Again, the close thematic connections that tie 6:1–5 and 6:6–11 together create the need for assessing the function of 6:1–5 in light of its narrative developments being taken up and brought to the dramatic denouement in the scene that follows. Still, some observations can be made already at this point.

---

[26] S. E. RUNGE, *Discourse Grammar of the New Testament. A Practical Introduction for Teaching and Exegesis* (Lexham Bible Reference Series; Peabody, MA 2010) 145, notes that the redundant quotative marker that reintroduces the same speaker within a single speech has a "pragmatic effect of highlighting a discontinuity in the text, specifically within the context of the speech," as well as an effect of "attracting more attention to the speech or segment of speech that follows."

[27] ROWE, *Early Narrative Christology*, 109–110, points to Exod 20:8–11 ["Remember the Sabbath day ... For in six days the Lord (יהוה/κύριος) made heaven and earth, the sea and all that is in them, but rested the seventh day; therefore the Lord (יהוה/κύριος) blessed the Sabbath day and consecrated it"] and aptly notes that Jesus does not just claim authority but provides the source of this authority by the use of *kyrios*. The Sabbath is God's Sabbath (τὰ σάββατά μου) in Exod 31:13; Lev 19:3,30; Ezek 20:12; cf. TAIT, *Jesus, The Divine Bridegroom*, 111.

All the characters in the scene are familiar, not just because they have appeared before but also because they play roles in which they have already been seen. The disciples behave in accordance with their master's norms; the Pharisees object to it. Jesus is the one who resolves the tension between the competing views.

Jesus is clearly the protagonist. He leads the disciples through the fields and, as their master, he acts in their defense. As he defends his disciples, he continues in his attempt to persuade the Pharisees of their need to accept him. He partially confirms their view by acknowledging that plucking grain on the Sabbath is unlawful. On the whole, he points out their ignorance, which is ultimately not an ignorance of the law but of Jesus' authority. This is where the central point of the story is made. Jesus is the Lord of the Sabbath, and so any allegiance to the Sabbath must be an allegiance to the Sabbath as interpreted by Jesus. Just as he was presented as a criterion of repentance (repentance as a turn to him), a criterion of fasting and feasting (as appropriate reactions to his absence and to his presence), he is now a criterion for determining Sabbath observance.[28] The accent is not on relaxation of legal observance in the face of human need; the accent is on the need to subordinate the Sabbath observance to the authority of Jesus.[29] The disciples eat not because hungry people can eat but because they are disciples of Jesus.

The indirect references to sinfulness can be detected at two points. When the disciples are accused of breaking the Sabbath law, they are categorized as sinners, the violators of God's law.[30] Jesus' authoritative perception affirms that this categorization is wrong. As before, the reader can correctly view the sinfulness (or lack thereof) only through the perception of Jesus. The second reference to sinfulness is simply carried over from the previous scene. Through his ministry to the Pharisees, Jesus continues his mission of bringing

---

[28] Jesus does not abrogate the Sabbath observance, (against SCHÜRMANN, *Das Lukasevangelium*, I, 305); he makes himself its ultimate criterion. The claim of M. KLINGHARDT, *Gesetz und Volk Gottes. Das lukanische Verständnis des Gesetzes nach Herkunft, Funktion und seinem Ort in der Geschichte des Urchristentums* (WUNT 2.R 32; Tübingen 1988) 229, that the story is primarily about the early Christian missionaries' right to sustenance (cf. 1 Cor 9:13–14) can be accepted only if the right in question is derived from the story's central Christological claim about Jesus' authority to regulate Sabbath observance.

[29] BOCK, *Luke*, I, 510: "Jesus functions in this passage as an authority in interpreting the law's scope." Similarly, NOLLAND, *Luke*, I, 257, agrees that the point is not that Jesus like David is free from restrictions of the law but that Jesus like David has authority to interpret the divine intention in the law.

[30] Exod 31:14; 35:2 prescribes the death penalty for breaking the Sabbath. Similarly *Jub.* 2.25–28. In CD XII, 3–6, however, the penalty is not death but a seven-year period of exclusion from the community. Josephus, *Ant.* 11.346, recounting how Alexander the Great permitted the construction of the temple on Mount Gerizzim, mentions how those accused of eating things unclean, or breaking the Sabbath, or committing any such crime (ἁμάρτημα) would flee to Samaria claiming they were unjustly accused.

sinners to repentance. They thus continue to be indirectly characterized as sinners. The irony, detectable already in 5:17–26, is that those who accuse others of sinfulness are themselves confirming their own self-characterization as sinners. The references to sinfulness function in a familiar way: the reader is being led to decipher and assimilate Jesus' view of what makes one sinful, or for that matter, of what cannot make one a sinner. Acting in obedience to Jesus cannot count as a sin. Rather, acting in obedience to Jesus counts as acting in obedience to the Lord of the Sabbath. It satisfies the obligation of the Sabbath law.

## 7.5. The Initial Situation (6:6–7)

Like in 6:1 so in 6:7, the new episode is announced by the ἐγένετο δέ formula followed by the chronological marker. In 6:1, the time marker was the Sabbath (ἐν σαββάτῳ). In 6:7, it is "another Sabbath" (ἐν ἑτέρῳ σαββάτῳ). Jesus, the Lord of the Sabbath (6:5), is now seen on the Sabbath day. As Luke announces a new episode in the life of Jesus, he immediately binds it with the central theme of the previous story. The location in time is followed by the space indication: Jesus is in the synagogue. In full coherence with his typical behavior,[31] he is there teaching.

In 6:6b and 6:7, Luke brings to light two types of characters that, as could be expected, will interact with Jesus. The first character is a man with a withered right hand. His characterization is limited to the description of his illness. By introducing someone who is ill, Luke sets up the expectation of healing. It is also possible to see a vague reference to the theme of Sabbath in that the withered right hand means that the man cannot work,[32] and thus cannot rest from work either.[33] The second type of personage is a group character consisting of scribes and Pharisees. The role they have played in the prior three episodes suggests that their presence now will again occasion a dispute with Jesus. Indeed, Luke clearly points in this direction when he unveils the inner disposition of the scribes and the Pharisees. They are watching (παρατηρέω) Jesus to see if he would cure on the Sabbath so they might find[34] an accusation against him (6:7). In 6:6b–7, Luke not only creates the conditions

---

[31] See Lk 4:15,16,31,44.

[32] Cf. GRASSO, *Luca* 182; KLEIN, *Das Lukasevangelium*, 235. For ERNST, *Das Evangelium nach Lukas*, 204, to specify that it was the right hand creates an impression of exactness.

[33] MEYNET, *L'Évangile de Luc*, 268.

[34] The expression ἵνα εὕρωσιν κατηγορεῖν is not an aramaism, as FITZMYER, *Luke*, I, 610–611, suggests. The verb εὑρίσκω without an object and linked directly with an infinitive, in the sense of "find a way (to)," "be able (to)," is well attested in Greek. See J. A. L. LEE, "A Non-Aramaism in Luke 6:7", *NT* 33 (1991) 28–34.

for two types of narrative development, the healing and the controversy stories,[35] but he also interlocks these two possible story lines by presenting the Sabbath healing as a controversial act, at least by the standards of Jesus' opponents. But there is more to be drawn from Luke's exposition of the scribes and Pharisees' intentions than just an expectation of a dispute.

First of all, the expressed intent of the scribes and Pharisees fills the gap created at the end of the previous episode. Their reaction to Jesus' claim to authority over the Sabbath was not reported. We discover that reaction only now. They must have found Jesus' claim unacceptable.[36] This is why they plan a legal action against him.[37]

Secondly, to describe their intent Luke uses the verb "to watch closely" (παρατηρέω) which in the present context takes on the meaning of malicious watching, of lying in wait for.[38] When one considers how in Ps 36:12 LXX, Dan 6:12[Theod.], and *DanSus* 12:15–16[Theod.] the verb παρατηρέω is used to express the sinner's conduct toward the righteous,[39] and when one recalls that in the Calling of Levi, the Pharisees and scribes' opposition to Jesus has been indirectly characterized as sinful, the use of παρατηρέω in the sense of malicious watching becomes significant. It advances the portrayal of the "sinfulness" of Jesus opponents. It is not just resistance but active opposition that characterizes their attitude toward Jesus.

Thirdly, many Sabbath healings must have taken place since the Pharisees are hoping to see one now.[40] The fact that the prior Sabbath healings reported in the Gospel caused no controversy[41] does not mean that the prohibition of Sabbath healings is a frivolous invention of the Pharisees to be used against Jesus only now. As we shall see, Jesus' argument will not question the existence of such a prohibition;[42] it will point rather to Jesus' unique authority to

---

[35] WOLTER, *Das Lukasevangelium*, 236.

[36] "They have clearly failed to recognize Jesus as Lord of the Sabbath, for they seek to submit him to it." DARR, *On Character Building*, 98.

[37] Although the general meaning for κατηγορέω is to "speak against," according to BDAG, 533, it functions "nearly always as legal technical term: bring charges in court."

[38] On παρατηρέω taking on this meaning, see LSJ, 1327; BDAG, 771.

[39] Cf. BOVON, *Luke* 1, 203; WOLTER, *Das Lukasevangelium*, 237.

[40] ERNST, *Das Evangelium nach Lukas*, 204; C. F. EVANS, *Saint Luke*, 316. In addition, the use of the present tense (θεραπεύει) "likely portrays the action as customary here." CULY – PARSONS – STIGALL, *Luke*, 186.

[41] SCHÜRMANN, *Das Lukasevangelium*, I, 307.

[42] As MEIER, *A Marginal Jew*, IV, 248, notes, "the one offense of which Jesus is directly accused in the sabbath dispute stories – namely, healing the sick – is never mentioned as a breach of Sabbath law in any Jewish source written from 2d century B.C. to the end of the 1st century A.D." This lack of evidence regarding the halakhic status of the Sabbath healings is interpreted differently by different scholars. DOERING, *Schabbat*, 449–450 thinks the prohibition was current among the pre-70 Pharisees. MEIER, *A Marginal Jew*, IV, 251 argues that it was first developed only by the post-70 rabbis. Meier's conclusion

override it. That the prior Sabbath healings caused no controversy must be due, instead, to the fact that there were no Pharisees around to instigate a dispute.


## 7.6. Jesus' Triple Response (6:8–10)

The explicit fronted personal pronoun αὐτός at the beginning of 6:8 shifts the attention back to Jesus.[43] In 6:8–10, Jesus will be the only one addressing others in direct speech, though always in reaction to their thoughts and actions. Thus Luke will leave it to Jesus to respond to the expectations raised in 6:6–7.

Before Jesus commands the sick man to get up and stand in the middle (6:8b), the narrator states that Jesus is aware of his opponents' thoughts (6:8a). This prophetic ability of Jesus, by which he knows what others think, is familiar. It was foretold by Simeon in 2:35 and exercised by Jesus in 5:22.[44] This time it is used to depict not just Jesus' willingness to confront the controversial issue but also his readiness to risk giving to his opponents a cause for legal accusation against him. If any reasons for Jesus' openness to his opponents can be adduced, they must be seen in 5:31–32, that is, in Jesus'

---

partially rests on his claim that, even in the light of the post-70 mishnaic standards, the healing performed by Jesus was not a breach of law since no action was performed. Jesus used only words. The Pharisees would have had nothing to object to. Cf. *ibid.* 255. (See a similar claim by G. VERMÈS, *The Religion of Jesus the Jew* [London 1993] 23, and E.P. SANDERS, *Jewish Law*, 21.) Arguing against these views, BACK, "Jesus and the Sabbath", 2610–2613, shows that, in the rabbinic prohibitions against Sabbath healings, an otherwise normal activity of eating and drinking is not permitted if the sole purpose thereof is to bring healing (*m. Šabb.* 14:3–4). In other words, in the mishnaic thinking, it is the intended effect that constitutes the breach of Sabbath rest, not just an act that otherwise is normal. By analogy, an argument that talking is not regarded as work is unconvincing since it fails to take into account the intention of talking, which in this case is to effect healing. This, as Black rightly notes, does not prove the existence of the prohibition of Sabbath healing in first-century Palestine, but it presents such a possibility as a likely antecedent to later rabbinic practice. It would mean that the Gospel presents a historically plausible setting for Sabbath healing conflict.

[43] CULY – PARSONS – STIGALL, *Luke*, 187.

[44] M. B. DINKLER, *Silent Statements. Narrative Representations of Speech and Silence in the Gospel of Luke* (BZNW 191; Berlin – Boston 2013) 114–121, discusses various ways in which, within his Galilean ministry, Jesus exercises control over others' speech. Noting, in particular, how Jesus exposes others' unspoken speech, Dinkler avers: "Considering the instances of unspoken speech in the narrative underscores Jesus' control not only over who can and cannot speak, but also over who can and cannot remain silent" (*ibid.* 118).

mission to call sinners to repentance. By engaging the scribes and the Pharisees, Jesus acts like a physician attempting to treat the sick.

Secondly, combining Jesus' awareness of his opponents' intentions (6:8a) with his turning to the sick man (6:8b) brings the two story lines, the healing and the controversy, together. The dissimilarity between their respective actors can be observed. The negative intentions of the scribes and the Pharisees are contrasted now with the positive disposition of the sick man. He immediately performs what Jesus commands.[45] The verbal correspondence between the command – "get up" (ἔγειρε) and "stand" (στῆθι) – and its realization – "he rose and stood" (ἀναστὰς ἔστη) – illustrates his trusting obedience to Jesus' word.[46]

With the sick man in front of all those gathered, Jesus turns to his opponents. Before he heals the man in 6:10, he explains and justifies his action in 6:9. He does it in the form of a question. "Is it lawful (ἔξεστιν) on the Sabbath to do good (ἀγαθοποιῆσαι) or to do evil (κακοποιῆσαι),[47] to save life (ψυχὴν σῶσαι) or to destroy it (ἀπολέσαι)?" First of all, by putting a question to his opponents Jesus appoints them as judges of the proper Sabbath observance. Secondly, he makes their task appear easy because there is only one answer that could be given to his question. One should not do evil on the Sabbath, that is, one should rescue human life, not destroy it. The difficulty lies in identifying the referents of the two opposing operations of doing good and saving life on the one hand, and of doing evil and destroying it on the other. The context points to the healing of the withered hand as the action being considered in Jesus' question. To save life (ψυχὴν σῶσαι) would mean to deliver the sick man from his affliction.[48] And yet, the condition is

---

[45] Jesus is the only one speaking; "on a nonverbal level, however, the sick man does give a response through his trusting motion." BOVON, *Luke 1*, 202.

[46] Cf. ECKEY, *Das Lukasevangelium*, I, 274.

[47] BDAG, 501, conjectures the sense of "to harm, to injure" for κακοποιέω in Lk 6:9. DOERING, *Schabbat*, 450, however, is right in claiming that a transitive meaning for κακοποιῆσαι is unlikely because of its correspondence with ἀγαθοποιῆσαι. He points to 1 Pet 3:17; 3 John 11; 1 Pet 2:14 and 1 Pet 3:11 where the contrasting notions of κακοποιέω and ἀγαθοποιέω refer to the ethical quality of the action. Our narrative analysis of the scene will give further support to considering the verbs in question in their intransitive sense.

[48] Both ψυχή and σῴζω are capable of conveying a wide range of meanings. The former can mean, among other things, the soul as opposed to the body (for such a meaning see, for instance, Matt 10:28), earthly life, or a human person as a living entity. Since in Lk 6:9 its referent is someone with a physical ailment (a withered hand), ψυχή must be taken as standing for the entire person. See BDAG, 1098; G. DAUTZENBERG, *Sein Leben bewahren. Ψυχή in den Herrenworten der Evangelien* (StANT 14; München 1966) 158–160. The general meaning of σῴζω is to rescue from danger; the more specific religious meaning refers to preserving from transcendent danger or destruction such as eternal death or sin.

not life threatening, and thus to refrain from doing it cannot be considered a destruction of someone's life. If not healed on the Sabbath, the man with the withered hand will live and, possibly, look for a healing on another day. The "save life – destroy life" disjunction[49] puts limits on both terms. Saving life can only mean saving it from destruction.[50] The healing of the withered hand, as such, does not fall into that category. Jesus' question must be understood in another way.

One could argue that Jesus is expanding the notion of saving life to any amelioration of human living (not just rescuing from death) and that he is defining any postponement of doing good as doing evil. Not to do good is to do evil; not to heal a person is to destroy his existence.[51] But if that were the case, Jesus would effectively erase any notion of rest-from-work from the Sabbath observance.[52] If doing any kind of good is permitted on the Sabbath, the Sabbath is no different than any other day.[53] The problem with this line of interpretation is that in the end it departs from the stance Jesus took vis-à-vis Sabbath in the previous scene. Jesus did not abrogate the Sabbath; he made himself the criterion of what is allowed and what is not allowed on the Sabbath. To say that any kind of good deed is now allowed, that is, as some

---

See BDAG, 982. Again, in reference to a healing, it conveys the general meaning of delivering the sick man from his affliction. Cf. BOCK, *Luke*, I, 529.

[49] Jesus' rhetorical question is not comparative (against BDR, §245,3b₄); it is disjunctive, "separating opposites, which are mutually exclusive," BDAG, 432. Cf. BDF §446,1; WOLTER, *Das Lukasevangelium*, 238.

[50] The view that one can save life on the Sabbath when it is in mortal danger is reflected in the Qumran and later rabbinic writings. CD XI, 16–17a discusses a case of a human being who falls into water. It prohibits pulling such a person up with the help of ladder, rope, or tool. What is implied is that saving an endangered human life on the Sabbath is permissible as long as one does not use any kind of tool. 4Q265 fragment 6 lines 6–8 allows using one's own garment to help a person who has fallen into water on the Sabbath. See MEIER, *A Marginal Jew*, IV, 245, 263; DOERING, *Schabbat*, 201–204, 232–235; W. KAHL, "Ist es erlaubt, am Sabbat Leben zu retten oder zu töten? (Marc. 3:4) Lebensbewahrung am Sabbat im Kontext der Schriften vom Toten Meer und der Mischna", *NT* 40 (1998) 318–324. Later rabbinic halakha is less strict. *m. Yoma* 8:6 simply states that risk of loss of human life overrides the prohibitions of the Sabbath. This view is further elaborated in *t. Šabb.* 15:1.

[51] This seems to be the interpretation of L. BORMANN, *Recht, Gerechtigkeit und Religion im Lukasevangelium* (StUNT 24; Göttingen 2001) 247, who thinks that here, unlike in Mark 3:4, life is no longer understood as biological life but, as in the wisdom tradition, as a successful existence.

[52] As S. G. WILSON, *Luke and the Law* (MSSNTS 50; Cambridge 1983) 36, correctly observes, this logic "sets the requirement to do good above the requirement to rest in such a way that if the two conflict the former takes precedence."

[53] WOLTER, *Das Lukasevangelium*, 238, rightly observes that once the halakhic question is transposed into the ethical level, Sabbath is de facto suspended, because the ethical rule is valid for any day, including Sabbath.

commentators put it, to suppress the ritual dimension in the name of purely ethical considerations,[54] is to make ethics, not Jesus, the norm of the Sabbath observance.[55] The strong connection between 6:1–5 and 6:6–11 points toward a different understanding of Jesus' question about doing good and doing evil. To put it briefly, Jesus' argument must be understood Christologically. Jesus does not claim that any healing is lawful, but that the healing performed by the Lord of the Sabbath is. For Jesus, to continue his ministry of release from sickness is to do good, to save life. To give up his ministry, even temporarily, is to do evil, to destroy lives. The utmost urgency of Jesus' liberating mission is at stake here. It is not ethics but Jesus' ministry of release that governs the observance of the Sabbath. Other considerations give further support to this line of interpretation.

The prior scene culminated with a strong Christological claim about the Son of Man being the Lord of the Sabbath. This claim did not serve to suggest that Jesus' disciples broke no rule by plucking the grain on the Sabbath. This claim showed rather that, by virtue of their connection with their leader, the disciples were allowed to do what is otherwise forbidden on the Sabbath. Implicit in Jesus' argumentation was the claim that the proper observance of the Sabbath takes place within the bond that unites the Lord of the Sabbath with his followers. Now, by depicting the man with the withered hand in 6:8 and again in 6:10 as fully submissive and obedient to Jesus' command, Luke attributes traits to him that the prior narrative has connected with the good and lifesaving effects of Jesus' ministry. To recognize and to submit to Jesus' authority has been the hallmark of those who have been freed from Satan's power, illness, and sin. In the present context, Jesus' healing action implies a forging of a relationship within which Jesus' authority is recognized and acknowledged. As such, the healing constitutes a good and life-saving event. Furthermore, by bringing the man into a bond of relationship with the Lord of the Sabbath, Jesus enables him to celebrate the Sabbath in a proper way.[56]

Before the scribes and the Pharisees respond, Jesus continues his lesson. Looking around (περιβλεψάμενος) at all of them (6:10), he turns to the sick man, commanding him to stretch out his hand. The man obeys and his hand is

---

[54] So SCHÜRMANN, *Das Lukasevangelium*, I, 308: "Dabei ist die Frage im Grunde schon von der gesetzlichen Ebene auf die sittliche geschoben." Or JOHNSON, *The Gospel of Luke*, 102: "Jesus' question shifts the issue from ritual observance (however important) to moral discourse."

[55] See, for instance, a generalizing conclusion of GRASSO, *Luca*, 183: "Il criterio interpretativo non solo della legge del sabato, ma di ogni norma, diventa l'amore verso l'altro."

[56] The man is not accused of breaking the Sabbath. Jesus is. Still, the healing seems to imply some degree of cooperation on the part of the sick man. See the remark of the leader of the synagogue in Lk 13:14, who, while indignant at *Jesus'* act of healing, does not hesitate to implicate the people in the breaking of the law: "There are six days on which work ought to be done; come on those days to be cured, and not on the Sabbath day."

restored. To the reader, the use of the passive verbal form to describe the healing – the hand "was restored" (ἀπεκατεστάθη) – suggests that the true agent of the healing was God.[57] The controversy about Jesus' Sabbath healing becomes now a controversy about God. As in the case of the controversy regarding Jesus' power to forgive sins (5:17–26), it is God who acts through Jesus, and Jesus, who acts in God's place.

Turning with faith to Jesus has already been characterized as an encounter with the physician who heals the sickness of sin and as joining the wedding feast of the messianic bridegroom. Jesus has been presented as the criterion of repentance; his absence or presence as reason for fasting or feasting. The scribes and the Pharisees have been privileged to become addressees of all these self-revealing statements of Jesus. Now one more truth about Jesus is being communicated, namely, that the healing activity of the Lord of the Sabbath is both good and life-saving; its disruption is an evil act that destroys life. To repeat, it is not that the healing can be done because all healings are lawful; it is that the healing performed by the Lord of the Sabbath, the dispenser of God's liberating grace,[58] fulfills the Sabbath observance.[59]

Some commentators, perhaps in order to avoid the conclusion that not doing good amounts to doing evil, a conclusion that effectively erases the special character of the Sabbath day, postulate that in asking about doing good and doing evil Jesus contrasts his own activity with that of the scribes and the Pharisees.[60] Jesus' activity of healing is good; it saves life. The Pharisees and

---

[57] WOLTER, *Das Lukasevangelium*, 238.

[58] Against RADL, *Lukas*, I, 349, who claims that while earlier Jesus justified his acts by reference to his authority and mission (5:24,32,34; 6:5) now he uses a purely humanistic, wisdom tradition argument. By extension, the claims that the scene is about the relation between love of neighbor and law (ERNST, *Das Evangelium nach Lukas*, 205), or that any deed of love expresses the true meaning of the Sabbath (SCHNEIDER, *Lukas*, I, 144), or that the Sabbath and holy days require concentration on works of love (SCHÜRMANN, *Das Lukasevangelium*, I, 309), do not capture the main point of Jesus' argument. More on target is the claim of GREEN, *The Gospel of Luke*, 252, that "Jesus is less concerned with abrogating Sabbath law, and more concerned with bringing the grace of God to concrete expression in his own ministry, not least on the Sabbath." Quite apart stands the view of KLINGHARDT, *Gesetz und Volk Gottes*, 230, who understands the scene, in light of the Jewish-Christian conflict, as a defense of the Christian right to preach the message of salvation in the synagogues during Sabbath gatherings.

[59] While the reference to *fulfillment* of the Sabbath observance implies here the satisfaction of the legal norm, it at the same time resonates with the eschatological character of Jesus' mission through which the Sabbath *as pointing toward and anticipating the final blessedness* is now being realized. See LOHSE, "σάββατον", *TDNT* VII, 8: "The day of the rest which the patriarchs celebrated grants a foretaste already of eternal glory, which will be an unending Sabbath."

[60] BOVON, *Luke* 1, 203, n. 28, does not reject "an intentional conceptual connection between the evil action of the scribes and Pharisees and the words κακοποιῆσαι ("to do harm") and ἀπολέσαι ("to destroy") in Jesus' saying." A similar interpretation can be

the scribes, on the other hand, dedicate their Sabbath to doing evil. They come to the synagogue with malicious intent and they, in the end, plan to do something against Jesus. This way of reading is not unjustified. One can easily detect a contrast between the actions of Jesus and those of his opponents. The question is whether this is the primary contrast the story creates. It seems that the difference between the good action of Jesus and the evil plans of the Pharisees is just a manifestation of a more fundamental disparity, namely, their antithetical view of sin. What the Pharisees see as doing good and doing evil is the exact opposite of Jesus' view. For them not to heal on the Sabbath is good, to perform a healing is evil. For the reader, the evil actions of the Pharisees, in particular the foolishness (ἄνοια) to which they succumb, confirm that their view is wrong and that the true distinction between good and evil is presented by Jesus.

## 7.7. Reactions of the Pharisees and the Scribes (6:11)

As a result of their first encounter with Jesus, the scribes and the Pharisees were filled (ἐπλήσθησαν) with fear (5:26), recognizing the manifestation of God's glory in the acts of Jesus.[61] In subsequent scenes, 5:27–39 and 6:1–5, their reactions to Jesus' self-revelatory statements were not reported. It is only now, at the culmination of their fourth encounter with Jesus, that their reaction is described. They are again filled (ἐπλήσθησαν), but this time with "unreason" (ἄνοια).

Some commentators take ἄνοια not as a cognitional quality but as an affective one, understanding it to mean fury,[62] or blind fury[63], or fury combined with other designations such as madness,[64] or rage born of incomprehension.[65] The affective sense of ἄνοια appears to go back to Plato, who said in

---

found in BOCK, *Luke*, I, 530; CULPEPPER, *The Gospel of Luke*, 135; ECKEY, *Das Lukasevangelium*, I, 274; C. F. EVANS, *Saint Luke*, 316; KLEIN, *Das Lukasevangelium*, 234; MEYNET, *L'Évangile de Luc*, 267–268; and J. ROLOFF, *Das Kerygma und der irdische Jesus*. Historische Motive in den Jesus-Erzählungen der Evangelien (Göttingen 1970) 65, 80. Among those who reject this line of interpretation are MARSHALL, *The Gospel of Luke*, 233; RADL, *Lukas*, I, 347, n. 399; and SCHÜRMANN, *Das Lukasevangelium*, I, 308, n. 62.

[61] On this reaction constituting a formal element of the synoptic miracle stories, see G. THEISSEN, *Urchristliche Wundergeschichten*. Ein Beitrag zur formgeschichtlichen Erforschung der synoptischen Evangelien (StNT 8; Gütersloh 1974) 78–80. On the role of a fear motif in Luke, see HOLZ, "Zur christologischen Relevanz des Furchtmotivs im Lukasevangelium", 484–505.

[62] C. F. EVANS, *Saint Luke*, 317.

[63] BOVON, *Luke* 1, 204.

[64] FITZMYER, *Luke*, I, 611.

[65] GREEN, *The Gospel of Luke*, 257.

*Tim.* 86b that there were two kinds of ἄνοια, madness (μανία) and ignorance (ἀμαθία).[66] Still, considering the use of ἄνοια in the cognitional rather than affective sense among ancient classical authors[67] and Jewish Hellenistic writers,[68] one must ask if Luke provides any grounds for taking ἄνοια not in its generally attested sense of ignorance but in the sense of fury. In 4:28, the citizens of Nazareth were filled with rage (θυμός) at the words of Jesus, and attempted to throw him off the cliff. One could view this event as a prototype of a highly emotional negative reaction to Jesus to be emulated now by the Pharisees and the scribes in 6:11. But the more immediate context of 6:6–11 provides other, more directly connected, models of reaction to the miracles of Jesus. In 5:17–26, a scene involving the same characters (the scribes and the Pharisees) and describing reactions to the same kind of miracle (healing), they all are filled with reverential fear (φόβος), recognizing the manifestation of God's power in the miracles of Jesus (5:26). This reaction repeats and reinforces the prior reactions of astonishment (θάμβος) reported in 4:36 and in 5:9 in response to Jesus' exorcism and the miraculous catch. The healing performed in 6:10 creates an expectation of a similar reverential fear and astonishment. What comes instead is a surprising frustration of that expectation. The scribes and the Pharisees are said to be unable to recognize God's work in Jesus. They lack reason. It is not fury leading to murderous plans, as in 4:28–29; it is lack of understanding leading to deliberations as to what they might possibly do[69] to Jesus.

By describing the scribes and the Pharisees as lacking in understanding, Luke connects their characterization as sinners with the motif of ignorance. On the one hand, such connection makes their sin forgivable,[70] keeping open the possibility of their future conversion and narratively justifying Jesus' fu-

---

[66] That, however, did not prevent Plato from making a distinction between ἄνοια and μανία in his other writings. See *Resp.* 382c, 382e; cf. LSJ, 145.

[67] See references in BUSSE, *Die Wunder*, 138; RADL, *Lukas*, I, 348, n. 411.

[68] Philo, *Leg.* 3.164,211; *Ebr.* 93; *Conf.* 54; *Somn.* 2.115,169,191,200; *Mut.* 193; *Sobr.* 11; Josephus, *Ant.* 16.260; cf. BUSSE, *Die Wunder*, 138; WOLTER, *Das Lukasevangelium*, 239; MAYER-HAAS, *„Geschenk aus Gottes Schatzkammer" (bSchab 10b)*, 311. Of particular importance, as pointed out by WOLTER, *Das Lukasevangelium*, 239, is the use of ἄνοια as the antithesis of wisdom (σοφία) in Prov 14:8, and of sagacity (ἀγχίνοια) in Philo, *Mut.* 193, or its distinction from madness (μανία) in Josephus, *Ant.* 16.260. Wolter goes as far as to say that "in der hellenistischen Umwelt des frühen Christentums wird ἄνοια immer nur im Sinne von ἀμαθία gebraucht" (*ibid.* 239).

[69] The use of the potential optative (ἂν ποιήσαιεν) denotes what is merely thought. See BDF, §385,1.

[70] See Lev 5:17–19; Num 15:22–31 on the possibility of forgiveness for those who sin unwittingly, and denial of forgiveness for those who sin "high-handedly." Ignorance makes offences forgivable in *T. Jud.* 19.3; Philo, *Mos.* 1.273; Thucydides, *The Peloponnesian War* 3.40.1; Xenophon, *Cyr.* 3.1.38; Epictetus, *Diatr.* 2.22.36; cf. WOLTER, *Das Lukasevangelium*, 757. See other references in MARSHALL, *The Gospel of Luke*, 867.

ture interactions with the Pharisaic party. On the other hand, Luke does not exculpate the Pharisees and the scribes.[71] Their ἄνοια is just another way of characterizing their evil plans and intentions,[72] this time, however, in a language reminiscent of a wisdom discourse. Indirectly, Jesus and those who submit to him are characterized as wise; those who oppose him as foolish.[73]

## 7.8. The Theme of Sinfulness and the Likely Effects of Lk 6:6–11

The scene is populated by three categories of characters. Other than Jesus, the protagonist, there are the scribes and the Pharisees, acting as a group character, and there is the man with the withered right hand. The Pharisaic party and the sick man are presented in relation to Jesus. They either react to him or are addressed by him. While the sick man does not interact with the Pharisaic party, his relation with Jesus becomes an element of Jesus' interaction with the scribes and the Pharisees. The sick man is a plot functionary whose only role is to display the life-saving effects of Jesus' ministry. The characterization of the scribes and the Pharisees is more complex in that they enter the scene with traits acquired in prior episodes. Their interaction with Jesus stands in the center of the narrative attention. The final stage of the story is dedicated solely to their reactions. When it comes to the narrator, his voice is more pervasive than before. Other than offering a description of the sick man's gestures or the Pharisaic party's reactions, he reveals the intentions of the scribes and the Pharisees and discloses Jesus' knowledge of these intentions. Still, the narrator leaves it to Jesus to engage both his opponents and the reader in an interpretive effort aimed at comprehending his teaching and its demands. Jesus appears as a teacher par excellence, not just by what he says but also by how he redirects the flow of dramatic tensions in ways suitable to his agenda. Let us retrace the strategy responsible for this effect.

---

[71] For the notion of culpable ignorance see Dan 9:15 (LXX); *T. Levi* 3.5; *T. Zeb.* 1.5; 1 Cor 15:34. Ignorance does not eliminate the need for repentance in Acts 3:17–19; 17:30.

[72] For the use of ἄνοια in reference to evil actions, plans or intentions, see 2 Macc 4:6; 2 Macc 15:33; 3 Macc 3:16; Wis 19:3. Philo, *Leg.* 3.211, speaks of repentance for deeds of folly (ἄνοια) and iniquity (ἀδικία). Josephus, *Ant.* 8.318, describes king Ahab's evil deeds as exceeding in folly (ἄνοια) and wickedness (πονηρία) those of the kings before him.

[73] For BORMANN, *Recht, Gerechtigkeit und Religion*, 248, this allows Luke to avoid the charge of promoting lawlessness. He observes: "Die Differenzen in der Sabbathalakha sind nach Lukas nicht die Folge einer gemeinschaftsschädigenden Gesetzesverachtung Jesu, die den *consensus iuris* des jüdischen Volkes infragestellt, sondern erwachsen aus der Verschlossenheit der jüdischen Gesetzesinterpreten, die in ihrer ἄνοια gefangen sind."

The story narrated in 6:6–11 has an appearance of straightforwardness. Its setup prepares the reader for two plots, the plot of healing and the plot of controversy. And indeed this is what the story delivers. By the end, the sick man receives the gift of healing, while the opponents of Jesus receive an authoritative answer to their questions. But as the reader discovers, this simplicity is deceptive. The healing does not serve to win the controversy, as one would expect. It creates the controversy. Jesus' answer does not satisfy his opponents; it confuses them. Yes, Jesus again proves himself to be a compassionate healer. But neither his ability to heal nor his compassion are being questioned. What is being question is his conformity with the Sabbath halakha. His answers, however, only appear to engage the halakhic mode of discussion. In reality, both in 6:1–5 and 6:6–11, he moves the controversy to another level so that it is no longer about him being able to observe halakhic norms, but about this opponents being able to accept him as the norm of the Sabbath halakha. Jesus' skill as a debater is evident. He reverses perspectives from which the problems are debated. He chooses the categories through which he can be comprehended. He reframes the controversial issue, forcing his opponents into an ultimate decision of being either with him or against him. Although differing in terms of their expectations, both the reader and the opponents of Jesus are faced here with surprising reversals orchestrated and executed by Jesus.

It is significant how Jesus, the teacher – "he entered the synagogue and taught" 6:6 – maneuvers his opponents into the recognition dynamic very familiar to the reader. To repeat, the reader has learned to move from (1) the statements about Jesus, through (2) the realization that Jesus is the only one capable of authoritative interpretation of himself, to (3) submission to Jesus' didactic of piecemeal revelation of the truth about his redemptive mission. Elements of the same dynamic can be seen in Jesus' dealings with the Pharisees. He teaches them that the authoritative interpretation of his person comes only from him, not from their preconceived categories. They have to put aside the categories of halakhic dispute and accept his mode of argumentation. He subjects them, thanks to his ability to read their minds and to the indirectness with which he reveals his own stance, to a process of seeking the logic of his claims. In the end, they either fail to execute the search or refuse to grasp the inevitable conclusions of that search.

To the reader, who by now is thoroughly familiar with the need to recognize and to submit to Jesus' normative point of view, this scene communicates a sense of pressing seriousness. On the one hand, the continuation or suspension of Jesus' ministry of release is presented as a matter of life and death. On the other hand, the persistent refusal of Jesus' authority by his opponents appears to have disastrous consequences. The reader equipped with outlooks and categories cultivated by the prior discourse on sin and sinners, concludes that in the Lukan world one either accepts Jesus' view of sin or he remains dangerously ignorant, even of his own sin. Let us spell out this conclusion in more detail.

The increasingly negative attitude of the scribes and the Pharisees toward Jesus gives the impression of a radicalization of their sin. They do not just exclude themselves from the community of those who accept Jesus with faith; they create a community of evildoers. As a result, they destroy their life in that they forgo their ability to understand.[74] In the episodic plot of Lk 5:1–6:11, their rejection of Jesus is a counter image of the initial acceptance of him by Simon Peter. Simon responded to the miraculous catch with astonishment. He recognized the Lord in Jesus, and he acknowledged himself as a sinner. The scribes and the Pharisees fail in both regards. In response to the miracle of healing, they succumb to foolishness that blinds them from seeing the Lord of the Sabbath in Jesus and from seeing themselves as sinners whose sinfulness Jesus wants to forgive.

Notably, Luke's recourse to ἄνοια means that the same category that designates the radicalization of their sin lays the ground for its potential forgiveness. In the end, they can be said to act against Jesus out of ignorance. As the disputes (5:17–6:11) are brought to their climax, the note of perplexity – what the Pharisees *might do* to Jesus – combined with their potentially redeemable ignorance, creates a strong narrative suspense.

Finally, the ἄνοια of the scribes and the Pharisees evokes the theme of the misunderstanding of Jesus, that is, it discloses the gap between what Jesus reveals and the human ability to grasp it. Many characters have grappled with a certain opacity or apparent absurdity of Jesus' statements and commands. But while others in such circumstances have treasured the words (2:51), or trustfully acted on them (5:5), the scribes and the Pharisees resist Jesus' explanations to the point that defies logic. They become foolish.

## 7.9. Concluding Remarks on Luke's Portrayal of Sinners in 5:1–6:11

Before we summarize our conclusions regarding the portrayal of sinners in Lk 5:1–6:11, let us briefly return to the problem of the segmentation of the Lukan text. Our initial decision to concentrate on Lk 5:1–6:11 was motivated by the assumption that the text under consideration represents a self-

---

[74] This furnishes some realization of Simeon's prediction in 2:34 about Jesus' ministry being the cause of the falling and the rising of many in Israel. It could also be seen as a parodic realization of Jesus' disjunctive alternatives of saving or destroying life. Accordingly, "to destroy life" would mean to destroy one's own life. For the use of ψυχή in the absolute state, without the possessive pronoun, and in the reflexive sense (one's own ψυχή), see Heb 10:39; 2 Pet 2:8; Josephus, *Ant.* 4.294; *J.W.* 2.141; *Sib. Or.* 14.103–104.

contained literary unit. This unit marks the beginning of the section known as the Galilean ministry of Jesus which, together with the travel narrative and the activity of Jesus in Jerusalem, comprises the narrative proper of the Gospel. Within the Galilean ministry of Jesus, 5:1–6:11 represents the first of the three successive stages in Jesus' relationship to his disciples: Jesus gathers his disciples in 5:1–6:11; he chooses and prepares the twelve in 6:12–8:56; he entrusts to them a mission in 9:1–50.[75]

As a structuring element, Jesus' relation with his disciples does not exclude but rather combines with other indicators of literary arrangement. In the case of 5:1–6:11, an obvious criterion of segmentation is the theme of opposition to Jesus. It reaches its initial climax in 6:11. Another factor is the unfolding of Jesus' ministry of release. Announced in Nazareth and programmatically enacted in Capernaum, it now takes the concrete form of release from sin (5:1–11; 17–26; 27–39), and sickness (5:12–16; 17–26; 6:6–11). Our study of the strategies by which Luke guides the reader's understanding of sin and sinners offers now another criterion in support of the literary unity of 5:1–6:11. The narrative cycle opens with Jesus' encounter with a self-confessed sinner and concludes with his ministry to those whose actions betray their characterization as sinners. In between, the discourse on sin and sinners informs and is formed by every major step the story takes. The disciples are chosen from sinners; sin is what Jesus releases from; the opponents are indirectly characterized as sinful. The discourse on sin binds 5:1–6:11 together.

Having uncovered the strategies by which Luke makes the characteristic of sinfulness emerge in the consciousness of the reader, we are ready to ask about the Lukan portrayal of sinners in 5:1–6:11. Who are the sinners? What functions does Luke ascribe to the various components of their characterization? The following points summarize and systematize our findings:

1. Luke redirects his readers from the question "Who are the sinners?" to the question "Who are the sinners in Jesus' eyes?" We have detected this effect in our analysis of the preliminary narrative of Luke 1–4. Our study of 5:1–6:11 confirms that the basic dynamic of recognizing and submitting to Jesus' authoritative view includes as its integral part the recognition of and submission to Jesus' view of sinners.

2. Once redirected, that is, judged in terms of Jesus' normative view, the characterization of sinners becomes thoroughly relational. They are depicted *in relation* to Jesus. Sinners are those whose sinfulness Jesus sees, whose recognition of sinfulness he triggers, whose recognition of sinfulness he invites, whose sins he forgives in response to faith in him; they are the ones

---

[75] As expounded in § 1.5 above, in proposing this segmentation of the narrative we follow Ó FEARGHAIL, *The Introduction*, 44.

from among whom he forms his disciples. Finally, those who reject Jesus' mission toward them become sinners.

3. Within the dynamic of relation, by which the characters known as sinners reflect the profile of Jesus' mission, Luke places an element of confrontation. As seen already in the discrepancy between the expectations set by John the Baptist's ministry to sinners and Jesus' actual realization of these expectations, Jesus' relation to sinners runs against the expectations of other characters and the reader. These expectations, voiced by Peter, the Pharisees and the scribes, or simply deduced by the reader from the cultural background of the narrated world, are never superficial or irrational. Rather, they serve to highlight Jesus' supreme authority in establishing new norms of conduct reflective of his unique status.

4. Both in its relational and confrontational function, the characteristic of sinfulness is used in repetitive ways. Similarities in the characterizations of Peter, the paralytic, Levi, or for that matter the leper and the man with the withered hand, consolidate the image of Jesus reflected in his dealings with these characters. Even the recurring disputes with the scribes and the Pharisees bear the mark of Jesus' continuing mission to sinners. At the same time, repetitions slow down the forward movement of the story, inviting the study of coherence and nuances in the presentation of Jesus. They force the reader to revisit, reconsider and re-appropriate what appears to be known.

5. Luke builds coherence in the reader's perception of sin and sinners not just by repetition but also by conformity with his use of other traits. Jesus' ministry of release from sin stands in parallel to his ministry of release from sickness, or satanic power. Similarly, Jesus' status as the criterion of repentance parallels his status as the criterion of fasting and Sabbath observance.

6. Both relational and confrontational use of the characteristic of sinfulness invites an interpretive effort on the part of the reader. Jesus does not so much explain his ministry to sinners as display it through interactions that involve conflicts of view, shifts of perspective, use of elusive titles and indirectness. He does it repeatedly and in connection with other controversial issues such as Sabbath observance or fasting. This strategy has its calculated effect on the reader. Luke deploys the references to sinfulness so as to engage the reader in a search for the normative view of Jesus. By untangling crisscrossing viewpoints formed around sinfulness – implied, inferred, directly stated, overcome, or rejected – the reader's *coming* to know Jesus is enacted.

Let us conclude with a comment meant to contextualize the final point just made (number 6). Christopher Bond's study of Milton's *Paradise Regained* occasions a clever observation: Milton's Jesus "is not tempted so he can become perfectly virtuous and free from sin, as a conventional epic hero might be; rather he is tempted to demonstrate – to the reader, to Satan, and to himself – in what way he is to be understood as perfect and virtuous."[76] Although the product of a different literary investigation, this perceptive statement captures to a certain extent the effects of the Lukan presentation of Jesus in 5:1–6:11. As a hero, Jesus is not growing in perfection; rather he is demonstrating how his perfection is to be understood. We do not see him go through trials and adventures so as to achieve a stature demanded of him by the divinely appointed mission. Rather, through his trials and activities Jesus discloses the perfection of God's redemptive plan. That said, the redemptive purpose of God's eschatological visitation, which the story of Luke 1–4 has inextricably bound with the person and mission of God's agent, is not thereby fully transparent. Despite many straightforward traits that dominate Jesus' characterization – he is prophet, teacher, healer, interpreter of the law – his complete theological profile, reflected as much by the postures of those who accept him as by the criticisms of those who oppose him, emerges only indirectly through the interpretive effort of the reader. We have noted how Jesus' reference to the divine necessity (4:43) that governs his otherwise unaccounted for movement through Galilee reveals as much as it conceals about the plan he is following. Jesus' self-referential use of the Son of Man title works in a similar way. It names an aspect of Jesus' activity without explaining why this and not some other name should capture that aspect. The riddle-speech of Jesus' self-designations confirms for the reader that Jesus knows more than the narrator, more than other characters and more than the reader. This peculiar opacity of the protagonist Jesus perpetuates the gap between God's redemptive visitation and the human ability to grasp it. It also justifies Luke's strategy of engaging the reader in an active search for the mystery of Jesus' person and mission. In fact, in the Lukan story it is Jesus himself who orchestrates the search.

In the end, then, as we have often observed, Jesus is a static character whose characterization remains dynamic. He does not develop, but the reader's acquaintance with him does. The sinners as characters cannot be said to be either static or dynamic. They are not an easily identifiable category of characters squarely captured by the stable lexical marker, ἁμαρτωλός. Rather, they are what could be called fluid characters whose principal characteristic, their sinfulness, enters the narrative world forming relations, confrontations, and repetitions, all aimed at engaging the reader in a search for Jesus' person and mission. Naturally, there is nothing remarkable in the fact that the category of sin, that is, the category that captures one's (negative) stance in relation to God, is so extensively used by Luke. What is remarkable, though, is that Luke so highly problematizes the issue of the what, the how, and the

---

[76] C. BOND, *Spenser, Milton, and the Redemption of the Epic Hero* (Plymouth 2011) 195.

why that constitutes a negative stance toward God. This, I believe, is his way of bringing the reader to the certainty (ἀσφάλεια; cf. 1:4) of faith.

Chapter 8

# Sin and Sinners in Lk 6:12–9:50

In our study of the Lukan portrayal of sinners in 5:1–6:11, we have identified the variety of strategies that prompt the reader to infer the characteristic of sinfulness, even in the absence of its direct textual referent. Interested in the maximal realization of these strategies, we have analyzed and explained the functions Luke ascribes to various components of the portrayal of sinners as they emerge in the temporal unfolding of the first cycle of episodes narrating Jesus' public ministry. We have concluded that, in the end, Luke's deployment of both direct and indirect references to sinfulness engages the reader in a search for the normative view of Jesus: the reader's *coming to know* Jesus is enacted. As Jesus, the agent of God's redemption and the unique interpreter of his own person and mission, progressively enacts God's plan, the reader not only grows in familiarity with the primary roles Jesus assumes in his ministry (exorcist, healer, teacher, miracle worker, prophet, etc.) but also comes to experience the often indirect and enigmatic mode of Jesus' self-revelation as a demand for an active search of Jesus' theological profile. For the reader, to search for Jesus' normative view is to acknowledge this view as authoritative and yet not easily attainable. Conversely, the reader's submission to Jesus' view is enacted as a search for that which in the end escapes full assimilation. We have shown that the progressive emergence of an attitude of searching on the part of the reader is structured and sustained by Luke's deployment of the characteristic of sinfulness.

A deeper understanding of the complexity of the Lukan portrayal of sinners and the ensuing increased appreciation of what Luke's construction of this portrayal ultimately effects for the reader of 5:1–6:11 constitute the main achievements of our study. That said, the Lukan narrative continues to unfold, and so does the theme of sinfulness. We now propose to follow the arc of the narrative up to 9:50, that is, to the finale of the section within which 5:1–6:11 forms an essential component. While attending to the Lukan discourse on sin and sinners in Lk 6:12–9:50, we wish to utilize the interpretive potential Luke's portrayal of sinners in 5:1–6:11 holds for the subsequent sinner texts. In particular, we wish to demonstrate how certain exegetical problems that emerge in the interpretation of the "sinner texts" in Lk 6:12–9:50 can be now illuminated and resolved in light of our reading of 5:1–6:11. Our understanding of what Luke achieves in 5:1–6:11 will be confirmed and advanced when employed to clarify the issues that otherwise evade simple explanation. Two more comments are in order before we extend our analysis of the Lukan narrative up to 9:50.

As already mentioned, we do not propose a thoroughgoing investigation of the Galilean portion of the ministry of Jesus, let alone of other remaining portions of Luke-Acts. Still, by contributing to the clarification of the Lukan discourse on sin and sinners in 6:12–9:50, we hope to exhibit the coherence of Luke's portrayal of sinners and, in effect, of the narrative section within which they come into view as characters. In agreement with our methodological assumption postulating mutual dependence between the formal segmentation of the text and the determination of the ordering principle,[1] a proof of coherence of Luke's presentation of sinners in 5:1–9:50 offers additional justification for the presumed compositional unity of 5:1–9:50.[2] Our initial decision to view Lk 5:1–6:11 as a component of Lk 5:1–9:50, shall be confirmed.

The hermeneutic circle, which upholds the part and the whole in a mutually interpretive relationship, would ultimately invite a consideration of the entire Lukan oeuvre as the whole to which Lk 5:1–6:11 could be meaningfully related. Nevertheless, our methodological assumption regarding the temporal production of the narrative's effects on the reader, and the concomitant decision to reconstruct the effects of a first-time reading by the implied reader, privilege the immediate context as most pertinent to the reader who grasps the text successively. Of the many Lukan "sinner texts," the ones that follow immediately after 5:1–6:11 are most applicable when it comes to assessing the understanding of sinners produced by 5:1–6:11. Hence, given both the literary composition the reader is expected to assume in the text and the temporal production of the narrative effects on the reader, extending our analysis to Lk 9:50 presents itself as the most productive way to confirm and advance our understanding of what Luke achieves in 5:1–6:11.

---

[1] See §1.3.4.

[2] This is not to say that the portrayal of sinners constitutes the ordering principle behind the compositional unity of 5:1–9:50. The principle of division of Jesus' ministry into three stages – the Galilean ministry, the travel narrative, and the final events in the city of Jerusalem – remains geographical, though it is supported by many other literary and thematic considerations. See Ó FEARGHAIL, *The Introduction*, 39–40.

# 8.1. Choice and Preparation of the Twelve (6:12–8:56)

### 8.1.1. Choice of the Twelve and the Sermon on the Plain (6:12–49)

In 6:32–34, the reader of the Sermon on the Plain encounters a radically negative categorization of sinners. They appear as the ones who not only stand outside the community of Jesus' disciples, but also as the ones from whom the disciples *should* differ.[3] This might strike the reader as rather unusual when compared with the earlier favorable presentation of sinners as recipients of Jesus' salvific mission.[4] So far, Jesus' stance toward sinners appears to have been largely positive. He suppressed the mention of God's vengeance in his inaugural Isaianic self-presentation and stressed the notion of release; he associated with sinners and forgave them; he defended his ministry toward them against the objections of the Pharisees. How are we now to understand his negative categorization of sinners? Does Luke's presentation of sinners become incoherent at this point?

Neale's omission of 6:32–34 from the number of "sinner texts" he studies in detail (5:27–32; 7:28–50; 15:1–32; 18:9–14; 19:1–10) seems to be symptomatic of the apparent difficulty of reconciling Luke's presentation of sinners in the Sermon on the Plain with his depiction of them in the scenes that Neale does analyze. Neale's overall solution is to postulate an intentional development of a sympathetic view of the sinner in Luke's Gospel. For Neale, Luke presents sinners as a despised element of society in 3:12; 5:29 and 6:32–34 only to transform them into "a sympathetic figure with whom the reader is encouraged to identify" in 7:36–50; 13:1–5; 15:1–32.[5] Our analysis of the portrayal of sinners in Luke 1–4 and 5:1–6:11 discourages such an interpretation. As we have seen, from the very beginning of the Gospel, God's redemptive intervention is meant to address the sinful state of the people of Israel. Sinners are the object of God's – and his agent's – salvific action. If Jesus' harsh words about sinners in 6:32–34 are surprising, it is precisely because they depart from the sympathetic presentation of sinners already established by Luke's presentation of Simon Peter, Levi and others who have welcomed Jesus' gracious ministry. As we shall see, the solution to the problem posed by 6:32–34 is found not in the alleged reinterpretation of the "sinner" term in the later parts of the Gospel but in the Christological

---

[3] As W. C. VAN UNNIK, "Die Motivierung der Feindesliebe in Lukas VI 32–35", *NT* 8 (1966), 287, observes, while verses 27–31 depict the positive behavior of Christians toward their enemies, verses 32–34 offer "Motivierung dieses Liebesverhältnisses, weil die Christen sich von den Sündern abheben sollen."

[4] GREEN, *The Gospel of Luke*, 273, simply notes the difference between these and the earlier uses of the term "sinner" in the Third Gospel.

[5] NEALE, *None but the Sinners*, 164.

definition of sin – opposition to Jesus being qualified as sinful – first detected in Jesus' dealings with those indirectly characterized as sinners in 5:27–39. Before we spell out the details of this solution let us identify and place in context all the references to sin and sinners within 6:12–49.

After the night long prayer (6:12b), Jesus chooses and appoints the twelve (6:13–16), whom he names apostles and who, together with a great crowd of his disciples and a great multitude of people, will form the audience of Jesus' sermon. Although the Pharisees and the scribes are no longer present, the theme of opposition to Jesus is not completely absent. In a narrative aside,[6] Luke informs the reader that Judas Iscariot, a disciple from the inner circle of apostles, will become a traitor (προδότης). It is not specified whom or what Judas will betray, let alone how the betrayal will take place;[7] still, coming from the narrator, this evaluation is credible. The prior narrative aligned the Pharisaic party's growing opposition to Jesus with the increasingly marked designation of them as sinners. If Judas' betrayal turns out to be the betrayal of Jesus, his status as a traitor will group him with those who actively oppose Jesus and thus prove themselves to be sinners. This possibility seems to be at least intimated by means of a curious *inclusio* between Simon Peter, a sinner turned disciple, listed as the first among the twelve, and Judas Iscariot, a disciple to become a traitor, closing the list of the twelve. When, in his sermon, Jesus goes on to elaborate on the proper treatment of one's enemies, his choosing of Judas, a potential enemy, receives some degree of justification.

Jesus' sermon (6:20–49) opens with a series of antithetically arranged blessings and woes (20–27), echoing the theme of reversal of fortunes from Mary's Song (1:46–55).[8] The remaining parenetic speech can be further divided into 6:27–38, a call to behavior not based on the ethic of reciprocity,[9]

---

[6] S. M. SHEELEY, *Narrative Asides in Luke-Acts* (JSNT.S 72; Sheffield 1992) 104. Asides of this type "remind the reader that the narrator has more information than the reader does" (*ibid.* 153–154).

[7] As R. L. BRAWLEY, *Centering on God.* Method and Message in Luke-Acts (Literary Currents in Biblical Interpretation; Louisville, KY 1990) 47, aptly notes, "because the notice leaves up in the air whether Judas will betray his country, his vows, his parents, his peers, God, or Jesus, it leaves the reader hanging."

[8] GREEN, *The Gospel of Luke*, 265.

[9] It is important to achieve precision in the use of the term "reciprocity". Following the work of M. SAHLINS, *Stone Age Economics* (New York 1972), many commentators of Luke distinguish between three types of reciprocity: general, balanced, and negative. A. KIRK, "Karl Polanyi, Marshall Sahlins, and the Study of Ancient Social Relations", *JBL* 126 (2007) 182, offers a succinct summary of Sahlin's taxonomy: "*General* reciprocity is characteristic of the intimate relationships of kinship and friendship. Its emblematic feature is generous sharing, which generates gratitude and an open-ended, diffuse obligation to make a return. *Balanced* reciprocity features overt concern for equivalence and timeliness of exchange. While it frames such transactions as labor exchanges among kin and friends, it is also characteristic of more distant relationships in which self-interest and material

and 6:39–49, a collection of images fittingly announced in verse 39 ("He also told them a *parable*").[10] Within this final section, verses 46–49 function as a conclusion of the entire speech, framing it, as they do, by a renewed emphasis on the verb ἀκούω (6:47,49), found initially in 6:18 and again in 6:28.

The opening blessings and woes are addressed to the disciples of Jesus (cf. 6:20a). That Jesus designates them first as "the poor" harmonizes with his Isaianic self-presentation (Lk 4:18; Isa 61:1). He is the one who brings good news to the poor, particularly through the ministry of release. They are the poor ones, that is, those who have received his gracious ministry.[11] The disciples' blessedness – one aspect of which is the assurance of future reversal of the present state of need (6:21) – appears as the direct result of Jesus' mission toward them. The Christological grounding of their blessedness is further confirmed by their suffering on account of the Son of Man (6:22). To the reader, who has seen Jesus being confronted by those who not only resist his ministry but also actively oppose it, the opposition to be experienced by the disciples aligns them with their master. Furthermore, if those who oppose Jesus have been increasingly characterized as sinful, those who oppose his disciples on account of their master must be viewed in the same way.

The woes against the rich, well-fed, laughing and well-spoken-of are formed antithetically to the blessings. Since both blessings and woes are ultimately addressed to the disciples, the "rich ones" are best seen as a fictive category employed by Jesus as a foil against which the true nature of discipleship can be discerned.[12] The poor ones receive the ministry of Jesus, suffer

---

concerns take priority over the human bond itself, as in market exchange. *Negative* reciprocity is the maximization of one's own benefit at the expense of another, in its pronounced forms amounting to exploitation." Jesus clearly rejects retaliation, that is, reciprocation of harm. What is questioned is his stance toward actions that are beneficial to others. As our analysis of Lk 6:20–49 will soon make clear, while speaking of Jesus' critique of the ethic of reciprocity, we mean his critique of both balanced and general reciprocity, since in both of them the sole orientation of the moral choice consists of either enacting or expecting reciprocation. One acts in order either to repay or to receive a benefit. Moral grounding of action exhausts itself within the bond of exchange between the doer and the receiver of an action. Furthermore, since the *patron-client* relations of the Greco-Roman world, even though unequal, were articulated in terms of friendship and fictive kinship, we understand them to be included in the category of general reciprocity. As such they fall under the reciprocal ethic critiqued by Jesus. Still, as Kirk aptly notes, although the *patron-client* relations were publicly presented as manifestations of "unselfish human relations (general reciprocity)," they were in fact "exploitative relations of exchange (negative reciprocity)" (*ibid.* 189).

[10] WOLTER, *Das Lukasevangelium*, 245.

[11] This is not to deny that by leaving everything in order to follow Jesus (cf. 5:11,28) the disciples were poor also in the material sense. On the term "poor" combining both spiritual and material nuances in 4:18 and 6:20, see C. M. HAYS, *Luke's Wealth Ethics. A Study in Their Coherence and Character* (WUNT 2.R 275; Tübingen 2010) 110–111.

[12] Cf. WOLTER, *Das Lukasevangelium*, 247.

on account of him, and are promised the eschatological reward. The rich ones do the opposite. Their consolation[13] is not grounded in their relationship with Jesus. They are the ones unaffected by his ministry.[14] No reward is promised to them.

By means of an antithetical arrangement of blessings and woes, Jesus' speech begins to form a bipolar ideological horizon. As we shall see, Jesus' references to sinners in 6:32–34 will assume and further confirm the existence of the ultimate dividing line defined by one's relation to Jesus. One either belongs to the category of Jesus' disciples or excludes himself or herself from the promised eschatological reward. The boundaries between disciples and non-disciples are drawn. Inasmuch as exclusion from eschatological reward is equivalent to the punishment to be allotted to sinners in the final judgment,[15] the characterization of the "rich ones" assumes the trait of sinfulness.

In 6:27–38, the central section of his sermon, Jesus urges his listeners to actions and attitudes that defy the logic of reciprocal social exchange. Two types of behavior stand out. Jesus urges his followers to love their enemies (6:27,35), that is, those who hate, curse, and abuse them (6:27b,28). Secondly, he encourages them to give (6:30). The giving includes giving to those who ask (6:30a), to those who take away by force (6:29b,30b), as well as offering the other cheek (6:29a), and lending (6:35a). Before he goes on to repeat the requirements of loving, doing good, and lending by means of three rhetorical questions (6:32–34), Jesus generalizes his ethical demands by means of the Golden Rule. As formulated by Jesus, the Golden Rule defines as the norm, not the limited actions of the other, but the limitless desires of the self.[16] The followers of Jesus are to do to others as they would *want* others to do to them (6:31). Just like the instructions contained in 6:27–30, this clearly means acting with a generosity beyond the constraints of the *do ut des* logic.[17]

---

[13] Pointing to Lk 2:25 as well as to Isa 40:1–5; 49:13; 61:2, P. KLEIN, "Die lukanischen Weherufe Lk 6, 24–26", *ZNW* 71 (1980) 155, notes: "Es ist deutlich, daß von hier aus der Begriff keineswegs unter einem seelsorgerlichen Aspekt zu sehen ist, sondern daß er streng theologisch zu interpretieren ist als *ein* Ausdruck der eschatologischen Hoffnung des Judentums."

[14] As WOLTER, *Das Lukasevangelium*, 253, correctly observes, "der entscheidenden Unterschied zwischen den Armen und den Reichen markiert darum einzig und allein Jesus."

[15] On the destruction of sinners in the final judgment see *1 En.* 1.1; 38.1; 81.7–8; *T. Ab.* A 12–13; *Sib. Or.* 3.669–701. On the Jewish criticism of the rich and riches, see HAYS, *Luke's Wealth Ethics*, 31–39.

[16] Cf. L. J. TOPEL, *Children of a Compassionate God. A Theological Exegesis of Luke 6:20–49* (Collegeville, MN 2001) 157–158.

[17] Against P. RICOEUR, "The Golden Rule: Exegetical and Theological Perplexities", *NTS* 36 (1990) 392–393, who perceives a tension between the Golden rule ("logic of

Having expounded his ethical demands through the categories of loving
and giving (6:27–30), and having pressed the Golden Rule to serve his ethical
ends (6:31), Jesus goes on to repeat the requirements of loving, doing good,
and lending by means of three rhetorical questions (6:32–34). They are identical in form, as the following disposition makes clear:

*Table 6:* Parallel structure of Lk 6:32–34

6:32 καὶ εἰ ἀγαπᾶτε τοὺς
ἀγαπῶντας ὑμᾶς,

ποία ὑμῖν χάρις
ἐστίν;

καὶ γὰρ οἱ ἁμαρτωλοὶ τοὺς
ἀγαπῶντας αὐτοὺς ἀγαπῶσιν.

6:33 καὶ [γὰρ] ἐὰν ἀγαθοποιῆτε
τοὺς ἀγαθοποιοῦντας ὑμᾶς,

ποία ὑμῖν χάρις
ἐστίν;

καὶ οἱ ἁμαρτωλοὶ τὸ αὐτὸ
ποιοῦσιν.

6:34 καὶ ἐὰν δανίσητε παρ᾽ ὧν
ἐλπίζετε λαβεῖν,

ποία ὑμῖν χάρις
[ἐστίν];

καὶ ἁμαρτωλοὶ ἁμαρτωλοῖς δα-
νίζουσιν ἵνα ἀπολάβωσιν τὰ
ἴσα.

And they describe behaviors said to be no different from the behavior of sinners. What are these behaviors? Some commentators see these actions in
terms of balanced reciprocity.[18] To act lovingly toward those from whom one
receives the same loving service amounts to no praiseworthy credit (χάρις).

---

equivalence") and love of enemies ("logic of superabundance") and with TOPEL, *Children
of a Compassionate God*, 157, who accurately observes that "by using θέλειν instead of
ἐλπίζειν, προσδέχεσθαι, προσδοκᾶν, the Golden Rule excludes the motive of *do ut des*."
For points of continuity between Jesus' ethical instruction and Hellenistic moral discourse
see H. D. BETZ, *The Sermon on the Mount*. A Commentary on the Sermon on the Mount,
Including the Sermon on the Plain: Matthew 5:3–7:27 and Luke 6:20–49 (Hermeneia;
Minneapolis, MN 1995) 590–619.
[18] See GREEN, *The Gospel of Luke*, 270–273. Similarly, for TOPEL, *Children of a Compassionate God*, 161, "in Luke 6:32–34 Jesus refers to a balanced reciprocity in which
anyone who gives a good or service to another expects a comparable return, and anyone
who receives a good is expected to make a return."

One is just repaying a debt.[19] To lend to those from whom one expects to receive involves no risk and implies no merit either.[20] Other commentators claim that the critique of Jesus goes beyond balanced reciprocity. They perceive the actions said to be carried out even by sinners as examples of the open-ended sharing between kin and friends. Regarded in this way, such actions would generate χάρις and operate in view of χάρις, that is, of granting and receiving favors, of evoking and demonstrating gratitude.[21] Jesus' rhetorical question – "What kind of credit (ποία χάρις) is that to you?" – and the denial of χάρις that it implies, would then produce a radical shift of perspective.[22] The χάρις Jesus has in mind in 6:32–34 must differ from the regular use of that term in Greek moral discourse. Jesus must be referring here to divine χάρις, that is, to the reward (μισθός) spoken of in the next verse.

The position Lk 6:32–34 occupies in the development of Jesus' ethical argumentation suggests that more is at stake than just Jesus' critique of balanced reciprocity. To assume that Jesus is criticizing only the kind of ethical behavior that limits itself to repaying favors or offering risk-free loans is to assume too little. This would leave the entire patron-client ethic based on exchange of χάρις intact. Jesus is doing much more. His criticism is directed to the entire ethic of reciprocity, balanced and generalized alike. The parallelism between ἀγαπᾶτε τοὺς ἐχθροὺς ὑμῶν // καλῶς ποιεῖτε τοῖς μισοῦσιν ὑμᾶς and εἰ ἀγαπᾶτε τοὺς ἀγαπῶντας ὑμᾶς // ἐὰν ἀγαθοποιῆτε τοὺς ἀγαθοποιοῦντας ὑμᾶς indicates that Luke's argument in 6:32–34 functions as a negative example of the love commandment announced in 6:27. In 6:32–34, Luke describes not just balanced reciprocity but reciprocity

---

[19] See VAN UNNIK, "Die Motivierung der Feindesliebe in Lukas VI 32–35", 296–297, who finds examples of similar reasoning in Thucydides 2.40.4 and Seneca, *Ben.* 4.11.

[20] Even though TOPEL, *Children of a Compassionate God*, 167, considers Lk 6:34 to refer to interest-free loans, and even though he admits that such loans would be considered χάριτες in the Greek thought-world, he claims that Jesus denies them that status (they contain no χάρις) because these loans are made with an expectation (ἐλπίζειν) of return, and so with very low risk for the lender.

[21] On χάρις as a key term for both favors given and received and gratitude shown and earned in the dynamic of generalized reciprocity, see A. KIRK, "'Love Your Enemies,' the Golden Rule, and Ancient Reciprocity (Luke 6:72–35)", *JBL* 122 (2003) 678–679, and references therein. See also SPICQ, "χάρις", III, 500–506, in particular 503–504 on χάρις as an expressed gratitude: "a person does not stop at merely feeling gratitude toward a benefactor but makes an effort to pay him back, as if paying off a debt by returning benefit for benefit."

[22] KIRK, "'Love Your Enemies'", 683, n. 77, captures well this effect: "The protasis of each of the rhetorical questions depicts 'the give and return' conventionally correlated to χάρις, while the apodosis suddenly alienates χάρις from that dynamic. The effect for those listening is a jarring defamiliarization of the term."

as such, that is, all the doing of good that does not reach the level established in 6:27.[23]

Finally, with a redefined χάρις a redefined reciprocity enters the picture. It is a reciprocity guaranteed by God who "is kind to the ungrateful and the wicked" (6:35) and who gives in an overflowing measure, pressed down, shaken, and running over (6:38). The followers of Jesus enact God's mercy (6:36) and generosity (6:35) manifesting themselves as his children (6:35). God and his way of acting become a norm that grounds and redefines the rules of human actions. In summary, according to Jesus' argumentation, the insufficiency of the ethics of human reciprocity is underlined by the fact that even sinners are capable of practicing it. In other words, Jesus places sinners among those whose action exhausts itself within the limits of reciprocity and so loses any claim to relation with God, understood here as the one who rewards those who love without expecting anything in return. Sinners stand outside God's logic of giving and receiving.

By grounding his ethical demands in God's way of acting, and by positioning the practitioners of the ethic of reciprocity in the same class as sinners, Jesus frames his ethical instructions in religious terms. What is more, he creates a bipolar world in which one is either on the side of God, or on the side of sinners. As we have noted at the beginning, this radically negative categorization of sinners might strike some as unusual when compared with the earlier favorable presentation of sinners as recipients of Jesus' salvific mission. And yet there is nothing inconsistent in Jesus' perception of sinners. He has never dismissed the notion of sin; nor has he denied that sinners were indeed sinful. Moreover, in his gracious ministry he did not hesitate to imply the sinfulness of others. In this sense, Jesus' world has always been marked by boundaries. But like God, who is kind to the ungrateful and the wicked (6:35), Jesus has reached out to sinners, not condemning them (cf. 6:37b) but instead offering forgiveness (cf. 6:37c). Jesus has already embodied the ethic he now proposes. The demarcation of the God-sinners boundary does not limit Jesus' mission; it highlights its limitless scope. At the same time it demonstrates, as any ethic should, that there is the right and the wrong side.

---

[23] For Kirk, Jesus does not abandon the principle of reciprocity as such but only the principle of discrimination by which the recipients of generous giving are selected in view of the gratitude (χάρις) they are likely to reciprocate. Kirk works with a broad notion of the principle of reciprocity. For him, even the divine giving described in 6:35b operates within the general reciprocity model simply because God's generosity, though not contingent on the response, desires it. See KIRK, "'Love Your Enemies'", 684. Our understanding of the principle of reciprocity is more restricted. That is why, while agreeing that χάρις is reinterpreted, we state that reciprocity *as the basis of ethics* is undone. The moral justification is no longer grounded in the bond of reciprocation but shifts toward a new evaluative horizon, namely, the imitation of divine, unrestricted generosity.

The disciples of Jesus need to be "fully schooled"[24] (κατηρτισμένος) in order to embody this ideal (6:40). At the same time, however, their commitment must be total; otherwise they will bring a great ruin upon themselves (cf. 6:49).

To recapitulate, in expounding his ethical demands, Jesus ultimately places his audience in front of a fundamental choice: they will either act the way God does or the way sinners do;[25] they will bring upon themselves either blessings or woes. In the ideological horizon of Jesus (and therefore of Luke) there is no neutral ground. Furthermore, Jesus' ministry to sinners – something first noted as early as 5:27–39 – consists not just in bringing the offer of forgiveness but also in identifying and defining sin in Christological terms. Not to commit to Jesus' way of loving and giving is to remain on the side of sinners.

### 8.1.2. John the Baptist's Question and Jesus' Response (7:18–35)

Chapter 7 is a closely-knit unit. The miracles of Jesus (7:1–17) provoke the spread of his fame (7:17), which in turn triggers John the Baptist's inquiry about Jesus' messianic status (7:18–20). As Jesus defends his status against John's doubts (7:21–23), he moves to clarify John's status to the people (7:24–28), and to criticize those who reject his and John the Baptist's mission (7:29–35). Ironically, the critics' perception of Jesus as a friend of tax collectors and sinners (7:34) is correct; it describes the essential part of his mission. Jesus' encounter with the sinful woman (7:36–50) will prove this. The theme of sinfulness enters the flow of narration indirectly. It can be detected beneath John the Baptist's doubts about Jesus' messianic status. Jesus is not a fiery judge bringing about the destruction of the unrepentant sinners. As Jesus responds to John's doubts, the issues of repentance, sin, and sinners surface with more intensity. They dominate the story in 7:36–50.

D. P. Moessner has proposed to read various references to sin and sinners in 7:18–35 as intended to project an image of the entire generation's resistance to Jesus.[26] Whether John the Baptist's doubts or the lack of repentance on the part of the Pharisees and the scribes, all these reactions amount to

---

[24] FITZMYER, *Luke*, I, 626.

[25] To be exact, Jesus does not say that they will become sinners. He simply states that their ethical standards will be no different from the standards observed by sinners. Still, the rhetorical import of this statement is clear. The audience must choose between two mutually exclusive grounds of action: the ethic of reciprocity or God's unlimited giving.

[26] D. P. MOESSNER, "The 'Leaven of the Pharisees' and 'This Generation': Israel's Rejection of Jesus According to Luke", *JSNT* 34 (1988); idem, *Lord of the Banquet. The Literary and Theological Significance of the Lukan Travel Narrative* (Harrisburg, PA [2]1998) 98–110.

rejection of God's prophet, Jesus.[27] As we now analyze references to sin and sinners in 7:18–35, we shall question Moessner's view of a uniform resistance. We will argue that, in the Lukan world, the *movement* toward submission or rejection of Jesus is important. Luke does not so much paint characters who are simply sinners or non-sinners, but rather characters who are coming to know and accept Jesus and thereby no longer sinners, or who are becoming inimical to him and thus compounding their sinfulness, or who function as open-ended constructs, that is, their final reaction is solicited but left untold.

In answering John the Baptist's question with "a symphony of Isaianic echoes"[28] (Isa 26:19; 29:18–19; 35:5–6; 42:7,18; 43:8; 61:1), noticeably overlapping with his inaugural sermon (4:18–19), Jesus presents his activity as a realization of the prophetic promises of God's eschatological salvation. His self-presentation departs from the image of the fiery judge foretold by John the Baptist (3:16–17). This serves to highlight Jesus' autonomy in articulating his mission. Not even John the Baptist is capable of conclusively delineating the profile of God's agent. The ultimate interpretation of God's plan can come only from Jesus.

Jesus' surprising originality as well as a certain indirectness with which he asserts his claims are, by now, familiar features of his characterization. John the Baptist's doubts are, then, not surprising. He is just another character in the story who is forced to cope with Jesus' indirectness. As we have seen, many characters have grappled with a certain opacity or with the apparent absurdity of Jesus' statements and commands. Some in such circumstances have treasured the words (2:51), or trustfully acted on them (5:5); others, like the scribes and the Pharisees in 6:11, have resisted Jesus' explanations to the point of succumbing to foolishness. The final reaction of John is not reported. Still, the Isaianic self-description and the macarism Luke places on Jesus' lips – "And blessed is the one who is not scandalized by me (ὃς ἐὰν μὴ σκανδαλισθῇ ἐν ἐμοί)" (7:23) – function primarily as a call to faith, not a

---

[27] MOESSNER, "The 'Leaven of the Pharisees'", 27, argues for the following dynamic of response to Jesus in 7:18–35: "(1) The questioning or doubt on the part of a smaller group, viz. John and his disciples, regarding Jesus' identity as expressed in his healings and exorcisms (7.10, 11–17, 21–22) is transmuted by Jesus into a charge of offense against the whole crowd. It is the 'folk of this generation' who, like children in the market place, do not know how to respond to either John's or Jesus' movement (7.31–32). (2) The blanket charge against the whole generation is conceived and formulated as that offense displayed in the resistance of the Pharisees-scribes ('eating and drinking with tax collectors and sinners', 7.34, 5.30). That is to say doubting or disenchantment with Jesus' activities is perceived by Jesus as a *direct* affront to his authority. Desire for further demonstration of Jesus' credentials is tantamount to rejection. It is rather the submission of repentance or faith in the 'little ones' or 'least' that vindicates God's purpose (βουλή) in Jesus." Emphasis original.

[28] GREEN, *The Gospel of Luke*, 297.

pronouncement of condemnation.[29] Correspondingly, Jesus' appraisal of John as someone "more than a prophet" (7:26), the greatest among those born of women and yet smaller than the least in the kingdom of God (7:28), aims – just like the rhetorical import of the John-Jesus comparison in Luke 1–4 – not at belittling John but at showcasing the greatness of Jesus' mission. Luke does not present John as someone who rejects Jesus but as someone called to advance in his recognition of Jesus' unique status.

The references to sin and sinners continue as Jesus, having defined the preparatory role of John the Baptist (7:24–28), assesses the divergent reactions his ministry elicited among the people and the elites of Israel (7:29–30).[30] Those who received the baptism, including the tax collectors, acknowledged the justice of God (ἐδικαίωσαν τὸν θεόν); the Pharisees and the lawyers rejected God's purpose for themselves. Jesus characterizes the Pharisees and the scribes[31] as sinners by virtue of their rejection of God's will. But more is at stake in this characterization. Ironically, the Pharisees and the scribes reject being baptized, that is, they refuse to undergo the ritual of repentance. Their sinfulness then is compounded by their refusal to

---

[29] See the following observation by G. STÄHLIN, "σκάνδαλον, σκανδαλίζω", *TDNT* VII, 349: "These passages [Matt 26,31.33; 11,6 par. Lk 7,23; Matt 13,57 par. Mark 6,3] show that σκανδαλίζεσθαι ἐν αὐτῷ can be the opposite of πιστεῦσαι εἰς αὐτόν". In other words, the call not to be scandalized functions as a call to faith.

[30] Some commentators, for instance NOLLAND, *Luke*, I, 342; BOCK, *Luke*, I, 676–677, treat verses 29–30 as a narratorial comment. Others, such as RADL, *Lukas*, I, 477; ERNST, *Das Evangelium nach Lukas*, 251, consider it part of Jesus' speech. The decisive argument in favor of the latter view is that it is unlikely for πᾶς ὁ λαός in verse 29 to refer to the ὄχλοι who in verse 24 form an audience of Jesus' words about John the Baptist. When verses 29–30 are assumed to come from Jesus, πᾶς ὁ λαός has its natural referent in the audience John the Baptist had addressed during his ministry. Cf. ERNST, *Das Evangelium nach Lukas*, 251; WOLTER, *Das Lukasevangelium*, 284. R. MARTÍNEZ, *The Question of John the Baptist and Jesus' Indictment of the Religious Leaders. A Critical Analysis of Luke 7:18–35* (Eugene, OR 2011) 134, puts forward another suggestion that tries to reconcile the above mentioned opposing views. According to him, "the fact that Luke has not deliberately emphasized the change of narrative voice suggests that he may have intended to synchronize unobtrusively his own point of view with that of Jesus. [...] Luke and Jesus speak in unison."

[31] "The term *nomikos* is probably only a synonym for *grammateus*, 'scribe.'" FITZMYER, *Luke*, I, 675.

acknowledge their sin.[32] In that, they stand in contrast to the tax collectors and the people who acknowledged their need for penance.[33]

Jesus' negative judgment of the people of "this generation"[34] (7:31) is then best seen as aimed at the perversion of the Pharisees and the lawyers who refused to accept the call to repentance, finding fault with both John the Baptist and Jesus. To include all the contemporaries of Jesus and John in the criticism leveled at "this generation" would have to contend with the fact that the crowds Jesus is addressing did heed John's preaching, as confirmed by Jesus in 7:24–28 ("He began to speak to the crowds about John: 'What did you go out into the wilderness to look at?'") and 7:29.[35] The sinful state of the Pharisees and the scribes, who reject God's plan by refusing to acknowledge their sins, is even more tragically ironic in that they reject Jesus on the grounds of his friendly attitude toward sinners (7:34). Jesus is rejected by the religious leaders on the grounds on which he should be accepted all the more: he is a friend of tax collectors and sinners, and thus, ironically, their friend. The story to begin in verse 36 proves his friendliness toward them.

---

[32] ERNST, *Das Evangelium nach Lukas*, 251, offers a perceptive interpretation. He notes how, opposite the people and the tax collectors, there are "die Unbußfertigen, Pharisäer und Gesetzeslehrer (Lk 10,25; 11,45.46.52; 14,3), welche sich gegen die Bußpredigt sperren, da sie ja die »Gerechten« sind. Die Taufe ist für sie, die vollwertigen Glieder des Heilvolkes (3,8), geradezu eine Beleidigung."

[33] This becomes all the more clear when one considers how in *Pss. Sol.* 3.5; 8.7–8,23–26; 9.2; LXX Ps 50:6 acknowledgment of God's justice (δικαιοῦν τὸν θεόν) is correlated with the confession of one's sins. Cf. WOLTER, *Das Lukasevangelium*, 285.

[34] For analogical use of this concept within Jewish apocalyptic writings, see *1 En.* 93.9; 1 QpHab 2.6; *Jub.* 23.16; cf. V. HASLER, "γενεά", *EWNT*, I, 579.

[35] Cf. WOLTER, *Das Lukasevangelium*, 284. In his attempt to bring John the Baptist, the crowds and the Pharisaic party together under the umbrella of "this generation", MOESSNER, "The 'Leaven of the Pharisees'", 25–26, discerns the main division among Jesus' addressees differently. In interpreting both 3:7–21 and 7:18–35, Moessner postulates a division between the crowds (ὄχλος in 3:7,10; 7:24) and the people (λαός in 3:15,18,21; 7:29). The crowds went to be baptized by John (3:7) and are now addressed by Jesus (7:24), but only the people (λαός) received baptism (3:21), the fact acknowledged now in 7:29. In 7:29, then, Jesus speaks to the crowds, who did not receive baptism, about λαός and tax collectors, who did receive baptism. Jesus' criticism of this generation (7:31–35) would then include the crowds but exclude the λαός (as well as tax collectors). However, it is dubious whether Luke intends the distinction between the crowds and the people in the sense outlined above. Given the parallelism between 3:7 (crowds coming to be baptized) and 3:21 (λαός being baptized) as well as between 3:10 (crowds asking what to do) and 3:12 (tax collectors asking what to do), the crowds appear as the crowds of those who did receive baptism. Once instructed and later baptized, they are appropriately called λαός (3:15,18,21). Besides, as we have seen, at the center of John's preaching is not the act of receiving baptism – and thus of being set apart from those who, allegedly, come to hear John but refuse to be baptized by him – but the need to move beyond the mere ritual of baptism by means of producing fruits of right ethical conduct.

As noted in our analysis of the Sermon on the Plain, Jesus' ethical instructions are firmly set within a religious worldview where the boundary between sinners and non-sinners is clearly marked. The boundary is fixed. One's position vis-à-vis the boundary is not. In his ministry, Jesus attempts to effect conversion, that is, to bring to his side those who are not yet there. It is not just being with or against Jesus that characterizes the inhabitants of the Lukan world. There is also the question of how deeply they are with him or against him. Their *moving* closer or farther from Jesus is one of the essential elements of their presentation.

Ultimately, in Lk 7:18–35 we find the contrast between two responses to God's call to repentance: the response given by the people and the tax collectors on the one hand, and by the Pharisees and the scribes on the other. The principal trait of John the Baptist, however, is not that he belongs to the repenting sinners or unrepentant ones. His main characteristic is that, as someone greater than a prophet, he still needs to grow in faith. Even the Pharisees are not presented as intransigent in their sinfulness. That some of them could, in principle, be converted will be made evident by the story to unfold in 7:36–50. For the reader, the characters' movements – actual or possible, farther from or closer to Jesus – contribute to the characterization of Jesus as someone who draws the boundary between sinners and non-sinners only to keep urging others, sinners and non-sinners alike, to advance in recognition and submission to his unique authority. The so-called fluid nature of the characteristic of sinfulness – repeatedly manifested throughout 5:1–6:11 – contributes to this effect.

### 8.1.3. Jesus and the Sinful Woman (7:36–50)

The story of the sinful woman in 7:36–50 constitutes a high point of the Lukan discourse on sin and sinners. Well fitted into the context of the preceding discussion of John the Baptist's and Jesus' ministry to sinners,[36] this story recreates the familiar dramatic triangle between Jesus, the Pharisees, and sinners. The present story surpasses all the previous ones in the degree of complexity with which the various points of view clash over the issue of sinfulness. The narrative strategy aimed at the reader's identification with Jesus' host will be more refined. Finally, Jesus' argumentation will be more striking – the language of love first introduced in the Sermon on the Plain will now express the workings of forgiveness.

---

[36] R. VON BENDEMANN, "Liebe und Sündenvergebung. Eine narrativ-traditionsgeschichtliche Analyse von Lk 7,36–50", *BZ* 44 (2000) 162, notes also the story's connection with the Sermon on the Plain: the woman comes to Jesus (cf. 6:47: πᾶς ὁ ἐρχόμενος πρός με καὶ ἀκούων μου τῶν λόγων...), she is another weeping woman (7:38; cf. 6:21b; 7:13: μὴ κλαῖε), her deed, just like that of the centurion (7:5), is qualified as an act of love (7:47; cf. 6:27–36).

The story is notorious for its apparent inconsistency. It presents the woman's love as a fruit of the forgiveness of her sins only to create an impression – with the declaration of forgiveness in 7:48 – that the gestures of love are actually the reason why the forgiveness is granted. The difficulty is compounded by the grammar of 7:47 where the causal sense of the conjunction ὅτι – "her sins, which were many, have been forgiven, ὅτι she loved much" – can be viewed as giving grounds for the state of affairs ("*because* she loved much") or the grounds for the inference of the state of affairs ("*the evidence of which is that* she loved much").[37] In what follows, it will be the interpretive potential of 5:27–39 – a scene in which Jesus' table fellowship with tax collectors and sinners signifies their status as already forgiven sinners – that will help us affirm a consistent presentation of love as a fruit of already received forgiveness throughout 7:36–50.

The very beginning of the story, where a Pharisee invites Jesus to dine (7:36), illustrates well the complex ways in which the references to sinfulness are woven into the fabric of the narrated world. Since by now the Pharisees are understood to be sinful (7:30) and the table fellowship with Jesus is viewed as a sign of sin-removing conversion (5:29–32), are we to expect the conversion of Simon the Pharisee? Has Simon the Pharisee already included himself among the "tax collectors and sinners" with whom Jesus shares his meals (7:34)?[38] The sheer possibility of a positive answer to these questions prohibits the reader from seeing the Pharisee in a negative light.

The very next verse (7:37) adds to the ambiguity of the situation. The narrator states that a certain woman "was in the city a sinner" (γυνὴ ἥτις ἦν ἐν τῇ πόλει ἁμαρτωλός). This phrase could simply mean that a certain woman,

---

[37] Cf. ZERWICK, *Biblical Greek*, § 422. FITZMYER, *Luke*, I, 686–687, lists some ancient and modern commentators who represent each of the two competing views: love as a condition versus love as a result of forgiveness. The authors of the monographs dedicated to Luke's portrayal of sinners disagree as well. For NEALE, *None but the Sinners*, 145, the gestures of the woman express repentance, while the parable of the two debtors shifts the emphasis to forgiveness. Verse 7:47 "attempts to synthesize the two disparate perspectives" (*ibid.* 145–146). ADAMS, *The Sinner in Luke*, does not really address the problem of apparent incoherence. As a result, his interpretation seems inconsistent: he describes the woman's gestures as repentance (*ibid.* 142, 145), only to state, while discussing 7:47, that her gestures are an expression of love evidencing the gift of forgiveness (*ibid.* 146). PESONEN, *Luke, the Friend of Sinners*, 127, notes the problem regarding the exact sequence of love and forgiveness, but does not attempt to solve it, claiming that "the text is unclear and contradictory about the sequence of love and repentance because it has no interest in the question." Finally, there are those who, like BOVON, *Luke 1*, 297, welcome this inconsistency as a sign of Luke's desire to show the interdependency between forgiveness and love.

[38] GOWLER, *Host, Guest, Enemy and Friend*, 219, asks similar questions: "Why would one who had rejected the purpose of God invite Jesus to dinner, an apparent act of friendship? Is there still hope for the Pharisees?"

who was in the city, was a sinner. But it is also possible to see in this phrase a restriction: the narrator is saying not that she was a sinner but that in the city she was considered to be a sinner.[39] The narrator's choice of words would create here a meaningful distance between public negative opinion and his own point of view: he reports the opinion without completely endorsing it. The tension between two possible readings of "was in the city a sinner" heightens the need for clarification, which – as can be by now expected – will come through Jesus' normative perception of both Simon the Pharisee and the woman. But this same tension also allows the narrator to trick the reader – without compromising the narrator's omniscient point of view – into seeing the woman as a sinner, that is, from a perspective common to that of the Pharisee, as will soon be made evident.

Ambiguity regarding the woman becomes heightened rather than resolved with the description of her unusual gestures in 7:38. What is the meaning of her gestures? The tears imply that there are no sexual overtones in the scene.[40] Are the woman's gestures a sign of repentance? Are they a sign of reverent gratitude? The ancient cultural script leaves the possibilities open: her behavior could be a sign of grieving, or grateful devotion, or of supplication.[41] The narrator describes the unusual gestures without clearly identifying their meaning. The reader is left in suspense waiting for the meaning of the shocking gestures to be revealed.

The Pharisee is the first one to clarify the situation. For him, the woman is a sinner and Jesus a false prophet (7:39). Thus the Pharisee unmasks himself. He did not invite Jesus because he counted himself among the tax collectors and sinners with whom Jesus was known to dine. Rather, by inviting Jesus he wished to bring in someone known to be a prophet (cf. 7:16). Since Jesus

---

[39] J. J. KILGALLEN, "Forgiveness of Sins (Luke 7:36–50)", *NT* 40 (1998) 106. See also observations made by PLUMMER, *Gospel According to S. Luke*, 110: "The exact meaning is not quite clear: either, 'which was a sinner in the city,' *i.e.* was known as such in the place itself; or possibly, 'which was in the city, a sinner.'"

[40] Some commentators interpret the gesture as erotic. See K. E. CORLEY, "The Anointing of Jesus in the Synoptic Tradition: an Argument for Authenticity", *JSHS* 1 (2003) 68–71, or GREEN, *The Gospel of Luke*, 310, who goes as far as to maintain that "letting her hair down in this setting would have been on a par with appearing topless in public." But, as C. H. COSGROVE, "A Woman's Unbound Hair in the Greco-Roman World, with Special Reference to the Story of the «Sinful Woman» in Luke 7:36–50", *JBL* 124 (2005) 688, shows, "a first-century audience would be unlikely to form this impression of the woman for several reasons. First, the woman has not been supplied by the host. Second, the setting is a Pharisee's dinner party, not a morally lax Greco-Roman banquet. Third, the woman is weeping." Besides, Simon does not find the woman's gestures sexually provocative. His objections have to do with who she is (a sinner), not with how she touches Jesus. See *ibid.* 688–689.

[41] COSGROVE, "A Woman's Unbound Hair", 688, who also provides ample evidence explaining the symbolism of women's hair in antiquity (678–686).

failed to recognize and keep away from a publicly known sinner, he cannot be a prophet. Like the Pharisees and the scribes in 5:30, Simon disapproves of Jesus' socialization with a sinner. One can expect that, like the Pharisees and the scribes before, Simon will now stand corrected by Jesus. Inasmuch as the initial narratorial comments allowed the reader to see the woman as a sinner, the reader will stand corrected alongside Simon the Pharisee.

In 7:40–47 Jesus announces his authoritative view, manifesting at the same time his prophetic knowledge of the woman's true status and of Simon's hidden thoughts. First, through the parable, the woman is identified with the greater debtor who shows greater love. She goes beyond what is extraordinary: tears instead of water, hair instead of a towel, kiss and anointing with ointment on the feet instead of kiss and anointing with oil on the head.[42] The one known in the city as a sinner and the one looked down upon by the Pharisee for being a sinner is now presented in a different light. Her sins have already been forgiven (ἀφέωνται). By placing a reference to forgiveness (ἀφέωνται αἱ ἁμαρτίαι αὐτῆς αἱ πολλαί) before the mention of the woman's love (ὅτι ἠγάπησεν πολύ), Jesus directly and emphatically counters the false opinion the Pharisee has about the woman: "that she is a sinner" (7:39). The label, which the Pharisee has attached to the woman, is redrawn. She is a forgiven sinner, the proof of which is the love she expresses through her gestures. Like the company of the tax collectors and others at Levi's table (5:29), who, inaccurately categorized as sinners by the Pharisees and the scribes (5:30), were revealed to be the forgiven participants of the messianic banquet, the woman is no longer a sinner; her gestures are a celebration of love. The sins of the sinful woman are not downplayed. Jesus stresses the fact that her *many* sins have been forgiven. The reality of her sinfulness is accounted for. But, astonishingly, it is her great sinfulness that occasions her great love. The forgiveness of sins generates a love relationship.

If the one to whom more is forgiven shows greater love to the creditor, and if the woman's gestures are an expression of love, then Jesus, to whom these gestures are directed, stands for the divine creditor. This is a logical conclusion from the parable and Jesus' affirmation of the woman's forgiveness in 7:47. Now this logical conclusion is made explicit in verses 48 and 49.

As already noted, the fact that Luke has Jesus declare forgiveness only now, in 7:48, could create an impression that the gestures of love have led to a declaration of forgiveness, and not the other way around. The impression of inconsistency, however, can be easily avoided. Respecting the "love as a fruit of forgiveness" interpretation produced so far by the story, we can see the declaration of forgiveness in 7:48, not as a temporal marker of forgiveness

---

[42] That hosts were not expected to provide water for foot-washing, kisses at the door, or oil for anointing, is persuasively argued by J. P. MULLEN, *Dining with Pharisees* (Interfaces; Collegeville, MN 2004) 120–122.

but as a statement of the present state of forgiveness. The perfect tense verb favors such a reading.[43] Jesus stresses that the woman stands forgiven. Even more, the narrative has created the need for such a statement. The public confirmation of forgiveness corresponds to the public opinion about her expressed at the very beginning of the story, namely, that "she was in the city a sinner" (7:37).[44] The ensuing question posed by the guests in 7:48 – "Who is this that even forgives sins?" – does not contradict this interpretation either. The use of the present tense (ἀφίησιν) is not meant to indicate *when* the forgiveness took place but to ask *who* is the one who possesses a permanent capacity to do so.[45]

The final words pronounced by Jesus – "Your faith has saved you, go in peace" (7:50) – point to the woman's faith as the ground of her freedom from sin, qualified now as salvation and peace. It is impossible to determine exactly what in the woman's behavior is categorized as faith. As readers we do not see her in the moments that led to her forgiveness. Jesus' comment is then

---

[43] Both in 5:20 and 7:48 the forgiveness of sins is announced in the perfect passive tense. As we have noted in the analysis of Lk 5:17–26, the use of the perfect tense does not point to the exact moment of forgiveness but rather stresses the continuance of the resulting state of freedom from sin. The exact moment of forgiveness must be deduced from the context. In the Healing of the Paralytic scene, the context suggests that the forgiveness coincides with Jesus' proclamation. In 7:36–50, the context suggests the timing of forgiveness prior to the beginning of the scene. KILGALLEN, "Forgiveness of Sins (Luke 7:36–50)", 110, n. 11, argues that Luke's use of the perfect tense in 5:20,23, as opposed to the present tense in Mark 2:5,9, "pushes back the moment of forgiveness to coincide with the act of faith in Jesus, as is the teaching of Luke throughout." It is true that in the Lukan narrative forgiveness of sins and faith in Jesus are connected. But to make this connection into the temporal coincidence of two acts – of faith and of forgiveness – seems to press the textual data beyond what they can yield. First of all, in the case of the Healing of the Paralytic, one cannot identify the particular moment at which the act of faith takes place. Rather, the prolonged effort at overcoming various obstacles in order to reach Jesus manifests an attitude of faith, perhaps even a deepening attitude in the face of mounting obstacles. Similarly, in the Calling of Simon Peter, we identified not just one but several moments in which faith was enacted. As a result, we spoke of Peter's itinerary of faith. Therefore, rather than speaking of the temporal coincidence of faith and forgiveness, it would appear more accurate to speak of forgiveness occurring as a response to faith in Jesus.

[44] See GREEN, *The Gospel of Luke*, 314, and in particular his sensible argumentation: "That Jesus' fundamental concern in these verses is with this woman's restoration to the community of God's people (and not with her individualistic experience of forgiveness or assurance of divine acceptance) is suggested, first, by the fact that she is presented as already behaving in ways that grow out of her new life."

[45] Cf. J. J. KILGALLEN, "What Does It Mean to Say That There Are Additions in Luke 7,36–50?", *Bib* 86 (2005) 532, n. 15, where he states: "The question is so written that one knows it to be a characteristic clause; that is, what is at stake here is not just that Jesus has forgiven the woman, but that forgiveness of sins is a characteristic of Jesus' person. In this, the question is akin to what is given in Luke 5,24, which affirms Jesus' enduring power to forgive."

best understood in light of the connection between faith and forgiveness established by the prior narrative. Like Peter, the paralytic, and Levi, the woman has received forgiveness of her sins because of her faith in Jesus.

Jesus takes the possibility of the Pharisee's transformation seriously
enough to propose to him a teaching that will aim at correcting the Pharisee's
perception. The Pharisee is not simply dismissed as an erroneous judge. He is
invited to transform his view. As in his dialogue with the Pharisees in 5:30–
39, here too Jesus attempts to win him over. Jesus invites Simon to enter the
trajectory of greater love, that is, to see the divine creditor in Jesus and to see
a sinner in himself. The specific nature of the Pharisee's sinfulness might be
outside the center of narrative attention, but the need to acknowledge this
sinfulness and to have it forgiven is not: the invitation to enter the relationship of greater love forms the core of Jesus' appeal to the Pharisee. If he re-
fuses Jesus' appeal, the Pharisee will remain among those who, in their own
eyes, are well (5:31), and so are little forgiven (7:47), but in reality exclude
themselves from the wedding guests (5:34–35) and great love (7:47).

The fact that the character of the Pharisee remains an open construct – his
characterization is silent about acceptance or rejection of Jesus' discourse –
invites the readers to entertain the possible outcomes of Jesus' efforts to win
over the Pharisee. The possibility of pondering the teaching of Jesus from the
Pharisee's point of view is augmented by the fact that the narrator delays the
clarification of the sinful condition of the woman long enough to have the
readers share the Pharisee's perception of the woman as a sinner: the readers
see her through the Pharisee's eyes before they see her through the eyes of
Jesus. Insofar as they share the Pharisee's perception the readers are now
forced to ponder their own need for transformation in seeing, including the
way they see themselves. In other words, because the story is so concerned
with *seeing* things in new way – seeing the woman not as a sinner, seeing
Jesus as a prophet who reconciles sinners, and seeing oneself as invited to
enter this new paradigm of interaction with God – it augments the potential
for the readers to see thier own seeing, that is, to take a self-reflexive
stance.[46] Ultimately, the correction of one's seeing implies submission to
Jesus' astonishing view of sin, that is, to the logic of greater love.

### 8.1.4. Teaching in Parables and the Miracles of Jesus (8:1–56)

In chapter 8, Luke redirects his readers' attention from the question of Jesus'
ministry to sinners to the issue of Jesus' relationship with the Twelve. He
appointed them in 6:12–16. They accompanied him during his subsequent
activities. But it is only now that their interaction with him intensifies, preparing them for participation in his mission in Luke 9.

---

[46] Which would fulfill the purpose announced in 2:35: "so that the thoughts (διαλογισ-
μοί) out of many hearts may be revealed."

After a short summary (8:1–3), which reaffirms Jesus' role as itinerant preacher of God's Kingdom and stresses the continuing presence of both the Twelve and the group of the female disciples around Jesus, the reader encounters two blocks of material: a set of Jesus' instructions centering on the theme of hearing the Word of God (8:4–21), and the presentation of Jesus' mighty deeds (8:22–56). The disciples are not just explicitly mentioned in every scene of this section, they also engage Jesus in conversation (8:9), come to him in their despair (8:24), inquire about his status (8:25), and respond, in the person of Peter, to his question (8:45). Finally, Peter, John, and James receive a privileged access to his healing ministry (8:51).

The move away from the issue of sin and sinners, so markedly present in 5:1–6:11 and then increasingly reintroduced in 7:18–50, does not signify the disappearance of interest in the effects produced by the Lukan discourse on sin. As it has been observed, Luke so deploys the references to sinfulness as to engage the reader in the process of deciphering Jesus' theological profile, that is, discovering and assimilating his normative view. The interaction between Jesus and his disciples in 8:1–56 is oriented toward the same goal. In the scenes recounted in Luke 8, Jesus so interacts with his disciples as to make evident their need for growth in faith, that is, for recognition and assimilation of his view.

In addition, the disappearance of sinners from the scene in Luke 8 does not imply a pause in Jesus' ministry of release. Luke has already presented acts of healings and acts of forgiveness of sins as essential, mutually interpretive aspects of Jesus' ministry of release. Jesus' acts of exorcism (8:26–39), healing (8:43–48), and resuscitation (8:40–42,49–56) are understood more fully when interpreted in the light of Jesus' prior acts of release, in particular the release from sin. Accordingly, in our analysis of Luke 8, we shall highlight two narrative developments for which the foundation has been laid prior to 6:12. First, we shall note how the reader's need for discovering and assimilating Jesus' normative view is now confirmed by the emergence of a similar need inside Jesus' relationship with his disciples. Secondly, we shall attend to elements of continuity and coherence in the portrayal of Jesus' mission of release.

Jesus' parable (8:4–8), together with its explanation (8:9–18), makes clear that the proper reception of the word of God is not a one-time event but a process, the continuation of which can be threatened by various exterior and interior forces (Satan, trials, worries, riches, pleasures of life). It is possible to receive the word with joy, believe for a while, and fall away (8:13). The familiar gap between God's visitation and the human ability to respond to it is now metaphorically conveyed as a time of growth that separates the sowing of the seed from the bearing of the fruits. Interestingly, as Jesus enacts what he depicts, that is, as he proclaims and explains the word of God (sows the seed), he provokes the question about its meaning. The disciples are invited to inquire about the word they hear (8:9). Their search for meaning functions as a dramatic enactment of their process of receiving the word with an honest and good heart (8:15). The growth of the word in them, however, is not yet accomplished.

In 8:22–25, threatened with the storm, the disciples[47] find themselves in danger of perishing. Jesus' question – "Where is your faith?" (8:25) – unmasks the insufficiency of their faith, but it also, in light of the need for growth expounded in the parable of the Sower, challenges their faith to grow.[48] Fear and astonishment (8:25), triggered by the display of Jesus' authority over the powers of nature, lead the disciples to inquire about the identity of Jesus. On the one hand, their question reveals their puzzlement regarding the identity of Jesus. They appear unable to fully grasp who he is. On the other hand, they ask the right question. This becomes evident not just when echoes from the LXX are heard in the question[49] but also when their reactions to the miracle are compared with those of the Gerasenes in the following scene (8:26–39). The Gerasenes' response to the display of Jesus' power over the demons is also fear (8:35,37). But this fear, a proper response to the manifestation of the divine power, does not lead to questions about Jesus' authority. Instead, it leads to their request for Jesus to depart. While the faith of the disciples is still growing, the faith of the Gerasenes has difficulty taking roots. Luke, however, does not depict their situation as hopeless. The healed demoniac's testimony about God's work through Jesus keeps open the possibility of their future positive response to God's word.

The final scene (8:40–55) offers further lessons about faith. The faith demonstrated by the hemorrhaging woman (8:48),[50] as well as Jesus' words encouraging Jairus to move from fear to faith (8:50),[51] depict the manifestations of Jesus' power over sickness and death as connected with faith.

---

[47] Considering the differences between the Marcan and Lukan accounts of the storm, X. LÉON-DUFOUR, "La tempête apaisée", *Études d'Évangile* (Parole de Dieu; Paris 1965) 164, concludes that, when it comes to Luke, "sa description est centrée moins sur l'événement que sur les disciples."

[48] In 8:4–21, the desired response to the word of God, and to Jesus as his proclaimer, is variously described as maturation of the fruit (τελεσφοροῦσιν; 8:14), production of the fruit (καρποφοροῦσιν; 8:15), the proper manner of hearing (πῶς ἀκούετε; 8:18), hearing and doing (ἀκούοντες καὶ ποιοῦντες; 8:21), but also as faith that leads to salvation (πισ-τεύσαντες σωθῶσιν; 8:12). The critique of the disciples' faith in 8:25 connects with the message of the parable. The need for growth is stressed in both places.

[49] LXX Ps 88:9; 106:29–30. Cf. C. H. TALBERT – J. H. HAYES, "A Theology of the Sea Storms in Luke-Acts", *Jesus and the Heritage of Israel*. Luke's Narrative Claim upon Israel's Legacy (ed. D. P. MOESSNER) (Harrisburg, PA 1999) 276.

[50] In 8:48, Jesus attributes the healing to the woman's faith: "Daughter, your faith has saved you (ἡ πίστις σου σέσωκέν σε)".

[51] "Do not fear (μὴ φοβοῦ). Only believe (μόνον πίστευσον), and she will be saved (σωθήσεται)."

Salvific rewards of genuine faith indicate the direction of growth for the faith of the disciples.

For the reader attuned to the diverse ways by which Luke effects the ascription of sinfulness to a given character in the story, the absence of such strategies in Luke 8 is very telling. Neither the lack of faith on the part of the disciples nor the negative reception of Jesus on the part of the Gentile citizens of Gerasa are worded in or meant to evoke the language of sin. This is particularly striking in the case of the Gentile Gerasenes. Even though the term sinner was sometimes used to describe the Gentile enemies of Israel,[52] Luke does not actualize this potentiality. Unlike his discussions with the scripturally versed Pharisees, Jesus is not trying to convince the Gerasenes of their sinfulness nor his ability to forgive it. Their encounter with him revolves around a much more basic issue. At stake is the question of overcoming their natural fear in the face of the manifestation of the holy. As we have seen, the fundamental concern that emerges in 8:22–25 and 8:26–39 is the need for continuing growth in responsiveness to the activity of Jesus. The Gerasenes and the disciples represent different stages in that process.

The main concern being the need to grow in faith, Luke makes it emerge while advancing the portrayal of Jesus' ministry of release. Luke's detailed description of the dehumanizing condition of the afflicted man (naked, living in tombs, breaking chains and shackles, driven into the wild cf. 8:27,29) throws into relief both the need for and the successful outcome of Jesus' exorcism. Still, the fact that Jesus' first deed in the Gentile territory is an act of exorcism brings to mind his very first mighty deed (4:33–37), by which he began to enact the programmatic sermon delivered in Nazareth. It is the same program of release that now brings Jesus to minister to the Gerasene demoniac. The reaction of the Gerasenes recalls the reaction of the citizens of Capernaum. While the former ask Jesus to leave and the latter desire to keep him, both groups respond in ways that fall short of the proper attitude of faith. The gap between God's redemptive visitation and human responsiveness persists.

The healing of the hemorrhaging woman – no words or gestures of Jesus are involved; the woman is healed upon touching the fringe of Jesus' clothes – suggests that, for those who turn toward him with faith, the sheer presence of Jesus produces liberating effects. This suggestion, in turn, confirms the depiction of Jesus as the one who by his very presence forms the new criterion of repentance: as we have seen in 5:27–39, sinners' repentance is accomplished by their turning in faith toward Jesus.

Lastly, we must note a short mention of Herod in 8:3. The fact that Joanna, one of the female disciples of Jesus, is identified as a wife of Herod's steward

---

[52] LXX Ps 9:15; 128:3; Isa 14:5; *Jub.* 23.24. Cf. ADAMS, *The Sinner in Luke*, 36–37, 60.

Chuza, illustrates in the first place her social status, and secondly the scope of Jesus' activity. Jesus' influence advances not just geographically but also socially, reaching higher social levels. Still, in light of the fact that, in 3:19–20, Luke depicted Herod as an embodiment of a wicked king, his mention in 8:3 may also intimate that Jesus operates in the world where unconverted sinners are active.[53]

## 8.2. The Twelve Entrusted with a Mission and with the Prediction of Jesus' Destiny (9:1–50)

Jesus' interaction with his disciples, so prominent in Luke 8, becomes even more so in Luke 9. The dramatic developments recounted in Luke 8 under-scored the need to grow in faith, understood as a cumulative and progressive recognition and assimilation of Jesus' normative view. In Luke 9, it is not just the disciples' need for growth but their continuing failure to grow that is showcased. As a result, there arises in Luke 9 a dramatic complication rooted in the problematic relationship between Jesus and his disciples. Three dra-matic movements structure the emergence of this complication.

First, Jesus the protagonist increases the level of involvement expected from his disciples. He engages them in his mission of healing and preaching (9:1–6). He imposes on them the task of feeding people (9:12–17). His ques-tions prompt a new articulation of their understanding of his identity (9:18–20). He reveals to them his destiny of death and resurrection (9:21–22), as well as his glorious status as the chosen Son of God (9:23–26). The reactions his initiatives meet – the second dramatic movement – are mixed. The disci-ples must have relied on Jesus' power and not on material means as they did the missionary work (cf. 9:10), but they seem to think only in terms of mate-rial resources when faced with Jesus' challenge to feed the crowds (9:13). While the revelation of Jesus' glory is not completely clear to the three of them (9:33), the remaining nine fail to exorcise an evil spirit, despite the au-thority to do so given to them by Jesus in 9:1. Jesus' second announcement of his destiny remains completely incomprehensible to them (9:45), and their quarrels about who is the greatest (9:46), and their negative perception of a successful ministry of someone from outside their group (9:49), demonstrate how deeply ingrained their misunderstanding of Jesus' program is. The third dramatic movement is formed by Jesus' consistent attempts to correct and challenge the mistaken perceptions of his disciples. He does it by reference to examples (9:24–25,48), direct denial of their view (9:50), repetition of his own teaching (9:44), reference to future judgment (9:26), or direct unmasking

---

[53] Darr, *Herod the Fox*, 162, notes: "That the wife of Herod's steward is in Jesus' en-tourage makes it likely that Herod knows or will soon know about Jesus."

of their faithlessness (9:41). Interestingly, their failures vis-à-vis Jesus' increasing attempts to conform them to his mission and destiny do not disqualify them. Quite the opposite, each of their failures is met with renewed emphasis on correction and explanation.

The emergence of this dramatic complication narratively justifies the need for the continuing formation of the disciples in the next major segment of the Gospel, the Journey to Jerusalem. The reader must ask how Jesus' plan, now known to contain a destiny of suffering and death, can be realized in collaboration with such non-collaborating disciples. This question will keep the reader in suspense.[54] Still, as Luke prepares the reader for the next segment of the story, he injects into the final scenes of the Galilean ministry of Jesus several references to sinfulness. We shall attend to the way they function within the dramatic complication just outlined. In particular, since D. P. Moessner has proposed to read various references to sin and sinners in Luke 9 as intended to form an image of one solid mass of sinful people, our analysis of Luke 9, somewhat similar to our reading of 7:18–35, will aim at contesting Moessner's view by bringing in the interpretive potential of Lk 5:1–6:11.

### 8.2.1. The Sending of the Twelve, Herod's Questions, and the Challenge to Feed the Crowds (9:1–17)

While instructing the Twelve prior to their first mission, Jesus tells them what to do in case there are some who do not welcome them. Jesus' disciples are to shake the dust off their feet as a testimony against the unwelcoming persons. The gesture implies a complete dissociation;[55] its intention – "in testimony against them (εἰς μαρτύριον ἐπ' αὐτούς)" (9:5) – seems to denote the condemnation to be allotted to them at the final judgment.[56] If correct, this inter-

---

[54] This is not to deny that Jesus' destiny of violent death announced in 9:22 is enough to keep the reader in suspense. As TANNEHILL, *The Narrative Unity of Luke-Acts*, 221, aptly notes: "While the course of the story may be clarified by 9:22, the reason why Jesus must be rejected and killed remains a puzzling mystery. The mystery deepens when we recognize that Jesus' suffering and death represent his violent rejection by the 'elders and chief priests and scribes.' Jesus' death is a crisis in the developing plot because it means that Israel's Messiah is rejected by the leaders of Israel, putting in doubt the salvation for Israel which Jesus came to bring."

[55] WOLTER, *Das Lukasevangelium*, 335, captures well the rhetorical thrust of the gesture: "Die so Handelnden demonstrieren, dass sie selbst mit so etwas Unbedeutendem und Unschuldigem wie mit dem Staub einer Stadt nichts mehr zu tun haben wollen – um wieviel weniger mit deren Bewohnern!"

[56] See É. DELEBECQUE, "'Secouez la poussière de vos pieds': Sur L'hellénisme de Luc 9:5", *RB* 89 (1982) 183, who asserts that "en usant de la préposition ἐπί + accusatif, Luc entend montrer que le geste des apôtres fait retomber la responsabilité sur ceux qui les repoussent, que le témoignage de la poussière servira devant Dieu *contre* eux le jour du

pretation points to the ultimate negative consequences of rejection of Jesus' ministry. Though not directly called sinners, those who turn down Jesus' preaching become functional equivalents of sinners as far as their negative standing in the final judgment is concerned.[57] The emergence of the eschatological horizon, with the final separation between the sinners and non-sinners that this horizon connotes, is significant. For one thing, it will be evoked again in 9:26. More importantly, however, it reminds the reader that Jesus' ministry of forgiveness of sins does not nullify the distinction between sinners and non-sinners. It rather assumes it. As was observed in our analysis of the Sermon on the Plain, in the ideological horizon of Jesus there is no neutral ground. In an indirect way, the mention of eschatological judgment, and particularly, the notion of the allocation of the sinners' lot that the judgment implies, evokes the final categorization of all into sinners and non-sinners. Jesus' ministry to sinners consists not just in bringing the offer of forgiveness but also in identifying and defining sin in Christological terms.

A much more direct reference to sinfulness appears in 9:7–9. Herod's interest in Jesus has a primary function of foregrounding the question about the identity of Jesus. Indirectly, however, it brings to mind not just the sins of which John the Baptist accused Herod in 3:19 but also Herod's most recent evil deed, the beheading of John the Baptist. Herod's interest in Jesus is ominous. He is a wicked king with the blood of one prophet already on his hands. Still, one cannot exclude the possibility that this sinner's encounter with Jesus, something that Herod seeks, could be the moment of his recognition and acceptance of Jesus' true identity, in particular his power to forgive sins.[58]

### 8.2.2. Peter's Confession, Transfiguration, and the Failures of the Disciples (9:18–50)

Responding to Peter's recognition of his messianic identity, Jesus announces an imperative component of his mission: he is to suffer rejection and death and be raised on the third day (9:22). The perpetrators of this violent act are identified as the elders, chief priests, and scribes, that is, the leadership of Israel. Since Jesus' innocence is beyond question, the ones to be responsible for his suffering and death must be seen as sinners. When in 9:44 Jesus

---

Jugement." This interpretive suggestion is strengthened when one considers how in Lk 11:31–32 the queen of the South and the people of Nineveh are said to condemn the evil generation at the future judgment. Cf. WOLTER, *Das Lukasevangelium*, 335.

[57] See LXX Mal 3:5, where God is said to come in judgment (ἐν κρίσει) and be a swift witness (μάρτυς ταχύς) against (ἐπί) sorceresses, adulteresses, those who swear falsely, defraud, or oppress.

[58] Cf. DARR, *Herod the Fox*, 211–212. See also Darr's helpful articulation of the reader's suspicions: "If there is indeed to be a confrontation, will Herod perceive the true significance of Jesus and respond to it, or will he be one of the many who see but do not see, and hear but do not hear?" (*ibid.* 170).

speaks about being delivered into human hands, it must be understood that he will be delivered into the hands of sinners.[59] Jesus' mission toward sinners (cf. 5:32) will bring him into the sinners' hands.

The most surprising reference to sinfulness appears in 9:41. The disciples' failure to exorcise a demon and thus to enact the authority given to them in 9:1, occasions Jesus' designation of them[60] as a faithless and perverse generation. Jesus' prior negative judgment of the people of "this generation" (7:31) aimed at the perversion of the Pharisees and the lawyers who refused to accept the call to repentance, finding fault with both John the Baptist and Jesus. This time Jesus' own disciples are described as the faithless and perverse generation. In the context of the Transfiguration, in which Moses and Elijah discuss Jesus' *exodus* (9:41), the notion of a faithless and perverse generation is likely to evoke the memory of the indictment pronounced by Moses against the people who had been enacting their *exodus* from Egypt to the Promised Land. In Deut 32:5, Moses calls them "crooked and perverse" (γενεὰ σκολιὰ καὶ διεστραμμένη), and in Deut 32:20 God describes them as "a perverse generation, sons who have no faithfulness in them" (γενεὰ ἐξεστραμμένη ἐστίν, υἱοί, οἷς οὐκ ἔστιν πίστις ἐν αὐτοῖς).[61] This negative judgment does not rupture the relation Jesus maintains with his disciples. He goes on to do what they were unable to, namely, to heal the man's son; they continue to consider themselves his followers (cf. 9:49). In this sense, he unmasks their sin only to forgive it.[62]

---

[59] This finds confirmation in the words of the angelic messengers in Lk 24:6–7: "Remember how he told you, while he was still in Galilee, that the Son of Man must be delivered into the hands of sinful men (δεῖ παραδοθῆναι εἰς χεῖρας ἀνθρώπων ἁμαρτωλῶν), and be crucified, and on the third day rise again"

[60] It is not immediately clear to whom Jesus directs his criticism. The context clarifies the issue. The father of the demoniac demonstrates faith in Jesus, despite being disappointed by the disciples. The crowds remain completely in the background. Only the disciples fit the profile of the addressees of Jesus' harsh criticism. Cf. GREEN, *The Gospel of Luke*, 388, n. 122; WOLTER, *Das Lukasevangelium*, 358.

[61] For a thorough analysis of the prophetic parallels of Moses in Deuteronomy to Jesus in Lk 9:1–50, see D. P. MOESSNER, "Luke 9:1–50: Luke's Preview of the Journey of the Prophet Like Moses of Deuteronomy", *JBL* 102 (1983) 575–605, as well as his *Lord of the Banquet*, 60–70, 77–79. R. F. O'TOOLE, "Luke's Message in Luke 9:1–50", *CBQ* 49 (1987) 79, n. 5, voices some reservations: "Moessner ("Luke 9: 1–50") may be correct that, according to Luke, Jesus is a prophet like Moses in Deuteronomy and thus leads the disciples on the journey to Jerusalem, but for Luke Jesus is likewise the Christ of God and the Son."

[62] WOLTER, *Das Lukasevangelium*, 358, suggests that the phrase "to bear with you" (ἀνέξομαι ὑμῶν) found in Jesus' complaint in 9:41b – "How long must I be with you and bear with you?" – should rather be understood in the sense in which it appears in Isa 46:4; 63:15, that is, in the sense of "to help you," "to deliver you from the plight." If correct, this interpretation would further support the conclusion that for Jesus the disciples' faults are not irredeemable.

In our study of references to sinfulness, this particular depiction of sin and forgiveness is very significant. When the characteristic of sinfulness is predicated of someone like the paralytic (5:17–26) or the sinful woman (7:36–50) – minor characters with only one-time appearance in the story – it serves, among other things, to demonstrate and confirm Jesus' power to forgive sins, or to point to Jesus' perception as the final evaluative view of who is and who is not a sinner. When, on the other hand, the sinfulness is predicated of the disciples – whose continual contact with Jesus forms the ordering principle behind the unity of 5:1–24:53 – it is inscribed in the journey of faith long enough to recount and account for many surprising, zig-zag-like movements and their corresponding effects on the reader. Jesus has called his disciples from among sinners, as Luke's depiction of Peter (5:8) and Levi (5:27) makes clear. By bringing them into his own company he effectively released them from their sins. But as the present incident in the relationship between Jesus and his disciples shows, their status as disciples does not make them immune to sin. Sinfulness is inscribed into their relation with Jesus not just at the beginning as something to be overcome once and for all. It reappears. Most importantly, however, it is remitted again, presenting Jesus as someone relentless in his ministry of release.

As Jesus' new destiny is revealed in Luke 9, heightening the tension between the increasing demands of Jesus' mission and the decreasing capabilities of his disciples, the reader notes that the narrative world is again marked by references to sin and sinners. There is the future sin of authorities who are to reject and kill Jesus; there is Herod, a wicked king, whose perplexity very likely hides his evil plans toward Jesus; and there are disciples whose failures reach the proportions of the faithless perversion typical of sinners. How are we to understand the presence of these references at this point in the narrative? As already indicated, we shall answer this question while considering David P. Moessner's view of Lk 9:1–50.

Moessner contends that through various references to sinfulness there emerges an image of one sinful generation. According to him, in 9:41, "Jesus lumps his disciples together with one solid mass of a disbelieving, perverse people."[63] Moreover, the "generation" mentioned in 9:41, and the "men" into whose hands Jesus is to be delivered (9:44), constitute the same group.[64] What Moessner thus wants to demonstrate is that "the grounding for the death of Jesus is thus the same as for Moses in Deuteronomy. Because of the intransigent sin of the people, a stiff-necked resistance so powerful that even

---

[63] MOESSNER, "Luke 9:1–50", 592; cf. *Lord of the Banquet*, 63; "Jesus and the 'Wilderness Generation'", *Society of Biblical Literature 1982 Seminar Papers* (ed. K. H. RICHARDS) (SBL.SPS 21; Chico, CA 1982) 328; "'The Christ Must Suffer': New Light on the Jesus–Peter, Stephen, Paul Parallels in Luke-Acts", *NT* 28 (1986) 237.

[64] MOESSNER, "Luke 9:1–50", 595–596: "It is not only the Sanhedrin that is going to kill Jesus, but so is this same twisted generation!"

gestures of redemption are spurned with twisted contempt, Moses/Jesus must suffer and die."[65] It could be that the Journey Narrative will bring the reader to such conclusions. At this point in the narrative, however, the dismissal of the differences between the particular groups – the disciples, the leaders of Israel, and the crowds – seems unjustified. For one thing, the fact that Jesus continues his ministry of forgiveness toward his disciples distinguishes them from other groups. The references to sinfulness are too variegated to form one solid bloc of characters, the sinful generation. There are sinners who are forgiven, a potential sinner, and those still to prove their sinfulness. To the reader primed to appreciate this variegation for the sake of disentangling and delineating Jesus' theological profile, these distinctions are significant.[66]

In the end, then, what 9:1–50 depicts is less the stubborn resistance by all of Jesus' contemporaries, forming a need for his atoning death,[67] and more Jesus' persistent ministry of release to those who are not always ready to receive it.[68] The reason for Jesus' death remains unknown. But if it is to happen at the hands of sinners, it will, ironically, bring Jesus into the hands of those who have the greatest need for his ministry (cf. 5:31). As the progression of Jesus' mission of release appears in danger of being thwarted by forces inim-

---

[65] MOESSNER, "Luke 9:1–50", 596; cf. MOESSNER, *Lord of the Banquet*, 67.

[66] Moessner's reading of Lk 9:1–50, and, in particular, his insistence on the monolithic sinfulness of the entire generation of Jesus' contemporaries, is related to the so-called fourfold structure of the deuteronomistc view of Israel's history, first brought to the attention of scholars by O. H. STECK, *Israel und das gewaltsame Geschick der Propheten. Untersuchungen zur Überlieferung des deuteronomistischen Geschichtsbildes im Alten Testament, Spätjudentum und Urchristentum* (WMANT 23; Neukirchen-Vluyn 1967): (A) rebellious people, (B) to whom God sends messengers, the prophets, to admonish them in ways of repentance, (C) reject, and even kill God's prophets, (D) bringing upon themselves God's judgment of destruction. Moessner uncovers the presence of this pattern not just in the Journey Narrative but already in Lk 9:1–50. See *Lord of the Banquet*, 91. In fact, for Moessner, it is "the disciples' solidarity with the faithless mass of the people (tenet A), so poignantly accented by Luke's carefully carved continuity in the crowds and scenery changes, which imprints 9:1–50 with the Deuteronomistc outlook" (*ibid.* 91). When we argue that Lk 9:1–50 does not exactly fit the deuteronomistic pattern of monolithic rebellion against the prophet (tenet A), it is not to say that no such pattern can be found in Luke's view of *Heilsgeschichte*, but rather that the presumed presence of this pattern makes Luke's departure from it even more significant.

[67] Although Moessner does not suggest that Deuteronomy offers a developed explanation of Moses' death as atoning, he considers Moses' death vicarious and redemptive. "Moses' death vis-à-vis the older generation is vicarious in the sense of a shared participation in their punishment, and it is redemptive for the younger generation as it finally enables or allows their deliverance to be consummated." MOESSNER, "Luke 9:1–50", 587, n. 52.

[68] Thus we agree with S. R. GARRETT, "Exodus from Bondage: Luke 9:31 and Acts 12:1–24", *CBQ* 52 (1990) 658, that "the reference in Luke 9:31 to an 'exodus' evokes notions, not of atonement, but of liberation."

ical or, at least, unfavorable to his cause, it also seems to be headed, paradox-ically, in the right direction, that is, toward confrontation with the forces of ignorance and sin.

## 8.3. Concluding Remarks on the Interpretive Potential of Lk 5:1–6:11 for the "Sinner Texts" in Lk 6:12–9:50

To conclude, the interpretive potential Lk 5:1–6:11 holds for the subsequent narrative has proven useful in countering particular interpretations and for adjudicating certain exegetical problems related to the "sinner texts" in 6:12–9:50. The following presentation summarizes our results.

The negative characterization of sinners in Lk 6:20–49 is not out of place. It coheres with the conclusion first reached in 5:27–39, namely, that rejection of Jesus compounds one's sinful state. Consequently, to reject Jesus' way of loving and giving is to remain among sinners. That said, sinners may stand for those who oppose God's logic of acting, but the boundary they mark does not pose a limit to God's (and Jesus') merciful action toward them.

Luke 7 highlights the contrast between those who accept the call to repent-ance and those who reject it. Still, as Jesus draws the line between sinners and non-sinners he continues to draw to himself both sinners and non-sinners alike. The Pharisees in Luke 7 might be categorized as sinners, but it is to one of them that Jesus appeals with the prospect of greater love engendered by greater forgiveness. Thus the designation sinner evokes both tragic and hope-ful connotations: sinners exclude themselves from final salvation but it is also to them that Jesus directs his ministry. The fluid nature of the designation sinner, so prominent in 5:1–6:11, comes again into view: the boundary be-tween sinners and non-sinners is fixed but the characters in the story are free to cross it. The image of sinners forming one solid block of opposition to Jesus appears inadequate.

In Luke 8 and Luke 9, Jesus' disciples begin to play a more prominent role. First, their need to grow in faith is underscored. Then their limited ca-pacities for faith and understanding are displayed, contrasting sharply with the increasing demands for their participation in Jesus' mission. As the com-plications in Jesus' relationship with his disciples escalate, and as the predic-tion of Jesus' violent death turns the plot in a new direction, the references to sinfulness intensify. There are sinners who are forgiven, a potential sinner, and those still to prove their sinfulness. The reader can expect that, as the story progresses, references to sin and sinners – as in 5:1–6:11 – will again need to be disambiguated into patterns, relations, and contrasts reflective of the normative, and yet not easily perceptible, view of Jesus, including the view of his own death at the hands of sinners.

Lastly, running the risk of repetitiveness, one could speak of three mutually related principles which, being established in 5:1–6:11, guide and determine the interpretation of the "sinner texts" in 6:12–9:50:

*Offer of forgiveness does not exclude attribution of sinfulness.* The reader who witnesses Jesus' ministry of forgiveness of sins in 5:1–6:11 also notes that the opposition to that ministry assumes the characteristics of aggravating sinfulness. The same reader is ready to conclude that, in the Sermon on the Plain and again in 9:1–7, rejection of Jesus amounts to exclusion from the eschatological reward – a destiny reserved for sinners.

*The tragedy of rejection does not exclude hope.* Luke's recourse to ἄνοια in 6:11 means that the same category that designates the radicalization of the Pharisees' and the scribes' sin lays the ground for its potential forgiveness. Thus, as their rejection of Jesus qualifies them as sinners, it paradoxically designates them as those to whom Jesus' ministry remains unwaveringly dedicated. Lk 7:36–50 highlights this point.

*The drawing of boundaries does not exclude the movement across them.* The so-called fluid nature of the characteristic of sinfulness, manifested repeatedly throughout 5:1–6:11, is the best way to describe the way references to sin and sinners function in Luke 7 and Luke 9. Far from forming one solid block of characters known as sinners, these references – reflecting a variety of Jesus' relations with forgiven sinners, potential sinners, or those yet to prove their sinfulness – engage the reader in the familiar search for the surprising profile of Jesus' person and mission.

Chapter 9

# Conclusions

It is impossible to understand who the Lukan sinners are without attending carefully to the *story world* within which they appear. Accordingly, our study of sinners in Lk 5:1–6:11 has endeavored to place them firmly in the configurations of plot, characters, setting, and point of view within which they come alive as literary personages. But it is also impossible to understand who the sinners are without attending carefully to *the way they appear* in the story, that is, without considering the metaphors, allusions, both direct and indirect references meant to evoke for the reader the notion of sinners. Our close reading of Lk 5:1–6:11 has attempted to account for a rich variety of modes through which the notions of sin and sinners emerge in the reader's consciousness. Ultimately, however, neither the static architecture of the world within which sinners come into view nor the variety of modes by which their presence is announced can fully account for their role. One must still attend to the *temporal unfolding* of the narrative in which sinners as characters emerge. Hence, our study, while attending to the temporal production of the narrative's effects on the reader, has reconstructed not so much a fixed category of the implied reader,[1] as the reader's continuous movement. The effects of Luke's narration and, by implication, the final explanation of the sinners' role in Luke's story, have been shown to consist in structuring the ideal reader's *movement* toward recognition and submission to Jesus' authoritative view. The text's meaning, or to put it in more Ricoeurian terms, the possibility of being opened up by the Lukan narrative,[2] is delineated by the steps the ideal reader takes. As we now bring together the results of our investigation, summarizing briefly each chapter's contribution to our overall project, we shall once more specify the successive steps of the implied reader.

Chapter One has an introductory nature. It spells out the methodological assumptions on which the study is based, in particular, the notions of the temporal ordering and the first time reading. It provides a reconstruction of

---

[1] On the heuristic notion of the implied reader, see §1.3.

[2] For Ricoeur, "understanding is not concerned with grasping a fact but with apprehending a possibility of being [...] to understand a text, we shall say, is not to find a lifeless sense which is contained therein, but to unfold the possibility of being indicated by the text." P. RICOEUR, "The Task of Hermeneutics", *Hermeneutics and the Human Sciences* (ed. and tr. J. B. THOMPSON) (Cambridge 1981) 56.

the implied reader's pre-existing beliefs pertaining to sinners, and it justifies concentration on Lk 5:1–6:11 on the grounds of its place in the composition of Luke-Acts.

Chapter Two accounts for the ways in which the preparatory narrative of Luke 1–4 frames the reader's understanding of sin and sinners. Throughout Luke 1–4, the ideal reader moves from seeing the sinful state of Israel as a condition to be addressed by God's eschatological intervention, to seeing Jesus, the agent of God's intervention, as the one who addresses sinfulness on his own terms. Gradually, as the reader observes Jesus, the embodiment of God's redemptive plan, he or she is persuaded to ascribe to Jesus the authority not just to enact but also to interpret God's plan. Particularly through the contrast with John the Baptist's mission to sinners, the reader comes to perceive in Jesus' ministry of release a divine initiative that asserts itself with surprising originality. The reader is moved to seek the logic of God's surprising intervention in Jesus' words and deeds; the need to turn to Jesus as the authoritative interpreter of God's action is established. Chapter Two concludes with the identification of a triple dynamic effect the reader of Luke 1–4 can be expected to undergo: the reader moves from (1) growing in the knowledge of God's agent, Jesus, through many revelatory statements about him, to (2) the realization that Jesus is the only one capable of authoritative interpretation of himself, to (3) becoming subjected to Jesus' didactic of piecemeal revelation of the truth about his redemptive mission. The reader's understanding of sinfulness becomes shaped by this triple dynamic. The reader moves from (1) perceiving sinfulness as a condition to be addressed by God's eschatological intervention, to (2) realizing that sinfulness can be properly perceived only from the perspective of God's eschatological agent.

In Chapters Three to Seven, a close reading of Lk 5:1–6:11 is conducted with a view to assessing its presentation of sinners. In the Calling of Peter (5:1–11), the reference to the sinfulness of Simon Peter is not just simply made explicit, it is also centrally staged – it coincides with the climax in the corresponding occurrences of Simon Peter's transformation and Jesus' revelation. Having asserted a distance between himself and Jesus on account of his own sinfulness, Simon ultimately submits to Jesus' call, indirectly recognizing Jesus' authority to cross and eliminate the alienation caused in Simon's mind by his sin. The reader notes how Simon Peter's itinerary of faith culminates not only in his recognition of Jesus as the Lord and of himself as a sinner, but also in acknowledging Jesus' lordship even over Peter's view of sin. Thus, Simon models for the reader the realization that sinfulness can be properly understood only on Jesus' terms. Like Peter, the reader cedes to Jesus the power over sin and the authority to define who is and who is not a sinner.

The subsequent scenes confirm for the reader the basic orientation of assessing sinners through Jesus' eyes and of deciphering Jesus' authoritative view – in effect, his view of sinners. In the Healing of a Leper (5:12–16), Luke presents as parallel the reactions of sinful Peter in 5:8 and the leper in 5:12. The issues of sinfulness and alienating disease, as reflected in these reactions, become related. Mirroring Simon's posture, the leper recognizes Jesus' power to eliminate alienation caused by disease. Jesus is not just resistant to the contagion of sin and sickness; he is capable of driving these oppressive and alienating forces away by virtue of his own words and gestures. Jesus' authority to define who is and who is not a sinner is matched and confirmed by his power to release from the forces of sickness and sin.

In 5:17–26, the paralytic experiences both healing and forgiveness as he demonstrates, in conjunction with his friends, a stubborn perseverance in placing himself at Jesus' disposal. As Jesus prophetically reveals and divinely remits the sins of the paralytic, he also challenges the mistaken notion that the scribes and the Pharisees have about his allegedly sinful conduct – according to them he blasphemes. It is Jesus, not the Pharisees, whose view of sin and sinners is validated by the miracle of healing. Both in the Calling of Peter and in the Healing of the Paralytic, Jesus remains the one who chooses to trigger the revelation, or simply chooses to reveal sin. At the same time, he corrects the mistaken understanding of sin's consequences, or of its attribution. The operations seen in 5:1–11 are repeated in 5:17–26 with an added emphasis on Christological explicitness, in particular on Jesus' power to forgive sins.

The Call of Levi (5:27–39) reinforces the characterization of Jesus as someone who reveals, correctly interprets, and frees from sin. His view of sin is authoritative. There is a new referential content of what is implied by sinfulness. Until now very little has been said about what concrete sin Peter, the paralytic, or even the tax collectors and sinners had fallen into. The only specific content of sinfulness is that attributed to the Pharisees: they are sinful because they fall into the rejection of Jesus. Such a Christological expansion of the content of sinfulness makes faith in Jesus an act of the highest religious import, since refusal of that faith amounts to sin.

In the Sabbath Disputes (6:1–11), Luke advances the portrayal of the sinfulness of Jesus' opponents. It is not just resistance but active opposition that characterizes their attitude toward Jesus. In response to the miracle of healing, they succumb to a foolishness that blinds them from seeing the Lord of the Sabbath in Jesus, and from seeing themselves as sinners whose sinfulness Jesus wants to forgive. They fail to see the sin the way Jesus sees it.

Throughout 5:1–6:11, as the reader's perception of sinners becomes aligned with Jesus' normative view of those sinners, their characterization turns out to be thoroughly relational. They are depicted *in relation* to Jesus. Sinners are those whose sinfulness Jesus perceives and identifies, whose recognition of sinfulness he prompts or invites, and whose sins he pardons in response to faith in him. Sinners are the ones from among whom he forms his disciples. Finally, those who reject Jesus' mission toward them become characterized as sinners.

Within the dynamic of relation, by which the characters known as sinners reflect the profile of Jesus' person and mission, the reader detects an element of confrontation. As the Pharisees and the scribes enter the scene, the reader's relation to the protagonist, Jesus, is problematized. It is not so much the fact that Jesus encounters opposition as the fact that this opposition is, initially, justifiable: Jesus does depart from the norms the Pharisees accept as binding. To solve this tension, the reader must move deeper into his recognition of who Jesus is. Like the scribes and the Pharisees, he or she is invited to view in Jesus the new criterion by which correct performance of religious practices is to be assessed. As the disputed practices (repentance, fasting, Sabbath observance) again revolve around sinners, or to be more exact, around the expected ways of both removing sin and falling into sin, the reader must again advance in deciphering and appropriating Jesus' view of what makes one a sinner. Not unlike the Pharisees, he or she must struggle here with Jesus' indirectness in delineating his authoritative vision.

Both in its relational and confrontational function, the characteristic of sinfulness is used in repetitive ways. These repetitions consolidate the image of Jesus reflected in his dealings with various characters. They also slow down the forward movement of the story, inviting the study of consistency and distinctiveness in the presentation of Jesus.

Finally, both relational and confrontational use of the characteristic of sinfulness invites an interpretive effort on the part of the reader. Throughout Lk 5:1–6:11, the ministry of Jesus becomes fully enfleshed, but not thereby fully transparent to the reader. Jesus does not so much explain his ministry to sinners as display it through interactions that involve divergences of view, shifts of perspective, recourse to elusive titles and indirectness. He does it repeatedly and in connection with other controversial issues such as Sabbath observance or fasting. This strategy has its calculated effect on the reader. Luke deploys multiple direct and indirect references to sinfullness so as to engage the reader in a search for the normative view of Jesus. By untangling crisscrossing viewpoints formed around sinfulness – implied, inferred, directly labeled, remitted, or rejected – the reader's *coming* to know Jesus is enacted.

In the final step, as the reader learns to categorize as sinners those who reject Jesus' ministry, he or she begins to note the paradox inherent in Jesus' ministry toward sinners. If the Pharisees reject Jesus because of his ministry to sinners, they reject him on the very grounds on which they need him all the more. This highlights their tragic blindness. But since Jesus' ministry is meant to reach sinners, their tragedy contains a seed of hope: it paradoxically makes them into addressees of his ministry of release. As the conflict between Jesus and the Pharisaic party reaches its initial climax in Lk 6:11, the reader reaches an important insight: if Jesus' mission seems to be in danger of being thwarted by confrontation with inimical, sinful forces, it also appears to be headed in the right direction, that is, toward an encounter with human sin.

Chapter Eight, following the arc of the narrative up to 9:50, demonstrates the interpretive potential Luke's portrayal of sinners in 5:1–6:11 holds for the subsequent sinner texts. Concomitantly, the remainder of the Galilean ministry confirms and advances the dynamic of the ideal reader's movement outlined above. In particular, Jesus' view of sinners, which the reader has been primed to discover and assimilate, continues to refer to the tragic and hopeful dimension of this designation. Both tragedy and hope are Christologically framed: allocation of eschatological condemnation for sinners results from their rejection of Jesus; their rejection of Jesus qualifies them as sinners, that is, as those to whom Jesus' ministry remains unwaveringly dedicated. The Story of the Sinful Woman in Lk 7:36–50 confronts the reader anew with Jesus' astonishing view of sinners. There the tragedy of sin is pressed to serve the logic of greater love. The prediction of Jesus' violent death at the hands of sinners ties again the mystery of his redemptive mission to his interactions with the characters known as sinners. The reader can expect that, as the story progresses, references to sin and sinners – as in 5:1–6:11 – will again need to be disambiguated into patterns, relations, and contrasts reflective of the normative, and yet not easily perceptible, view of Jesus, including the view of his own death at the hands of sinners.

The studies of Neale[3] and Adams[4] have paid sustained attention to the Lukan presentation of sinners. As it has already been noted, Neale affirms that the sinners of Luke are an ideological category employed in order to fuel the conflict with the Pharisees – the engine of the plot – and ultimately to exemplify "the right response to Jesus in counterpoint to the uncomprehending and bigoted 'Pharisees.'"[5] For Adams, sinners illustrate the far-reaching scope of Jesus' messianic mission through which the OT promises of salvation are fulfilled.[6] Both of these views can now be complemented.

Sinners indeed contribute to the conflict between Jesus and the Pharisees. But as our study has revealed, the engine of the story lies elsewhere. It is found in the gap between, on the one hand, Jesus' normative view and, on the other hand, both the characters' and the reader's willingness and ability to assimilate it. Even before the Pharisees enter the scene, the references to sin and sinners are deployed to delineate that gap, particularly as Jesus' ministry departs from the expectations set up by John the Baptist. Similarly, sinners indeed stand for the far-reaching limits of Jesus' messianic activity. Still, as it

---

[3] NEALE, *None but the Sinners*.

[4] ADAMS, *The Sinner in Luke*.

[5] NEALE, *None but the Sinners*, 193.

[6] ADAMS, *The Sinner in Luke*, 195–196.

has been observed, it is not just those bearing the lexical mark, but the ones indirectly characterized as sinners, such as the Pharisees, who illustrate the depth of Jesus' relentless ministry of release. Ultimately, the story is not about the reversal of expectations which the reader would have had regarding the black-and-white religious categories of sinners and the Pharisees. The reader is not led to simply identify with some characters (tax collectors and sinners) and to dismiss others (the Pharisees). The reader is rather led to follow all the references to sinfulness and to glean from them the proper shape of his or her own relationship with the protagonist, Jesus.

The last observation has a bearing on the issue of the historical identity of Luke's opponents. The scribes and the Pharisees, although not deprived of some positive features, receive an increasingly negative characterization.[7] Their opposition to Jesus marks them in the end as sinners, that is, as those who oppose God. It would seem natural to explain this literary phenomenon as an attempt to legitimize the Lukan community relative to any opposition, real or imagined, coming from certain Jewish or Jewish-Christian circles. In light of our study, however, such an explanation would have to be either questioned or further elaborated. Without deciding whether the Pharisees represent certain outside religious groups (Jewish or Jewish-Christian) or simply function as ahistorical foils meant to teach the audience by negative example, one must admit that the fluid nature of the characteristic of sinfulness discourages any fixed identification of religious outsiders as sinners. The demarcation line between sinners and non-sinners is clear, but one's positioning relative to this line is not. Jesus' mission, and the ideal reader's conceptual framework which it informs, privilege the possibility of transformation in one's stance toward God. In other words, religious outsiders are potential insiders. Still, for Luke, any religious transformation remains univocally Christocentric.[8]

Finally, the results of this study seem to be reaffirmed by the demands created by the macro-narrative of Luke-Acts. What sustains the main drama of the macro-narrative of Luke-Acts is the relationship between Jesus and his disciples. As the story unfolds, the increasing demands of Jesus' mission are met with the decreasing capabilities of his disciples, in particular with their inability to understand the suffering destiny of their master (see Lk 9:44–45;

---

[7] Generally, the studies of the Lukan Pharisees based on redaction criticism postulate a positive view of the Pharisees (see, for instance, BRAWLEY, *Luke-Acts and the Jews*, 84–106; ZIESLER, "Luke and the Pharisees"). The studies following the narrative approach tend to argue for a negative image of the Pharisees (see DARR, *On Character Building*, 85–126) or at least a more negative image of them in the Gospel than in the Acts (so GOWLER, *Host, Guest, Enemy, and Friend*).

[8] As pointedly expressed by A.-J. LEVINE "Luke and the Jewish Religion", *Interp.* 68 (2014) 399: "Whatever practice, theology, ritual, salvation history, or hermeneutic is available must, for Luke, culminate in Jesus. If it does not, it is incomplete or illegitimate."

18:31–34). In what is narrated between Luke 24 and Acts 2, a turning point takes place. The encounter with the Risen One who "opened the Scriptures" to them (24:32), the gift of the Spirit who inspired interpretation of the Scripture (as manifested by the Apostles' preaching in Acts), and the ability to understand Scriptures (24:45), constitute the experience of enlightenment.[9] The disciples receive categories through which they can comprehend and fully align themselves with God's plan enacted through Jesus' death and resurrection. The new understanding, however, is given to them but not to the readers. As readers, we do not know which Scriptures Jesus opened to them (24:27,32), or what kind of scriptural proof for the suffering and resurrection of the Messiah he gave them (24:46). As readers, we must keep searching for this new understanding in the Scriptures and in the words of Jesus, remembering in particular what he said "while he was still in Galilee" (24:6), and count on the help of the Spirit and of the Risen One. Thus the need to search for the profile of Jesus' person and mission is reaffirmed as the key demand formed not just in the initial chapters of the Gospel but also instilled by the logic of meta-narrative as such.

Interestingly, in the narration of Jesus' suffering, death, and resurrection, the direct and indirect references to the sinfulness of the leaders of Israel and of the disciples intensify as does the offer of forgiveness: pronounced on the cross (23:34), implied by the gift of peace (24:36), and foretold as the content of apostolic witness to be recounted in the Book of Acts, namely, "that repentance and forgiveness of sins is to be proclaimed in his name to all nations, beginning from Jerusalem" (24:47). It will fall to the Apostles to proclaim Jesus' authoritative view of sin, by both imputing guilt and offering forgiveness in Jesus' name.[10] To the reader, it is the same authoritative view of sin, discovered and recognized as such in the initial chapters of the Gospel, that now enters the narrative of Acts through the mediation of the Apostles. Conversely, the persistence of the sinfulness theme in the Book of Acts

---

[9] See J. B. GREEN, "Learning Theological Interpretation from Luke", *Reading Luke*. Interpretation, Reflection, Formation (ed. C. BARTHOLOMEW – J. B. GREEN – A. THISELTON) (Scripture and Hermeneutics Series 6; Grand Rapids, MI 2005) 70–72, who describes the removal of the disciples' ignorance as "a theological transformation", that is, "a deep-seated conversion in their conception of God and, thus, in their commitments, attitudes, and everyday practices. [...] The resolution of 'ignorance' is not simply 'the amassing of facts,' but a realignment with God's ancient purpose, now coming to fruition" (*ibid.* 71).

[10] See, for instance, Peter's forthright accusation directed to his Jerusalem audience in Acts 2:23 ("this man ... you crucified and killed") followed by an offer of forgiveness in Acts 2:38 ("be baptized every one of you in the name of Jesus Christ so that your sins may be forgiven") or Paul's proclamation of forgiveness in 13:38 ("through this man forgiveness of sins is proclaimed to you") followed by a reference to sins "from which you could not be freed by the law of Moses."

points to the importance of its initial presentation at the beginning of the narrative proper of the Gospel.

This study was motivated by a simple methodological observation that the role of sinners in Luke is properly assessed not just by examining sinner texts, that is, the pericopae containing the word sinner or its cognates, but also by uncovering and assessing all the textual strategies that prompt the reader to infer the characteristic of sinfulness, even in the absence of its direct textual referent. As a result, this study has revealed that the sinners are not an easily identifiable category of characters squarely captured by the stable lexical marker, ἁμαρτωλός. Rather, they are what could be called fluid characters: their defining characteristic – their sinfulness – is often found inadequate, rendered inapplicable, or transferred to another character. In the final analysis, interpretive effort implied by the task of sorting through the conflicting, ambiguous, or seemingly inconsistent understandings of sin and sinners engages the reader in the basic dynamic of recognizing and submitting to Jesus' authoritative view. The reader's *coming* to know Jesus is enacted. A future research in this field would naturally involve the study of direct and indirect references to sin and sinners in the remaining portions of the Gospel as well as in the Book of Acts. It could also include comparative study of Luke vis-à-vis other NT understandings of sin and sinners. Finally, it is also possible to envision an expansion of our investigation into the field of Lukan anthropology, captured not just at the level of the characters the Gospel depicts but also of the ideal reader it tends to form.

The last remark invites one more observation. Lukan anthropology, or the possibility of being opened up by the Lukan narrative, seems to allow for one more step in the ideal reader's movement toward recognition and acceptance of God's redemptive intervention. It creates conditions for incorporating the recognition of one's own sinfulness into the ideal reader's *coming* to know Jesus. After all, it is significant that in structuring the reader's itinerary Luke deploys references to *sinfulness*. The structuring function of references to sinfulness does not deprive them of their semantic import.[11] Quite the opposite, it highlights the fact that it is through one's sinfulness, recognized and remitted, that the bond of relation with the protagonist is formed. In the Lukan world, the tension-fueling gap betweeen God's visitation and the human willingness and ability to accept it is both disclosed and bridged by frequent recourse to the literary trait of sinfulness.

---

[11] That in the act of interpretation structural analysis is never foreign to the realm of meaning, is argued by P. RICOEUR, "What Is a Text? Explanation and Understanding", *Hermeneutics and Human Sciences* (ed. and tr. J. B. THOMPSON) (Cambridge 1981) 155–162.

# Bibliography

## Ancient Sources

1QIs$^a$; 1QpHab, *The Dead Sea Scrolls of St. Mark's Monastery* (ed. M. BURROWS) (New Haven, CT 1950).

1QM, 1QSa (ed. D. BARTHÉLEMY – J. T. MILIK) (DJD I; Oxford 1955).

1QS, *Scrolls from Qumran Cave I* (ed. J. C. TREVER) (Jerusalem 1972).

4Q242 (ed. G. BROOKE et al.) (DJD XXII; Oxford 1996).

4Q265 (ed. J. M. BAUMGARTEN et al.) (DJD XXXV; Oxford 1999).

4Q266, 4Q269, 4Q272 (ed. J. M. BAUMGARTEN et al.) (DJD XVIII; Oxford 1996).

4Q434 (ed. E. CHAZON et al.) (DJD XXIX; Oxford 1999).

11Q5 (ed. J. A. SANDERS) (DJD IV; Oxford 1965).

11Q13 (ed. F. GARCÍA MARTÍNEZ – J. C. TIGCHELAAR – A. S. VAN DER WOUDE) (DJD XXIII; Oxford 1998).

*1 (Ethiopic Apocalypse of) Enoch*, in CHARLESWORTH, J. H. (ed.), *The Old Testament Pseudepigrapha*. I. Apocalyptic Literature and Testaments (Garden City, NY 1983) 5–89.

*3 Maccabees*, CHARLESWORTH, J. H. (ed.), *The Old Testament Pseudepigrapha*. II. Expansions of the "Old Testament" and Legends, Wisdom and Philosophical Literature, Prayers, Psalms and Odes, Fragments of Lost Judeo-Hellenic Works (Garden City, NY 1985) 509–529.

AESCHINES, *The Speeches of Aeschines* (ed. C. D. ADAMS) (Cambridge, MA – London 1919; Repr. 1968).

ARETAEUS, *The Extant Works of Aretaeus, The Capadocian* (ed. F. ADAMS) (London 1856).

*The Assumption of Moses*, in CHARLES, R. H. (ed.), *The Apocrypha and Pseudepigrapha of the Old Testament in English*. With Introductions and Critical and Explanatory Notes to the Several Books (Oxford 1913) II, 407–424.

*The Bible in Aramaic Based on Old Manuscripts and Printed Texts*. The Latter Prophets According to Targum Jonathan (ed. A. SPERBER) (Leiden 1962).

*Biblia Hebraica Stuttgartensia* (ed. K. ELLIGER – W. RUDOLPH) (Stuttgart $^5$1997).

CD (Damascus Document), *Documents of Jewish Sectaries*. Vol. 1. Fragments of a Zadokite Work (ed. S. SCHECHTER) (Cambridge 1910; New York 1970).

*Corpus Medicorum Grecorum II*. Aretaeus (ed. C. HUDE) (Berlin $^2$1958).

DEMOSTHENES, *Demosthenis Orationes* (ed. W. RENNIE) (SCBO; Oxford 1931; Repr. 1985) III.

DIONYSIUS HALICARNASSUS, *Dionysi Halicarnasensis Antiquitatum romanarum quae supersunt* (ed. C. JACOBY) (BSGRT; Leipzig 1885–1905) I–IV.

EPICTETUS, *Epicteti Dissertationes ab Arriano digestae* (ed. H. SCHENKL) (BSGRT; Leipzig 1898).

EURIPIDES, *Euripidis Fabulae* (ed. J. DIGGLE) (SCBO; Oxford 1994) III.

*The Fourth Book of Ezra*, in CHARLESWORTH, J. H. (ed.), *The Old Testament Pseudepigrapha*. I. Apocalyptic Literature and Testaments (Garden City, NY 1983) 517–559.

The Greek Versions of the Testaments of the Twelve Patriarchs (ed. R. H. CHARLES) (Oxford 1908).

*Hesychii Alexandrini Lexicon* (ed. K. ALPERS – H. ERBSE – A. KLEINLOGEL) (Sammlung Griechischer und Lateinischer Grammatiker 11/3; Berlin – New York 2005) III.

HIPPOCRATES, *Hippocrates* (ed. P. POTTER) (LCL; Cambridge, MA – London 2012) X.

HIPPOCRATES, *Hippocrates* (ed. P. POTTER) (LCL; Cambridge, MA – London 1995) VIII.

HIPPOCRATES, *Hippocrates* (ed. W. D. SMITH) (LCL; Cambridge, MA – London 1994) VII.

JOSEPHUS, *Flavii Iosephi opera* (Edidit et apparatu critico instruxit B. NIESE) (Berlin 1887–1895) I–III, V–VI.

*Jubilees*, in CHARLESWORTH, J. H. (ed.), *The Old Testament Pseudepigrapha*. II. Expansions of the "Old Testament" and Legends, Wisdom and Philosophical Literature, Prayers, Psalms and Odes, Fragments of Lost Judeo-Hellenic Works (Garden City, NY 1985) 35–142.

*Letter of Aristeas*, in CHARLESWORTH, J. H. (ed.), *The Old Testament Pseudepigrapha*. II. Expansions of the "Old Testament" and Legends, Wisdom and Philosophical Literature, Prayers, Psalms and Odes, Fragments of Lost Judeo-Hellenic Works (Garden City, NY 1985) 7–34.

LUCIAN, *Luciani Opera*. III. Libelli 44–68 (ed. M. D. MACLEOD) (SCBO; Oxford 1980).

*Mishnayoth*, (ed. P. BLACKMAN) (New York [2]1963–1964) II, IV.

*Novum Testamentum Graece* (ed. E. & E. NESTLE – B. & K. ALAND – J. KARAVIDOPOULOS – C. M. MARTINI – B. M. METZGER) (Stuttgart [28]2012).

PHILO, *Philo*. With an English Translation by F. H. COLSON and G. H. WHITAKER. In Ten Volumes (LCL; Cambridge, MA – London 1929–1939; Rep 1984–1991) I, III–VIII.

PLATO, *Platonis Opera* (ed. J. BURNET) (SCBO; Oxford 1900–1907) I, IV.

PLUTARCH, *Plutarch's Moralia* (ed. B. EINARSON – P. H. DE LACY) (LCL; Cambridge, MA – London 1967) XIV.

*Prayer of Manasseh*, in CHARLESWORTH, J. H. (ed.), *The Old Testament Pseudepigrapha*. II. Expansions of the "Old Testament" and Legends, Wisdom and Philosophical Literature, Prayers, Psalms and Odes, Fragments of Lost Judeo-Hellenic Works (Garden City, NY 1985) 625–637.

Prophetarum vitae fabulosae indices apostolorum discipulorumque Domini Dorotheo Epiphanio Hippolyto aliisque vindicate (ed. T. SCHERMANN) (BSGRT; Leipzig 1907).

*Psalms of Solomon*, in CHARLESWORTH, J. H. (ed.), *The Old Testament Pseudepigrapha*. II. Expansions of the "Old Testament" and Legends, Wisdom and Philosophical Literature, Prayers, Psalms and Odes, Fragments of Lost Judeo-Hellenic Works (Garden City, NY 1985) 639–670.

QUINTILIAN, *The Institutio Oratoria of Quintilian* (ed. H. E. BUTLER) (LCL; London – New York 1922) III.

SENECA, *L. Annaei Senecae opera quae supersunt* (ed. C. HOSIUS) (BSGRT; Leipzig 1900) I.2.

*Septuaginta* (Editio Altera). I. Leges et historiae. II. Libri poetici et prophetici (ed. A. RAHLFS – R. HANHART) (Stuttgart 2006).

*Sibylline Oracles*, in CHARLESWORTH, J. H. (ed.), *The Old Testament Pseudepigrapha*. I. Apocalyptic Literature and Testaments (Garden City, NY 1983) 317–472.

*Testament of Abraham*, in CHARLESWORTH, J. H. (ed.), *The Old Testament Pseudepigrapha*. I. Apocalyptic Literature and Testaments (Garden City, NY 1983) 871–903.

*Testament of Isaac*, in CHARLESWORTH, J. H. (ed.), *The Old Testament Pseudepigrapha*. I. Apocalyptic Literature and Testaments (Garden City, NY 1983) 903–911.

*Testaments of the Twelve Patriarchs*, in CHARLESWORTH, J. H. (ed.), *The Old Testament Pseudepigrapha*. I. Apocalyptic Literature and Testaments (Garden City, NY 1983) 775–828.

THUCYDIDES, *History of the Peloponnesian War* (ed. C. F. SMITH) (LCL; Cambridge, MA 1975–1980) I–IV.

*The Tosefta*. Moed (ed. J. NEUSNER) (New York 1981).

XENOPHON, *Cyropaedia*. Books I–IV (ed. W. MILLER) (LCL; Cambridge, MA – London 1914; Repr. 1983).

XENOPHON, *Memorabilia* (ed. C. HUDE) (BSGRT; Stuttgart 1985).

# *Modern Authors*

ADAMS, H., *The Sinner in Luke* (The Evangelical Theological Society Monograph Series; Eugene, OR 2008).

ALETTI, J.-N., *L'art de raconter Jésus Christ*. L'écriture narrative de l'évangile de Luc (Parole de Dieu; Paris 1989).

ALETTI, J.-N., *Le Jésus de Luc* (Jésus et Jésus-Christ 98; Paris 2010).

ALEXANDER, L., *The Preface to Luke's Gospel*. Literary Convention and Social Context in Luke 1,1–4 and Acts 1,1 (MSSNTS 78; Cambridge 1993).

ANDERSON, G. A., *Sin*. A History (New Haven, CT 2009).

AVALOS, H., *Illness and Health Care in the Ancient Near East*. The Role of the Temple in Greece, Mesopotamia, and Israel (HSM 54; Atlanta, GA 1995).

BACK, S.-O., "Jesus and the Sabbath", *Handbook for the Study of the Historical Jesus*. Volume 3. The Historical Jesus (ed. T. HOLMÉN – S. E. PORTER) (Leiden – Boston 2011) 2597–2633.

BADEN, J. S. – MOSS, C. R., "The Origin and Interpretation of ṣāraʿt in Leviticus 13–14", *JBL* 130 (2011) 543–662.

BAILEY, J. N., "Looking for Luke's Fingerprints: Identifying Evidence of Redactional Activity In 'The Healing of the Paralytic' (Luke 5:17–26)", *RestQ* 48 (2006) 143–156.

BARNET, J. A., *Not the Righteous but Sinners*. M. M. Bakhtin's Theory of Aesthetics and the Problem of Reader-Character Interaction in Matthew's Gospel (JSNT.S 246; London 2003).

BASSET, L., "La culpabilité, paralysie du cœur. Réinterprétation du récit de la guérison du paralysé (Lc 5/17–26) ", *ETR* 71 (1996) 331–345.

VON BENDEMANN, R., "Liebe und Sündenvergebung. Eine narrativ-traditionsgeschichtliche Analyse von Lk 7,36–50", *BZ* 44 (2000) 161–182.

BERGSMA, J. S., *The Jubilee from Leviticus to Qumran*. A History of Interpretation (VT.S 115; Leiden 2007).

BETZ, H. D., *The Sermon on the Mount*. A Commentary on the Sermon on the Mount, Including the Sermon on the Plain: Matthew 5:3–7:27 and Luke 6:20–49 (Hermeneia; Minneapolis, MN 1995).

BISHOP, E. F. F., "Jesus and the Lake", CBQ 13 (1951) 398–414.

BIVIN, D., "The Miraculous Catch: Reflections on the Research of Mendel Nun", Jerusalem Perspectives 5/2 (1992) 7–10.

BLUMENTHAL, C., "Augustus' Erlass und Gottes Macht: Überlegungen zur Charakterisierung der Augustusfigur und ihrer erzählstrategischen Funktion in der lukanischen Erzählung", NTS 57 (2011) 1–30.

BOCK, D. L., Luke (BECNT 3; Grand Rapids, MI 1994) I.

BODA, M. J., *A Severe Mercy.* Sin and Its Remedy in the Old Testament (Siphrut, Literature and Theology of the Hebrew Scriptures 1; Winona Lake, IN 2009).

BÖHLEMANN, P., *Jesus und der Täufer.* Schlüssel zur Theologie und Ethik des Lukas (MSSNTS 99; Cambridge 1997).

BOND, C., *Spenser, Milton, and the Redemption of the Epic Hero* (Plymouth 2011).

BOOTH, W. C., *The Rhetoric of Fiction* (Chicago ²1983).

BORMANN, L., *Recht, Gerechtigkeit und Religion im Lukasevangelium* (StUNT 24; Göttingen 2001).

BOVON, F., *Luke 1.* A Commentary on the Gospel of Luke 1:1–9:50 (tr. C. M. THOMAS) (Hermeneia; Minneapolis, MN 2002).

BRAND, M. T., *Evil Within and Without.* The Source of Sin and Its Nature as Portrayed in Second Temple Literature (Journal of Ancient Judaism. Supplements 9; Göttingen 2013).

BRANDENBURGER, E., "Gerichtskonzeptionen im Urchristentum und ihre Voraussetzungen. Eine Problemstudie", *Studien zur Geschichte und Theologie des Urchristentum* (SBAB 15; Stuttgart 1993) 289–338.

BRAWLEY, R. L., *Luke-Acts and the Jews.* Conflict, Apology, and Conciliation (SBL.MS 33; Atlanta, GA 1987).

BRAWLEY, R. L., *Centering on God.* Method and Message in Luke-Acts (Literary Currents in Biblical Interpretation; Louisville, KY 1990).

BRINK, L., *Soldiers in Luke-Acts* (WUNT 2.R 362; Tübingen 2014).

BROCCARDO, C., *La Fede Emarginata.* Analisi narrativa di Luca 4–9 (Studi e ricerche; Assisi 2006).

BROWN, M. L., *Israel's Divine Healer* (Grand Rapids, MI 1995).

BROWN, R. E., The Gospel According to John (XIII–XXI). Introduction, Translation, and Notes (AncB 29A; New York 1970).

BURNETT, F. W., "Characterization and Reader Construction of Characters in the Gospels", *Semeia* 63 (1993) 1–26.

BURROWS, E., "The Gospel of the Infancy: the Form of Luke Chapters 1 and 2", *The Gospel of the Infancy and Other Biblical Essays* (ed. E. F. SUTCLIFFE) (Bellarmine Series 6; London 1940) 1–58.

BUSSE, U., *Die Wunder des Propheten Jesus.* Die Rezeption, Komposition und Interpretation der Wundertradition im Evangelium des Lukas (FzB 24; Würzburg ²1979).

CADBURY, H. J., "Commentary on the Preface of Luke", *The Acts of the Apostles*, Vol. 2. Prolegomena II: Criticism (ed. F. J. FOAKES JACKSON – K. LAKE) (The Beginnings of Christianity 1; London 1922) 489–510.

CARROLL, J. T., "Luke's Portrayal of the Pharisees", *CBQ* 50 (1988) 604–621.

CHANCE, J. B., *Jerusalem, the Temple, and the New Age in Luke-Acts* (Macon, GA 1988).

CHATMAN, S., *Story and Discourse.* Narrative Structure in Fiction and Film (Ithaca, NY – London 1980).

CHILTON, B. D., "Jesus and the Repentance of E. P. Sanders", *TynB* 39 (1988) 1–18.

CHILTON, B. D., "The Purity of the Kingdom as Conveyed in Jesus' Meals", *Society of Biblical Literature 1992 Seminar Papers* (ed. E. H. LOVERING) (SBL.SPS 31; Atlanta, GA 1992) 437–488.

CHILTON, B. D., review of D. H. ADAMS, *The Sinner in Luke* (The Evangelical Theological Society Monograph Series; Eugene, OR 2008), *RBLit* 1 (2009) 369–371.

CHILTON, B. D., "Jesus and Sinners and Outcasts", *Handbook for the Study of the Historical Jesus*. Volume 3. The Historical Jesus (ed. T. HOLMÉN – S. E. PORTER) (Leiden – Boston 2011) 2801–2833.

COHN-SHERBOK, D. M., "An Analysis of Jesus' Arguments Concerning the Plucking of Grain on the Sabbath", *JSNT* 2 (1979) 31–41.

COLERIDGE, M. B., *The Birth of the Lukan Narrative*. Narrative as Christology in Luke 1–2 (JSNT.S 88; Sheffield 1993).

CORLEY, K. E., "The Anointing of Jesus in the Synoptic Tradition: an Argument for Authenticity", *JSHS* 1 (2003) 61–72.

COSGROVE, C. H., "The Divine ΔΕΙ in Luke-Acts. Investigations into the Lukan Understanding of God's Providence", *NT* 26 (1984) 168–190.

COSGROVE, C. H., "A Woman's Unbound Hair in the Greco-Roman World, with Special Reference to the Story of the «Sinful Woman» in Luke 7:36–50", *JBL* 124 (2005) 675–692.

CRADDOCK, F. B., *Luke* (Interpretation, a Bible Commentary for Teaching and Preaching; Louisville, KY 1990).

CREED, J. M., *The Gospel According to St. Luke* (London 1930).

CRIMELLA, M., *Marta, Marta!* Quattro esempi di 'triangolo drammatico' nel 'grande viaggio di Luca' (Assisi 2009).

CULPEPPER, R. A., *Anatomy of the Fourth Gospel*. A Study in Literary Design (Foundations and Facets. New Testament; Philadelphia 1983).

CULPEPPER, R. A., *The Gospel of Luke*. Introduction, Commentary, and Reflections (The New Interpreter's Bible Volume IX; Nashville, TN 1995).

CULY, M. M. – PARSONS, M. C. – STIGALL, J. J., *Luke*. A Handbook on the Greek Text (BHGNT; Waco, TX 2010).

DANOVE, P., *The Rhetoric of Characterization of God, Jesus, and Jesus' Disciples in the Gospel of Mark* (JSNT.S 290; New York 2005).

DARR, J. A., *On Character Building*. The Reader and the Rhetoric of Characterization in Luke-Acts (Literary Currents in Biblical Interpretation; Louisville, KY 1992).

DARR, J. A., *Herod the Fox*. Audience Criticism and Lukan Characterization (JSNT.S 163; Sheffield 1998).

DAUBE, D., "Responsibilities of Master and Disciples in the Gospels", *NTS* 19 (1972–73) 1–15.

DAUTZENBERG, G. *Sein Leben bewahren*. Ψυχή in den Herrenworten der Evangelien (StANT 14; München 1966).

DELEBECQUE, É., "Les moissonneurs du Sabbat (6,1)", *Études grecques sur l'Évangile de Luc* (Paris 1976).

DELEBECQUE, É., "La vivante formule KAI ΕΓΕΝΕΤΟ", *Études grecques sur l'Évangile de Luc* (Paris 1976) 123–165.

DELEBECQUE, É., "'Secouez la poussière de vos pieds': Sur L'hellénisme de Luc 9:5", *RB* 89 (1982) 177–184.

DELORME, J., "Luc 5,1–11: analyse structurale et histoire de la redaction", *NTS* 18 (1972) 331–350.

DENAUX, A., "The Delineation of the Lukan Travel Narrative within the Overall Structure of the Gospel of Luke", *Studies in the Gospel of Luke*. Structure, Language and Theology (Tilburg Theological Studies; Berlin 2010) 3–37.

DIETRICH, W., *Das Petrusbild der Lukanischen Schriften* (BWANT 94; Stuttgart 1972).

DILLON, R. J., "The Benedictus in Micro- and Macrocontext", *CBQ* 68 (2006) 457–480.

DINKLER, M. B., *Silent Statements*. Narrative Representations of Speech and Silence in the Gospel of Luke (BZNW 191; Berlin – Boston 2013).

DOERING, L., *Schabbat*. Sabbathalacha und -praxis im antiken Judentum und Urchristentum (TSAJ 78; Tübingen 1999).

DONAHUE, J. R., "Tax Collectors and Sinners. An Attempt at Identification", *CBQ* 33 (1971) 39–61.

DOWNING, F. G., "Ambiguity, Ancient Semantics, and Faith", *NTS* 56 (2009) 139–162.

DRURY, J., *Tradition and Design in Luke's Gospel*. A Study in Early Christian Historiography (London 1976).

DUNN, J. D. G., "Sprit-and-Fire Baptism", *NT* 14 (1972) 81–92.

DUNN, J. D. G., *Baptism in the Holy Spirit*. A Re-examination of the New Testament Teaching on the Gift of the Spirit in Relation to Pentecostalism Today (London [2]2010).

DUPONT, J., "Vin vieux, vin nouveau", *CBQ* 25 (1963) 286–304.

ECKEY, W., *Das Lukasevangelium*. Unter Berücksichtigung seiner Parallelen (Neukirchen-Vluyn [2]2006) I.

ERIKSSON, A., "The Old is Good: Parables of Patched Garment and Wineskins as Elaboration of a Chreia in Luke 5:33–39 about Feasting with Jesus", *Rhetoric, Ethic, and Moral Persuasion in Biblical Discourse* (ed. T. H. OLBRICHT – A. ERIKSSON) (Emory Studies in Early Christianity; London 2005) 52–72.

ERNST, J., *Das Evangelium nach Lukas* (RNT 3; Regensburg [6]1993).

EVANS, C. A., *Luke* (NIBC 3; Peabody, MA 1990).

EVANS, C. F., *Saint Luke* (TPI New Testament Commentaries; London 1990).

FEENEY, D. "Criticism Ancient and Modern", *Ancient Literary Criticism* (ed. A. LAIRD) (Oxford Readings in Classical Studies; Oxford 2006) 440–454.

FERNGREN, G. B., *Medicine and Health Care in Early Christianity* (Baltimore, MD 2009).

FEUILLET, A., "L'*Exousia* du fils de l'homme (d'après Mc. II, 10–28 et parr.)", *RSR* 42 (1954) 161–192.

FIEDLER, P., *Jesus und die Sünder* (BET 3; Frankfurt – Bern 1976).

FISCHER, B., "Dialogic Engagement between the Birth Stories in Luke 1 and 2 and selected Texts from the Hebrew Bible: A Bakhtinian Investigation", *Scriptura* 94 (2007) 128–142.

FITZMYER, J. A., *The Gospel According to Luke I–IX*. Introduction, Translation, and Notes (AncB 28; New York 1981).

FLEBBE, J., "Alter und neuer Wein bei Lukas: zum Verständnis der sogenannten 'Weinregel' Lk 5,39", *ZNW* 96 (2005) 171–187.

FLUSSER, D., "Do You Prefer New Wine?", *Imm* 9 (1979) 26–31.

FREDRIKSEN, P., "Did Jesus Oppose the Purity Laws?", *BR* 11/3 (1990) 20–25, 42–47.

FREIN, B. C., "The Literary and Theological Significance of Misunderstanding in the Gospel of Luke", *Bib* 74 (1993) 328–348.

FREVEL, C. – NIHAN, C., "Introduction", Purity and the Forming of Religious Traditions in the Ancient Mediterranean World and Ancient Judaism (ed. C. FREVEL – C. NIHAN) (Leiden 2013) 1–46.

FREY, J., "New Testament Eschatology – An Introduction. Classical Issues, Disputed Themes, and Current Perspectives", *Eschatology of the New Testament and Some Related Documents* (ed. J. G. VAN DER WATT) (WUNT 2.R 315; Tübingen 2011), 3–32.

FRICKENSCHMIDT, D., *Evangelium als Biographie*. Die vier Evangelien im Rahmen antiker Erzählkunst (TANZ 22; Tübingen 1997).

GARCÍA SERRANO, A., *The Presentation in the Temple*. The Narrative Function of Lk 2:22–39 in Luke-Acts (AnBib 197; Rome 2012).

GARRETT, S. R., "Exodus from Bondage: Luke 9:31 and Acts 12:1–24", *CBQ* 52 (1990) 656–680.

GERBER, D., *"Il vous est né un Sauveur."* La construction du sens sotériologique de la venue de Jésus en Luc-Actes (Genève 2008).

GELDENHUYS, N., *Commentary on the Gospel of Luke* (NICNT; Grand Rapids, MI 1954).

GLOMBITZA, O., "Die Titel διδάσκαλος und ἐπιστάτης für Jesus bei Lukas", *ZNW* 49 (1958) 275–278.

GOOD, R. S., "Jesus, Protagonist of the Old, in Lk 5:33–39", *NT* 25 (1983) 19–36.

GOWLER, D. B., *Host, Guest, Enemy, and Friend*. Portraits of the Pharisees in Luke and Acts (Emory Studies in Early Christianity 2; New York 1991).

GRASSO, S., *Luca* (Roma 1999).

GREEN, J. B., *The Gospel of Luke* (NICNT; Grand Rapids, MI 1997).

GREEN, J. B., "Learning Theological Interpretation from Luke", *Reading Luke*. Interpretation, Reflection, Formation (ed. C. BARTHOLOMEW – J. B. GREEN – A. THISELTON) (Scripture and Hermeneutics Series 6; Grand Rapids, MI 2005) 55–78.

GRILLI, M., "Evento comunicativo e interpretazione di un testo biblico", *Gregorianum* 83 (2002) 655–678.

GRIMM, W., "θαμβέω, θάμβος", *EDNT*, II, 128–129.

GRUNDMANN, W., *Das Evangelium nach Lukas* (ThHK 3; Berlin [2]1961).

HABER, S., *"They Shall Purify Themselves."* Essays on Purity in Early Judaism (ed. A. REINHARTZ) (SBL Early Judaism and Its Literature 24; Atlanta, GA 2008).

HÄGERLAND, T., "Jesus and the Rites of Repentance", *NTS* 52 (2006) 166–187.

HÄGERLAND, T., *Jesus and the Forgiveness of Sins*. An Aspect of His Prophetic Mission (MSSNTS 159; Cambridge 2011).

HAHN, F., "Die Bildworte vom neuen Flicken und vom jungen Wein (Mk. 2,21f parr)", *EvTh* 31 (1971) 357–375.

HARRINGTON, H., *The Purity Texts* (Companion to the Qumran Scrolls 5; London 2004).

HASLER, V., "γενεά", *EWNT*, I, 579–581.

HAYS, C. M., *Luke's Wealth Ethics*. A Study in Their Coherence and Character (WUNT 2.R 275; Tübingen 2010).

HEATH, J. M. F., "Absent Presences of Paul and Christ: *Enargeia* in 1 Thessalonians 1–3", *JSNT* 32 (2009) 3–38.

HENGEL, M., *The Charismatic Leader and His Followers* (tr. J. C. G. GREIG) (Edinburgh 1981).

HERRENBRÜCK, F., *Jesus und die Zöllner*. Historische und neutestamentlich-exegetische Untersuchungen (WUNT 2.R 41; Tübingen 1990).

HIMMELFARB, M., "Impurity and Sin in 4QD, 1QS, and 4Q512", *DSD* 8/1 (2001) 9–37.

HOFIUS, O., "βλασφημία", *EWNT*, 527–532.

HOLMAN, S. R., "Healing the Social Leper in Gregory of Nyssa's and Gregory of Nazianzus's 'περὶ φιλοπτωχίας'", *HThR* 93 (1999) 283–309.

HOLZ, G., "Zur christologischen Relevanz des Furchtmotivs im Lukasevangelium", *Biblica* 90 (2009) 484–505.

HOLZ, G., "Purity Conceptions in the Dead Sea Scrolls: 'Ritual-Physical' and 'Moral' Purity in a Diachronic Perspective", *Purity and the Forming of Religious Traditions in the Ancient Mediterranean World and Ancient Judaism* (ed. C. FREVEL – C. NIHAN) (Leiden 2013) 519–536.

ISER, W., *Der implizite Leser*. Kommunikationsformen des Romans von Bunyan bis Beckett (UTB 163; München 1972).

ISER, W., *Der Akt des Lesens*. Theorie ästhetischer Wirkung (UTB 636; München 1976).

JEREMIAS, J., "Zöllner und Sünder", *ZNW* 30 (1931) 293–300.

JEREMIAS, J., *Neutestamentliche Theologie*. Erster Teil. Die Verkündigung Jesu (Gütersloh 1971).

JEREMIAS, J., *The Parables of Jesus* (London ³1972).

JOHNSON, L. T., *The Gospel of Luke* (SP 3; Collegeville, MN 1991).

JÜLICHER, A., *Die Gleichnisreden Jesu*. Zweiter Teil. Auslegung der Gleichnisreden der drei ersten Evangelien (Tübingen ²1910).

KAHL, W., "Ist es erlaubt, am Sabbat Leben zu retten oder zu töten? (Marc. 3:4) Lebensbewahrung am Sabbat im Kontext der Schriften vom Toten Meer und der Mischna", *NT* 40 (1998) 313–335.

KAUT, T., *Befreier und befreites Volk*. Traditions- und redaktionsgeschichtliche Untersuchung zu Magnifikat und Benediktus im Kontext der vorlukanischen Kindheitsgeschichte (BBB 77; Frankfurt am Main 1990).

KAZEN, T., *Jesus and Purity Halakhah*. Was Jesus Indifferent to Impurity? (CB.NT 38; Stockholm 2002).

KAZEN, T., *Issues of Impurity in Early Judaism* (CB.NT 45; Winona Lake, IN 2010).

KEE, A. "The Old Coat and the New Wine: A Parable of Repentance", *NT* 12 (1970) 13–21.

KILGALLEN, J. J., "Forgiveness of Sins (Luke 7:36–50)", *NT* 40 (1998) 105–116.

KILGALLEN, J. J., "What Does It Mean to Say That There Are Additions in Luke 7,36–50?", *Bib* 86 (2005) 529–535.

KINGSBURY, J. D., *Conflict in Luke*. Jesus, Authorities, Disciples (Minneapolis, MN 1991).

KINGSBURY, J. D., "The Pharisees in Luke-Acts", *The Four Gospels*. Festschrift Frans Neirynck (ed. F. VAN SEGBROECK – C. M. TUCKETT) (BEThL 100; Louvain 1992) II, 1497–1512.

KIRK, A., "'Love Your Enemies,' the Golden Rule, and Ancient Reciprocity (Luke 6:72–35)", *JBL* 122 (2003) 667–686.

KIRK, A., "Karl Polanyi, Marshall Sahlins, and the Study of Ancient Social Relations", *JBL* 126 (2007) 182–191.

KLAUCK, H.-J., "Die Frage der Sündenvergebung in der Perikope von der Heilung des Gelähmten (Mk 2,1–12 parr)", *BZ* 25 (1981) 223–248.

KLAUCK, H.-J., "Heil ohne Heilung? Zu Metaphorik und Hermeneutik der Rede von Sünde und Vergebung im Neuen Testament", *Sünde und Erlösung im Neuen Testament* (ed. H. FRANKEMÖLLE) (QD 161; Freiburg 1996) 18–52.

KLAWANS, J., *Impurity and Sin in Ancient Judaism* (New York 2000).

KLINGHARDT, M., *Gesetz und Volk Gottes*. Das lukanische Verständnis des Gesetzes nach Herkunft, Funktion und seinem Ort in der Geschichte des Urchristentums (WUNT 2.R 32; Tübingen 1988).

KLEIN, H., *Das Lukasevangelium* (KEK 1/3; Göttingen 2006).

KLEIN, P., "Die lukanischen Weherufe Lk 6, 24–26", *ZNW* 71 (1980) 150–159.

KUHN, K. A., "The Point of the Step-Parallelism in Luke 1–2", *NTS* 47 (2001) 38–49.

LAGRANGE, M.-J., *Évangile selon Saint Luc* (EtB; Paris 1948).

LAUSBERG, H., *Handbook of Literary Rhetoric*. A Foundation for Literary Study (tr. M. T. BLISS – A. JANSEN – D. E. ORTON) (ed. D. E. ORTON – R. D ANDERSON) (Leiden – Boston – Köln 1998).

LEE, J. A. L., "A Non-Aramaism in Luke 6:7", *NT* 33 (1991) 28–34.

LÉON-DUFOUR, X., "La tempête apaisée", *Études d'Évangile* (Parole de Dieu; Paris 1965) 149–182.

LEVINE, A.-J., "Luke's Pharisees" *In Quest of the Historical Pharisees* (ed. J. NEUSNER – B. D. CHILTON) (Waco, TX 2007) 113–130, 445–446.

LEVINE, A.-J., "Luke and the Jewish Religion", *Interp.* 68 (2014) 389–402.

LINDSTRÖM, F., *Suffering and Sin*. Interpretations of Illness in the Individual Complaint Psalms (CB.OT 37; Stockholm 1994).

LOHSE, E., "σάββατον", *TDNT* VII, 1–35.

LUZ, U., *Matthew 1–7*. A Commentary (tr. J. E. CROUCH) (Hermeneia; Minneapolis, MN 2007).

MACCOBY, H., *Ritual and Morality*. The Ritual Purity System and its Place in Judaism (Cambridge 1999).

MALINA, B. J. – NEYREY, J. H., "Honor and Shame in Luke-Acts: Pivotal Values of the Mediterranean World", *The Social World of Luke-Acts*. Models for Interpretation (ed. J. H. NEYREY) (Peabody, MA 1993) 25–65.

MAISCH, I., *Die Heilung des Gelähmten*. Eine exegetisch-traditionsgeschichtliche Untersuchung zu Mk 2,1–12 (SBS 52; Stuttgart 1971).

MARGUERAT, D. – BOURQUIN, Y., *How to Read Bible Stories*. An Introduction to Narrative Criticism (tr. J. BOWDEN) (London 1999).

MARGUERAT, D., "Le point de vue dans le récit: Matthieu, Jean et les autres", *Studien zu Matthäus und Johannes / Études sur Matthieu et Jean*. Festschrift für Jean Zumstein zu seinem 65. Geburtstag (ed. A. DETTWILER – U. POPLUTZ) (AThANT 97; Zürich 2009) 91–107.

MARSHALL, H., *The Gospel of Luke*. A Commentary on the Greek Text (NIGTC; Grand Rapids, MI 1978).

MARTÍNEZ, R., *The Question of John the Baptist and Jesus' Indictment of the Religious Leaders*. A Critical Analysis of Luke 7:18–35 (Eugene, OR 2011).

MATHIEU, Y., *La figure de Pierre dans l'oeuvre de Luc (Évangile et Actes des Apôtres)*. Une approche synchronique (Études bibliques. Nouvelle série, 052; Gabalda 2004).

MATHIEU, Y., "Pierre, Lévi et les douze apôtres en Luc 5,1–6,19. Les conséquences théologiques d'une mise en discours", *ScEs* 60 (2008) 101–118.

MAXWELL, K. R., *Hearing Between the Lines*. The Audience as Fellow-Worker in Luke-Acts and its Literary Milieu (LNTS 425; London 2010).

MAYER-HAAS, A. J., *„Geschenk aus Gottes Schatzkammer" (bSchab 10b)*. Jesus und der Sabbat im Spiegel der neutestamentlichen Schriften (NTA.NF 43; Münster 2003).

MEAD, A. H., "Old and New Wine: St Luke 5:39", *ET* 99 (1988) 234–235.

MEIER, J. P., *A Marginal Jew*. Rethinking the Historical Jesus. Volume IV Law and Love (AncBRL; New Haven, CT – London 2009).

MÉNDEZ-MORATALLA, F., *The Paradigm of Conversion in Luke* (JSNT.S 252, London 2004).

MEYNET, R., *L'Évangile de Luc* (Rhétorique sémitique 1; Paris 2005).

MILGROM, J., *Leviticus 1–16*. A New Translation with Introduction and Commentary (AncB 3; New York 1991).

MILLER, M., "The Function of Isa 61:1–2 in 11Q Melchizedek", *JBL* 88 (1969) 467–469.

MOESSNER, D. P., "Jesus and the 'Wilderness Generation'", *Society of Biblical Literature 1982 Seminar Papers* (ed. K. H. RICHARDS) (SBL.SPS 21; Chico, CA 1982) 319–340.

MOESSNER, D. P., "Luke 9:1–50: Luke's Preview of the Journey of the Prophet Like Moses of Deuteronomy", *JBL* 102 (1983) 575–605.

MOESSNER, D. P., "'The Christ Must Suffer': New Light on the Jesus–Peter, Stephen, Paul Parallels in Luke-Acts", *NT* 28 (1986) 220–256.

MOESSNER, D. P., "The 'Leaven of the Pharisees' and 'This Generation': Israel's Rejection of Jesus According to Luke", *JSNT* 34 (1988) 21–46.

MOESSNER, D. P., *Lord of the Banquet.* The Literary and Theological Significance of the Lukan Travel Narrative (Harrisburg, PA ²1998).

MOESSNER, D. P., "'Listening Posts' Along the Way: 'Synchronisms' as Metaleptic Prompts to the 'Continuity of the Narrative' in Polybius' Histories and in Luke's Gospel-Acts. A Tribute to David E. Aune", *New Testament and Early Christian Literature in the Greco-Roman Context.* Studies in Honor of David E. Aune (ed. J. FOTOPOULOS) (NT.S 122; Leiden 2006) 129–150.

MOLES, J., "Luke's Preface: The Greek Decree, Classical Historiography and Christian Redefinitions", *NTS* 57 (2011) 461–482.

MORGENTHALER, R., *Die lukanische Geschichtsschreibung als Zeugnis.* Gestalt und Gehalt der Kunst des Lukas (Zürich 1949) I.

MORLAN, D. S., *Conversion in Luke and Paul.* An Exegetical and Theological Exploration (LNTS 464; London 2013).

MULLEN, J. P., *Dining with Pharisees* (Interfaces; Collegeville, MN 2004).

MÜLLER, C. G., *Mehr als ein Prophet.* Die Charakterzeichnung Johannes des Täufers im lukanischen Erzählwerk (HBS 31; Freiburg 2001).

MÜLLER, K., "Gott als Richter und die Erscheinungsweisen seiner Gerichte in den Schriften des Frühjudentums. Methodische und grundsätzliche Vorüberlegungen zu einer sachgemäßen Einschätzung", *Weltgericht und Weltvollendung.* Zukunftsbilder im Neuen Testament (ed. H.-J. KLAUCK) (QD 150; Freiburg 1994) 23–53.

NASSAUER, G., "Gegenwart des Abwesenden. Eidetische Christologie in Lk 1.39–45", *NTS* 58 (2012) 69–87.

NAVE, G. D., *The Role and Function of Repentance in Luke-Acts* (SBL Academia Biblica 4; Atlanta, GA 2002).

NEALE, D., *None but the Sinners.* Religious Categories in the Gospel of Luke (JSNT.S 58; Sheffield 1991).

NEUSNER, J., *The Idea of Purity in Ancient Judaism.* The Haskell Lectures, 1972–1973; With a Critique and a Commentary by Mary Douglas (SJLA 1; Leiden 1973).

NEUSNER, J., "The Rabbinic Traditions about the Pharisees before 70 CE: An Overview", *In Quest of the Historical Pharisees* (ed. J. NEUSNER – B. D. CHILTON) (Waco, TX 2007) 297–311, 471.

NEYREY, J. H. "Ceremonies in Luke-Acts: The Case of Meals and Table Fellowship", *The Social World of Luke-Acts.* Models for Interpretation (ed. J. H. NEYREY) (Peabody, MA 1991) 361–387.

NOLLAND, J. L., *Luke 1–9:20* (WBC 35a; Dallas, TX 1989).

NUTTON, V., "Medicine", *The Cambridge Ancient History.* The High Empire, A. D. 70–192 (ed. A. K. Bowman – P. Garnsey – D. Rathbone) (Cambridge ²2008) XI, 943–966.

OBERHELMAN, S. M., "On the Chronology and Pneumatism of Aretaios of Cappadocia", *ANRW* 2 37 2 (1994) 941–966.

Ó FEARGHAIL, F., *The Introduction to Luke-Acts.* A Study of the Role of Lk 1,1–4,44 in the Composition of Luke's Two-Volume Work (AnBib 126; Rome 1991).

O'TOOLE, R. F., "Luke's Message in Luke 9:1–50", *CBQ* 49 (1987) 74–89.

O'TOOLE, R. F., "Jesus as the Christ in Luke 4,16–30", *Bib* 76 (1995) 498–522.

O'TOOLE, R. F., *Luke's Presentation of Jesus*. A Christology (SubBi 25; Rome 2004).

PAO, D. W. – SCHNABEL, E. J., "Luke", *Commentary on the New Testament Use of the Old Testament* (ed. G. K. BEALE – D. A. CARSON) (Nottingham 2007) 251–414.

PÉREZ RODRÍGUEZ, G., *La infancia de Jesús (Mt 1–2; Lc 1–2)* (Teología en diálogo 4; Salamanca 1990).

PERROT, C., *Les récits d'enfance de Jésus: Matthieu 1–2; Luc 1–2* (CEv 18; Paris 1976).

PERRY, M., "Literary Dynamics: How the Order of a Text Creates its Meanings", *Poetics Today* 1 (1979) 35–64, 311–361.

PESCH, R., *Jesu ureigene Taten?* Ein Beitrag zur Wunderfrage (QD 52; Freiburg 1970).

PESONEN, A., *Luke, the Friend of Sinners* (Diss. University of Helsinki; Helsinki 2009).

PILCH, J. J., *Healing in the New Testament*. Insights from Medical and Mediterranean Anthropology (Minneapolis, MN 2000).

PLUMMER, A., *A Critical and Exegetical Commentary on the Gospel According to S. Luke* (London 1896).

POLICH, J. C., *The Call of the First Disciples*. A Literary and Redactional Study of Luke 5:1–11 (Diss. Fordham University; New York 1991).

POWELL, M. A., "The Religious Leaders in Luke: A Literary-Critical Study", *JBL* 109 (1990) 93–110.

RABATEL, A., "Fondus enchaînés énonciatifs. Scénographie énonciative et point de vue", *Poétique* 126 (2001) 151–173.

RADL, W., *Das Evangelium nach Lukas*. Kommentar. Erster Teil: 1,1–9,50 (Freiburg im Breisgau 2003).

RAY, J. L., *Narrative Irony in Luke-Acts*. The Paradoxical Interaction of Prophetic Fulfillment and Jewish Rejection (Mellen Biblical Press Series 28; Lewiston, NY 1996).

RICE, G. E., "Luke's Thematic Use of the Call to Discipleship", *AUSS* 19 (1981) 51–58.

RICE, G. E., "Luke 4:31–44: Release For the Captives", *AUSS* 20 (1982) 23–28.

RICOEUR, P., *The Symbolism of Evil* (tr. E. BUCHANAN) (Religious Perspectives 17; New York 1967).

RICOEUR, P., "The Task of Hermeneutics", *Hermeneutics and the Human Sciences* (ed. and tr. J. B. THOMPSON) (Cambridge 1981) 43–62.

RICOEUR, P., "What Is a Text? Explanation and Understanding", *Hermeneutics and Human Sciences* (ed. and tr. J. B. THOMPSON) (Cambridge 1981) 145–164.

RICOEUR, P., "The Golden Rule: Exegetical and Theological Perplexities", *NTS* 36 (1990) 392–397.

RINDOŠ, J., *He of Whom It Is Written*. John the Baptist and Elijah in Luke (ÖBS 38; Frankfurt am Main 2010).

RINGE, S. H., *Jesus, Liberation, and the Biblical Jubilee* (Overtures to Biblical Theology 19; Philadelphia 1985).

RÖHSER, G., *Metaphorik und Personifikation der Sünde*. Antike Sündenvorstellungen und paulinische Hamartia (WUNT 2.R 25; Tübingen 1987).

ROLLAND, P., "Les prédécesseurs de Marc: Les sources présynoptiques de Marc II,18–22 et paralèles", *RB* 89 (1982) 370–405.

ROLLAND, P., "Jésus connaissait leurs pensées", *EThL* 62 (1986) 118–121.

ROLOFF, J., *Das Kerygma und der irdische Jesus*. Historische Motive in den Jesus-Erzählungen der Evangelien (Göttingen 1970).

ROSSE, G., *Il Vangelo di Luca*. Commento esegetico e teologico (Collana scritturistica di Città Nuova; Roma 1992).

ROWE, C. K., *Early Narrative Christology*. The Lord in the Gospel of Luke (BZNW 139; Berlin – New York 2006).

RUNGE, S. E., *Discourse Grammar of the New Testament*. A Practical Introduction for Teaching and Exegesis (Lexham Bible Reference Series; Peabody, MA 2010).

RUSSEL, D. A., "On Reading Plutarch's *Lives*", *Greece and Rome* 13 (1976) 139–154.

SABOURIN, L., *L'Évangile de Luc*. Introduction et commentaire (Roma 1985).

SAHLINS, M., *Stone Age Economics* (New York 1972).

SALDARINI, A. J., *Pharisees, Scribes and Sadducees in Palestinian Society*. A Sociological Approach (Wilmington, DE 1988).

SANDERS, E. P., *Jesus and Judaism* (Philadelphia 1985).

SANDERS, E. P., *Jewish Law from Jesus to the Mishnah* (Philadelphia 1990).

SANDERS, J. A., "Sins, Debts, and Jubilee Release", *Luke and Scripture*. The Function of Sacred Tradition in Luke-Acts (ed. C. A. EVANS – J. A. SANDERS) (Minneapolis, MN 1993) 84–92.

SANDERS, J. A., "From Isaiah 61 to Luke 4", *Luke and Scripture*. The Function of Sacred Tradition in Luke-Acts (ed. C. A. EVANS – J. A. SANDERS) (Minneapolis, MN 1993) 46–69.

SANDERS, J. T., "The Pharisees in Luke-Acts", *The Living Text*. Essays in Honor of Ernest W. Saunders (ed. D. GROH – R. JEWETT) (Lanham, MD 1985) 141–188.

SANDIYAGU, V. R., "Ἕτερος and Ἄλλος in Luke", *NT* 48 (2006) 105–130.

SCHNEIDER, G., *Das Evangelium nach Lukas*. Kapitel 1–10 (ÖTNT 3/1; Gütersloher – Würzburg 1977).

SCHOLZ, D. J., *Luke 5:1–11*. The Call and Commission of Simon Peter (Diss. Marquette University; Milwaukee, WI 1997).

SCHÜRMANN, H., *Das Lukasevangelium*. Kommentar zu Kap. 1,1–9,50 (HThK 3/1; Freiburg 1969).

SELLNER, H. J., *Das Heil Gottes*. Studien zur Soteriologie des lukanischen Doppelwerks (BZNW 152; Berlin – New York 2007).

SEYBOLD, K. – MUELLER, U., *Sickness and Healing* (Biblical Encounters Series; Nashville, TN 1981).

SHEELEY, S. M., *Narrative Asides in Luke-Acts* (JSNT.S 72; Sheffield 1992).

SHELLBERG, P., *From Cleansed Lepers to Cleansed Hearts*. The Developing Meaning of Katharizo in Luke-Acts (Diss. Marquette University; Milwaukee, WI 2012).

SIDER, J. W., "Proportional Analogy in the Gospel Parables", *NTS* 31 (1985) 1–23.

SLOAN, R., *The Favorable Year of the Lord*. A Study of Jubilary Theology in the Gospel of Luke (Austin, TX 1977).

SMITH, B. D., *The Tension Between God as Righteous Judge and as Merciful in Early Judaism* (Lanham, MD 2005).

SMITH, D. E. "Table Fellowship as a Literary Motif in the Gospel of Luke", *JBL* 106 (1987) 613–638.

SNODGRASS, K. R., *Stories with Intent*. A Comprehensive Guide to the Parables of Jesus (Grand Rapids, MI 2008).

SPICQ, C., "τίλλω", *Theological Lexicon of the New Testament* (tr. and ed. D. ERNEST) (Peabody, MA 1994) III, 379–380.

SPICQ, C., "χάρις", *Theological Lexicon of the New Testament* (tr. and ed. D. ERNEST) (Peabody, MA 1994) III, 500–506.

STANTON, G. N., *Jesus of Nazareth in the New Testament Preaching* (MSSNTS 27; New York 1974).

STÄHLIN, G., "σκάνδαλον, σκανδαλίζω", *TDNT* VII, 339–357.

STECK, O. H., *Israel und das gewaltsame Geschick der Propheten*. Untersuchungen zur Überlieferung des deuteronomistischen Geschichtsbildes im Alten Testament, Spätjudentum und Urchristentum (WMANT 23; Neukirchen-Vluyn 1967).

STEINHAUSER, M. G., *Doppelbildworte in den synoptischen Evangelien*. Eine form- und traditionskritische Studie (FzB 44; Würzburg 1981).

VON STEMM, S., *Der betende Sünder vor Gott*. Studien zu Vergebungsvorstellungen in urchristlichen und frühjüdischen Texten (AGJU 45; Leiden 1999).

STERLING, G. E., *Historiography and Self-definition*. Josephos, Luke-Acts and Apologetic Historiography (NT.S 64; Leiden 1992).

STERNBERG, M., *Expositional Modes and Temporal Ordering in Fiction* (Baltimore 1978).

STERNBERG, M., "Proteus in Quotation-Land", *Poetics Today* 3 (1982) 107–156.

STERNBERG, M., *The Poetics of Biblical Narrative*. Ideological Literature and the Drama of Reading (ISBL; Bloomington, IN 1987).

STRAMARE, T., *Vangelo dei misteri della vita nascosta di Gesù*. Matteo e Luca 1–2 (BeOS; Bornato in Franciacorta 1998).

STROBEL, A., "Die Ausrufung des Jubeljahres in der Nazarethpredigt Jesu. Zur Apokalyptischen Tradition Lc 4,16–30", *Jesus in Nazareth* (ed. W. ELTESTER) (BZNW 40; Berlin 1972) 38–50.

SUNG, C.-H., *Vergebung der Sünden*. Jesu Praxis der Sündenvergebung nach den Synoptikern und ihre Voraussetzungen im Alten Testament und frühen Judentum (WUNT 2.R 57; Tübingen 1993).

SUN-JONG, K., "Lecture de la parabole du fils retrouvé à la lumière du Jubilé", *NT* 53 (2011) 211–221.

TAEGER, J. W., *Der Mensch und sein Heil*. Studien zum Bild des Menschen und zur Sicht der Bekehrung bei Lukas (StNT 14; Gütersloh 1982).

TAIT, M., *Jesus, The Divine Bridegroom, in Mark 2:18–22*. Mark's Christology Upgraded (AnBib 185; Rome 2010).

TALBERT, C. H., *Reading Luke*. A Literary and Theological Commentary on the Third Gospel (New York 1986).

TALBERT, C. H. – HAYES, J. H., "A Theology of the Sea Storms in Luke-Acts", *Jesus and the Heritage of Israel*. Luke's Narrative Claim upon Israel's Legacy (ed. D. P. MOESSNER) (Harrisburg, PA 1999) 267–283.

TANNEHILL, R. C., "The Magnificat as Poem", *JBL* 93 (1974) 263–275.

TANNEHILL, R. C., *The Narrative Unity of Luke-Acts*. A Literary Interpretation. Volume One: The Gospel According to Luke (Philadelphia 1986).

TANNEHILL, R. C., *Luke* (ANTC; Nashville, TN 1996).

TAYLOR, J. E., *The Immerser*. John the Baptist Within Second Temple Judaism (Studying the Historical Jesus; Grand Rapids, MI 1997).

THEISSEN, G., *Urchristliche Wundergeschichten*. Ein Beitrag zur formgeschichtlichen Erforschung der synoptischen Evangelien (StNT 8; Gütersloh 1974).

THEOBALD, M., "Die Anfange der Kirche: zur Struktur von Lk 5:1–6:19", *NTS* 30 (1984) 91–108.

THYEN, H., *Studien zur Sündenvergebung im Neuen Testament und seinen alttestamentlichen und jüdischen Voraussetzungen* (FRLANT 96; Göttingen 1970).

TOPEL, L. J., *Children of a Compassionate God*. A Theological Exegesis of Luke 6:20–49 (Collegeville, MN 2001).

TRUDINGER, L. P., "Un cas d'incompabilité: Marc 2:21–22: Luc 5:39", *FV* 72/5–6 (1973) 4–7.

TURNER, M. B., "Holy Spirit", *Dictionary of Jesus and the Gospels* (ed. J. B. GREEN – S. MCKNIGHT) (Downers Grove, IL 1992) 341–351.

VAN UNNIK, W. C., "Die Motivierung der Feindesliebe in Lukas VI 32–35", *NT* 8 (1966) 284–300.

VERHEYDEN, J., "Creating Difference Through Parallelism: Luke's Handling of the Traditions on John the Baptist and Jesus in the Infancy Narrative", *Infancy Gospels. Stories and Identities* (ed. C. CLIVAZ – A. DETTWILER – L. DEVILLERS – E. NORELLI) (WUNT 281; Tübingen 2011) 137–160.

VERMÈS, G., *The Religion of Jesus the Jew* (London 1993).

VIGNOLO, R., "Una configurazione da non perdere. Il Vangelo come racconto di ricerca cristologica", *Non mi vergogno del Vangelo, potenza di Dio. Studi in onore di Jean-Noël Aletti SJ, nel suo 70° compleanno* (ed. F. BIANCHINI – S. ROMANELLO) (AnBib 200; Roma 2012) 371–389.

WEBB, R. L., "The Activity of John the Baptist's Expected Figure At the Threshing Floor (Matthew 3.12 = Luke 3.17)", *JSNT* 43 (1991) 103–111.

WEBB, R., *Ekphrasis, Imagination and Persuasion in Ancient Rhetorical Theory and Practice* (Farnham, UK 2009).

WEISS, H., "The Sabbath in the Synoptic Gospels", *JSNT* 38 (1990) 13–27.

WEISSENRIEDER A., *Images of Illness in the Gospel of Luke*. Insights of Ancient Medical Texts (WUNT 2.R 164; Tübingen 2003).

WELLS, L., *The Greek Language of Healing from Homer to New Testament Times* (BZNW 83; Berlin – New York 1998).

WERLINE, R. A., *Penitential Prayer in Second Temple Judaism*. The Development of a Religious Institution (SBLEJL 13; Atlanta, GA 1998).

WIARDA, T., *Peter in the Gospels*. Pattern, Personality and Relationship (WUNT 2.R 127; Tübingen 2000).

WIEFEL, W., *Das Evangelium nach Lukas* (ThHK 3; Berlin 1988).

WILKENS, W., "Die Theologische Struktur der Komposition des Lukasevangeliums", *TZ* 34 (1978) 1–13.

WILSON, S. G., *Luke and the Law* (MSSNTS 50; Cambridge 1983).

WINK, W., *John the Baptist in the Gospel Tradition* (MSSNTS 7; Cambridge 1968).

WITHERINGTON, B. III, "Salvation and Health in Christian Antiquity. The Soteriology of Luke-Acts in Its First Century Setting", *Witness to the Gospel. The Theology of Acts* (ed. H. I. MARSHALL – D. PETERSON) (Grand Rapids, MI 1998) 145–166.

WOLTER, M., "'Gericht' und 'Heil' bei Jesus von Nazareth und Johannes dem Täufer. Semantische und pragmatische Beobachtungen", *Der historische Jesus*. Tendenzen und Perspektiven der gegenwärtigen Forschung (ed. J. SCHRÖTER – R. BRUCKER) (BZNW 114; Berlin – New York 2002) 355–392.

WOLTER, M., *Das Lukasevangelium* (HNT 5; Tübingen 2008).

WOLTER, M., "Die Proömien des lukanischen Doppelwerks (Lk 1,1–4 und Apg 1,1–2)", *Apostelgeschichte im Kontext antiker und frühchristlicher Historiographie* (ed. J. FREY – C. K. ROTHSCHILD – J. SCHRÖTER) (BZNW 162; Berlin – New York 2009) 476–494.

WOLTER, M., "Die Rede von der Sünde im Neuen Testament", *Theologie und Ethos im frühen Christentum*. Studien zu Jesus, Paulus und Lukas (WUNT 236; Tübingen 2009) 471–499.

WOLTER, M., "Eschatology in the Gospel According to Luke", *Eschatology of the New Testament and Some Related Documents* (ed. J. G. VAN DER WATT) (WUNT 2.R 315; Tübingen 2011), 91–108.

WUELLNER, W. H., *The Meaning of the 'Fishers of Men'* (The New Testament Library; Philadelphia 1967).

YAMASAKI, G., *John the Baptist in Life and Death.* An Audience-Oriented Criticism of Matthew's Narrative (JSNT.S 167; Sheffield 1998).

YOUNG, N. H., "'Jesus and the Sinners': Some Queries", *JSNT* 24 (1985) 73–75.

ZERWICK, M., *Biblical Greek Illustrated by Examples* (English Edition Adapted from the Fourth Latin Edition by J. SMITH) (SPIB 114; Rome 1963).

ZIESLER, J. A., "Luke and the Pharisees", *NTS* 25 (1979) 146–157.

ZIMMERMANN, R., *Geschlechtermetaphorik und Gottesverhältnis.* Traditionsgeschichte und Theologie eines Bildfelds in Urchristentum und antiker Umwelt (WUNT 2.R 122; Tübingen 2001).

# Index of Ancient Sources

## Hebrew Bible / Old Testament

# New Testament

| | | | |
|---|---|---|---|
| 7:18–50 | 151 | 23:32,33,39 | 4 |
| 7:28–50 | 134 | 23:5 | 16 |
| 7:31 | 157 | 23:34 | 168 |
| 7:34 | 2 | 24:6 | 168 |
| 7:36–50 | 2, 134, 145–154, | 24:7 | 2 |
| | 158, 161, 166 | 24:27 | 168 |
| 8:1–56 | 150–154, 160 | 24:32 | 168 |
| 9:1–7 | 161 | 24:36 | 168 |
| 9:1–17 | 155–156 | 24:45 | 168 |
| 9:1–50 | 17, 128, 154–161 | 24:46 | 168 |
| 9:18–50 | 156–160 | 24:47 | 168 |
| 9:44–45 | 167 | 24:51 | 16 |
| 13:1–5 | 134 | 24 | 168 |
| 13:2 | 2 | | |
| 15:1,2,7,10 | 2 | *Acts* | |
| 15:1–32 | 134 | 1:21–22 | 16 |
| 18:9–14 | 134 | 2 | 168 |
| 18:13 | 2 | 4:25 | 10 |
| 18:31–34 | 168 | 10:37 | 16 |
| 19:1–10 | 2, 134 | 10:37–39 | 16 |

# Deuterocanonical Writings

| | | | |
|---|---|---|---|
| *Susanna* | | *Sirach* | |
| 12:56[Theod.] | 117 | 3:14 | 12 |
| | | 38:9,15 | 12 |
| | | 48:10 | 23 |

# Old Testament Pseudepigrapha and Dead Sea Scrolls

| | | | |
|---|---|---|---|
| *1 Enoch* | | *Testament of Isaac* | |
| 67.13 | 32 | 5.21–25 | 32 |
| | | | |
| *4 Ezra* | | *Dead Sea Scrolls* | |
| 13.10–11 | 32 | 1QS I, 22–25 | 13 |
| | | 1QS III, 6–9 | 32 |
| *Jubilees* | | 1QS IV, 21–22 | 32 |
| 23.24 | 11 | 4Q434 1 I, 2–4 | 13 |
| | | 11Q5 XXIV, 11– | 13 |
| *Testament of* | | 13a | |
| *Abraham* | | | |
| 13.11–14 | 32 | | |

# Philo, Josephus, and Classical Greek Sources

# Index of Modern Authors

# Wissenschaftliche Untersuchungen
# zum Neuen Testament

Edited by Jörg Frey (Zurich)

Associate Editors:

Markus Bockmuehl (Oxford) · James A. Kelhoffer (Uppsala)

Hans-Josef Klauck (Chicago, IL) · Tobias Nicklas (Regensburg)

J. Ross Wagner (Durham, NC)

*WUNT I* is an international series dealing with the entire field of early Christianity and its Jewish and Graeco-Roman environment. Its historical-philological profile and interdisciplinary outlook, which its long-term editor Martin Hengel was instrumental in establishing, is maintained by an international team of editors representing a wide range of the traditions and themes of New Testament scholarship. The sole criteria for acceptance to the series are the scholarly quality and lasting merit of the work being submitted. Apart from the specialist monographs of experienced researchers, some of which may be habilitations, *WUNT I* features collections of essays by renowned scholars, source material collections and editions as well as conference proceedings in the form of a handbook on themes central to the discipline.

*WUNT II* complements the first series by offering a publishing platform in paperback for outstanding writing by up-and-coming young researchers. Dissertations and monographs are presented alongside innovative conference volumes on fundamental themes of New Testament research. Like Series I, it is marked by a historical-philological character and an international orientation that transcends exegetical schools and subject boundaries. The academic quality of Series II is overseen by the same team of editors.

*WUNT I:*
ISSN: 0512-1604
Suggested citation: WUNT I
All available volumes can be
found at *www.mohr.de/wunt1*

*WUNT II:*
ISSN: 0340-9570
Suggested citation: WUNT II
All available volumes can be
found at *www.mohr.de/wunt2*

## Mohr Siebeck
www.mohr.de